# First World War
and Army of Occupation
War Diary
France, Belgium and Germany

21 DIVISION
Divisional Troops
Senior Supply Officer
15 September 1915 - 28 February 1919

WO95/2149/1

The Naval & Military Press Ltd
www.nmarchive.com
Published in association with The National Archives

Published by

## The Naval & Military Press Ltd

Unit 10 Ridgewood Industrial Park,

Uckfield, East Sussex,

TN22 5QE England

Tel: +44 (0) 1825 749494

www.naval-military-press.com

www.nmarchive.com

*This diary has been reprinted in facsimile from the original. Any imperfections are inevitably reproduced and the quality may fall short of modern type and cartographic standards.*

© **Crown Copyright**
**Images reproduced by permission of The National Archives, London, England, 2015.**

# Contents

| Document type | Place/Title | Date From | Date To |
|---|---|---|---|
| Heading | WO95/2149/1 | | |
| Heading | BEF 21 Division Senior Supply Officer 1915 Sep-1919 Feb | | |
| Heading | 21st Division SSO 21st Divl. Train Vol 2 Sept & Oct 15 | | |
| War Diary | | 15/09/1915 | 15/09/1915 |
| War Diary | | 16/09/1915 | 16/09/1915 |
| War Diary | | 17/09/1915 | 17/09/1915 |
| War Diary | | 18/09/1915 | 18/09/1915 |
| War Diary | | 19/09/1915 | 19/09/1915 |
| War Diary | | 20/09/1915 | 20/09/1915 |
| War Diary | | 21/09/1915 | 21/09/1915 |
| War Diary | | 22/09/1915 | 22/09/1915 |
| War Diary | | 23/09/1915 | 23/09/1915 |
| War Diary | | 24/09/1915 | 24/09/1915 |
| War Diary | | 25/09/1915 | 25/09/1915 |
| War Diary | | 26/09/1915 | 26/09/1915 |
| War Diary | | 27/09/1915 | 27/09/1915 |
| War Diary | | 28/09/1915 | 28/09/1915 |
| War Diary | | 29/09/1915 | 29/09/1915 |
| War Diary | | 30/09/1915 | 30/09/1915 |
| War Diary | | 01/10/1915 | 01/10/1915 |
| War Diary | | 02/10/1915 | 02/10/1915 |
| War Diary | | 03/10/1915 | 03/10/1915 |
| War Diary | | 04/10/1915 | 04/10/1915 |
| War Diary | | 05/10/1915 | 05/10/1915 |
| War Diary | | 06/10/1915 | 06/10/1915 |
| War Diary | | 07/10/1915 | 07/10/1915 |
| War Diary | | 08/10/1915 | 08/10/1915 |
| War Diary | | 09/10/1915 | 09/10/1915 |
| War Diary | | 10/10/1915 | 10/10/1915 |
| War Diary | | 11/10/1915 | 11/10/1915 |
| War Diary | | 12/10/1915 | 12/10/1915 |
| War Diary | | 13/10/1915 | 13/10/1915 |
| War Diary | | 14/10/1915 | 14/10/1915 |
| War Diary | | 15/10/1915 | 15/10/1915 |
| War Diary | | 16/10/1915 | 16/10/1915 |
| War Diary | | 17/10/1915 | 17/10/1915 |
| War Diary | | 18/10/1915 | 18/10/1915 |
| War Diary | | 19/10/1915 | 19/10/1915 |
| War Diary | | 20/10/1915 | 20/10/1915 |
| War Diary | | 21/10/1915 | 21/10/1915 |
| War Diary | | 22/10/1915 | 22/10/1915 |
| War Diary | | 23/10/1915 | 23/10/1915 |
| War Diary | | 24/10/1915 | 24/10/1915 |
| War Diary | | 25/10/1915 | 25/10/1915 |
| War Diary | | 26/10/1915 | 26/10/1915 |
| Heading | War Diary Oct 1st-31st 1915 S.S.O. 21st Division | | |
| War Diary | | 27/10/1915 | 27/10/1915 |
| War Diary | | 28/10/1915 | 28/10/1915 |
| War Diary | | 29/10/1915 | 29/10/1915 |

| | | | |
|---|---|---|---|
| War Diary | | 30/10/1915 | 30/10/1915 |
| Heading | 21st Division S.S.O. 21st Divl. Train vol 1 Nov 1 15 | | |
| Heading | War Diary of S.S.O 21st Division Nov 1st-30th 1915 | | |
| Miscellaneous | The Adjutant 21st Divl Train | 01/12/1915 | 01/12/1915 |
| War Diary | | 01/11/1915 | 01/11/1915 |
| War Diary | | 02/11/1915 | 02/11/1915 |
| War Diary | | 03/11/1915 | 03/11/1915 |
| War Diary | | 04/11/1915 | 04/11/1915 |
| War Diary | | 05/11/1915 | 05/11/1915 |
| War Diary | | 06/11/1915 | 06/11/1915 |
| War Diary | | 07/11/1915 | 07/11/1915 |
| War Diary | | 08/11/1915 | 08/11/1915 |
| War Diary | | 09/11/1915 | 09/11/1915 |
| War Diary | | 10/11/1915 | 10/11/1915 |
| War Diary | | 11/10/1915 | 11/10/1915 |
| War Diary | | 12/11/1915 | 12/11/1915 |
| War Diary | | 13/11/1915 | 13/11/1915 |
| War Diary | | 14/11/1915 | 14/11/1915 |
| War Diary | | 15/11/1915 | 15/11/1915 |
| War Diary | | 16/11/1915 | 16/11/1915 |
| War Diary | | 17/11/1915 | 17/11/1915 |
| War Diary | | 18/11/1915 | 18/11/1915 |
| War Diary | | 19/11/1915 | 19/11/1915 |
| War Diary | | 20/11/1915 | 20/11/1915 |
| War Diary | | 21/11/1915 | 21/11/1915 |
| War Diary | | 22/11/1915 | 22/11/1915 |
| War Diary | | 23/11/1915 | 26/11/1915 |
| War Diary | | 27/11/1915 | 27/11/1915 |
| War Diary | | 28/11/1915 | 30/11/1915 |
| War Diary | | 01/12/1915 | 31/01/1916 |
| War Diary | Pont Nieppe | 01/02/1916 | 29/02/1916 |
| Heading | S.S.O 21 Div Trench Vol 7 1916 Mar | | |
| War Diary | Pont Nieppe | 01/03/1916 | 24/03/1916 |
| War Diary | Strazeele | 25/03/1916 | 31/03/1916 |
| War Diary | Daours | 01/04/1916 | 16/04/1916 |
| War Diary | Ribemont | 17/04/1916 | 20/05/1916 |
| War Diary | Pms Daovrs | 20/05/1916 | 26/05/1916 |
| War Diary | Ribemont | 27/05/1916 | 21/06/1916 |
| War Diary | Ribemont | 22/06/1916 | 04/07/1916 |
| War Diary | Picquigny | 05/07/1916 | 06/07/1916 |
| War Diary | Cavillon | 07/07/1916 | 09/07/1916 |
| War Diary | Ribemont | 10/07/1916 | 19/07/1916 |
| War Diary | Cavillon | 20/07/1916 | 22/07/1916 |
| War Diary | Wamin | 23/07/1916 | 29/07/1916 |
| War Diary | Agnez-Les-Duisans | 30/07/1916 | 04/09/1916 |
| War Diary | Wamin | 05/09/1916 | 12/09/1916 |
| War Diary | Buire | 13/09/1916 | 16/09/1916 |
| War Diary | Fricourt | 17/09/1916 | 29/09/1916 |
| War Diary | Fricourt Chateau | 30/09/1916 | 30/09/1916 |
| War Diary | Fricourt | 01/10/1916 | 02/10/1916 |
| War Diary | St Sauveur | 03/10/1916 | 03/10/1916 |
| War Diary | Ailly-Le-Haut Clocher | 04/10/1916 | 07/10/1916 |
| War Diary | Noeux Les Mines | 08/10/1916 | 13/10/1916 |
| War Diary | Fouquieres | 14/10/1916 | 19/10/1916 |
| War Diary | Fouquieres Les-Bethune | 20/10/1916 | 25/10/1916 |
| War Diary | Fouquieres | 26/10/1916 | 27/01/1917 |

| | | | |
|---|---|---|---|
| War Diary | Wormhoudt | 28/01/1917 | 31/01/1917 |
| War Diary | Fouquieres | 01/01/1917 | 27/01/1917 |
| War Diary | Wormhoudt | 28/01/1917 | 12/02/1917 |
| War Diary | Bethune | 13/02/1917 | 13/02/1917 |
| War Diary | Noeux | 14/02/1917 | 28/02/1917 |
| War Diary | Wormhoudt | 01/02/1917 | 12/02/1917 |
| War Diary | Bethune | 13/02/1917 | 13/02/1917 |
| War Diary | Noeux | 14/02/1917 | 19/03/1917 |
| War Diary | Lucheux | 20/03/1917 | 31/03/1917 |
| War Diary | Bavincourt | 01/04/1917 | 04/04/1917 |
| War Diary | Pommiers | 05/04/1917 | 10/04/1917 |
| War Diary | Adinfer Wood | 11/04/1917 | 25/04/1917 |
| War Diary | Hamelincourt | 26/04/1917 | 10/05/1917 |
| War Diary | Adinfer Wood | 12/05/1917 | 30/05/1917 |
| War Diary | Hamelincourt | 31/05/1917 | 19/06/1917 |
| War Diary | Adinfer Wood | 20/06/1917 | 30/06/1917 |
| War Diary | Hamelincourt | 01/07/1917 | 12/08/1917 |
| War Diary | Moyenville | 14/08/1917 | 27/08/1917 |
| War Diary | Agnez-Les Duisans | 28/08/1917 | 31/08/1917 |
| War Diary | Avesne Le-Comte | 01/09/1917 | 14/09/1917 |
| War Diary | Avesne Le Comte Caestre | 15/09/1917 | 20/09/1917 |
| War Diary | Caestre | 21/09/1917 | 22/09/1917 |
| War Diary | Meteren | 23/09/1917 | 28/09/1917 |
| War Diary | Reninghelst | 29/09/1917 | 29/09/1917 |
| War Diary | Ouderdom Railhead | 30/09/1917 | 30/09/1917 |
| War Diary | Reninghelst | 01/10/1917 | 08/10/1917 |
| War Diary | Blaringhem | 09/10/1917 | 18/10/1917 |
| War Diary | Zevecoten | 19/10/1917 | 22/10/1917 |
| War Diary | Chateau Segard | 23/10/1917 | 15/11/1917 |
| War Diary | Vieux Berquin | 16/11/1917 | 17/11/1917 |
| War Diary | Barlin | 18/11/1917 | 21/11/1917 |
| War Diary | Madagascar | 22/11/1917 | 30/11/1917 |
| War Diary | Madagascar Camp | 01/12/1917 | 01/12/1917 |
| War Diary | Buire-Courcelles | 02/12/1917 | 02/12/1917 |
| War Diary | Tincourt | 03/12/1917 | 27/12/1917 |
| War Diary | Aizecourt Le-Bas | 28/12/1917 | 21/03/1918 |
| War Diary | Haut Allaines | 22/01/1918 | 22/01/1918 |
| War Diary | Clery & Maricourt | 23/01/1918 | 23/01/1918 |
| War Diary | Bray S/Somme | 24/01/1918 | 25/01/1918 |
| War Diary | Bresle | 26/01/1918 | 26/01/1918 |
| War Diary | Beaucourt Near Beaucourt | 27/03/1918 | 28/03/1918 |
| War Diary | Beaucourt | 29/03/1918 | 29/03/1918 |
| War Diary | Allonville | 30/03/1918 | 01/04/1918 |
| War Diary | Dranoutre | 02/03/1918 | 11/03/1918 |
| War Diary | Heksken | 12/04/1918 | 15/04/1918 |
| War Diary | Lissenthoek | 16/04/1918 | 18/04/1918 |
| War Diary | G14.a.9.8 | 19/04/1918 | 29/04/1918 |
| War Diary | L13.b.5.7 | 30/04/1918 | 30/04/1918 |
| War Diary | 27/L13.b.5.7 | 01/05/1918 | 01/05/1918 |
| War Diary | Rubrouck | 02/05/1918 | 04/05/1918 |
| War Diary | Romigny | 05/05/1918 | 15/05/1918 |
| War Diary | Prouilly | 16/05/1918 | 27/05/1918 |
| War Diary | Serzy | 28/05/1918 | 28/05/1918 |
| War Diary | Paradis | 29/05/1918 | 30/05/1918 |
| War Diary | Chaltrait Au-Bois | 31/05/1918 | 08/06/1918 |
| War Diary | La Noue | 09/06/1918 | 14/06/1918 |

| | | | |
|---|---|---|---|
| War Diary | Oisemont | 14/06/1918 | 21/06/1918 |
| War Diary | Gamaches | 22/06/1918 | 01/07/1918 |
| War Diary | Beauquesne | 02/07/1918 | 17/08/1918 |
| War Diary | Raincheval | 18/08/1918 | 23/08/1918 |
| War Diary | Acheux | 24/08/1918 | 24/08/1918 |
| War Diary | Mailly | 25/08/1918 | 29/08/1918 |
| War Diary | Grandcourt | 30/08/1918 | 03/09/1918 |
| War Diary | Le Sars | 04/09/1918 | 06/09/1918 |
| War Diary | Les Boeufs | 07/09/1918 | 18/09/1918 |
| War Diary | Rocquigny | 20/09/1918 | 23/09/1918 |
| War Diary | Les Boeufs | 24/09/1918 | 27/09/1918 |
| War Diary | Le Mesnil En-Arrouaise | 29/09/1918 | 04/10/1918 |
| War Diary | Near Equancourt | 06/10/1918 | 08/10/1918 |
| War Diary | West of Gouzeaucourt W.11.c.4.8 | 09/10/1918 | 09/10/1918 |
| War Diary | M32.b.7.2 (57b) | 10/10/1918 | 10/10/1918 |
| War Diary | Walincourt | 11/10/1918 | 22/10/1918 |
| War Diary | Beaumont by Inchy | 23/10/1918 | 26/10/1918 |
| War Diary | Inchy | 26/10/1918 | 04/11/1918 |
| War Diary | Poix du-Nord | 05/11/1918 | 06/11/1918 |
| War Diary | Locquignol | 07/11/1918 | 07/11/1918 |
| War Diary | Berlaimont | 08/11/1918 | 11/11/1918 |
| War Diary | Aulnoye | 12/11/1918 | 30/11/1918 |
| Heading | War Diary of Senior Supply Officer., 21st Division From December 1st. To December 31st 1918 | | |
| War Diary | Aulnoye | 01/12/1918 | 13/12/1918 |
| War Diary | Inchy | 14/12/1918 | 15/12/1918 |
| War Diary | Molliens Vidame | 16/12/1918 | 31/12/1918 |
| Heading | War Diary of Senior Supply Officer., 21st Division From 1st January 1919 To 31st January 1919 | | |
| War Diary | Molliens Vidame | 01/01/1919 | 31/01/1919 |
| Heading | War Diary of Senior Supply Officer., 21st Division From 1st February 1919 To 28th February 1919 | | |
| War Diary | Molliens Vidame | 01/02/1919 | 28/02/1919 |

WO95/2249/1

# BEF

# 21 DIVISION

## SENIOR SUPPLY OFFICER

1915 SEP — 1919 FEB

21st Khorasan

12/7608

S.S.O. 2pt Intl: Iran
Vol 2

SENT Oct 15

War Diary SSO 2nd Div

15/9/15

Division now concentrated —
Hd Qrs R.A. + 4 Bdes leave
the Divl area + are
noticed by me as a group
in themselves — (for consumption
16/9/15) —
This necessitates a re-grouping
of the Divn as follows —

No 1 Group — Hd Qrs R.A.
                4 Bdes R.F.A.
Refilling Point — The  } Portion Hd Qr Coy A.S.C.
cross Rds 1 mile SE }  (100 men + horses).
of MONNECOVE on
ST. OMER — CALAIS rd.

No 2 Group — Div H Q.
                No 1 Sec Signal Coy.
                Divl Cyclists
Refilling Point    Sanitary Section
                Mobile Vety Section
                Squadron Div Cavalry
Éperlecques       Hd Qrs R.E.
                Motor Repair Workshop Section
                Divsnal Bn.
                Portion H.Q. Coy. A.S.C.
                Ammn Sub Park
                62nd Bde Hd Qr + No 2
                8th East Yorks Section Signalling
                        (Cont'd)

15/9/15 (Cont'd).

{ 10th Yorkshire Regt.
12th Northumberland Fus
13th "
63rd Field Ambulance.
97th Field Coy. R.E.
No 2 Coy Train.

No 3 Group. { 63rd Bde H.Q.
3 Section Signal Coy
Refilling Point { 8th Somerset L.I.
8th Lincoln Regt
MONNECOVE { 12th W. Yorks
10th York & Lancs
64th Field Amb.
98th Field Coy R.E.
No 3 Coy Train.

No 4 Group { 64th Bde H.Q.
4 Section Signal Coy
9th K O Y L I
Refilling Point { 10th "
14th D. L. I.
LOSTRAT { 15th "
126th Field Coy R.E.
21st D. A. C.
65th Field Ambulance
No 4 Coy Train

15/9/15  (Cont:d).

Hay Ration for Div:n 10 lbs per Horse.

200 Gals of Rum received in Supply Column as a Reserve.

Coal purchased for Div:n by R.O. of 62nd Bde Group under my instructions

Railhead   ST - OMER.

[signature]
Major SSO

16/9/15.

No 1 Group (R.A) fed by me for 17/9/15.
Refilling Point CAESTRE.
15 Lorries remain at CAESTRE (Detached from Div<sup>n</sup>) - this place being their Rail Head for 17/9/15.

200 gals Pinum on Supply Column held as a reserve.

Peter O'Connor
Major
SSO

17/9/15.

No 1 Group (R.A) fed by 2nd Army for ~~this day~~ consumption tomorrow 18/9/15.

No: 2 Group's forage from Reserve forage on Supply Column for consumption on 19/9/15. No forage for this Group drawn from the Rail Head.

No issue to Supply Section made for consumption tomorrow to Amm^n Sub. Park, fed by Corps. (XI)

Issue to units made for tomorrow's consumption of M & V Rations, 25% of total.

10,000 Kilos. Coal bought by R.O. for 62nd Bde Group for whole Div^n

[signature]
Major
SSO

18/9/15

Issue made of 75% Fresh
25% ~~Dry~~
% Dried

R.M. Ceylan
Manager
SSD

19/9/15

Reserve Boxes of Iron Rations
(100 rations, 5 Boxes) have
been issued to S.O's
62nd, 63rd & 64th Bdes.
The Reserve Iron Rations for
S.O Divl Troops being held
by Supply Column till line
between
In addition Iron Rations to
adjust certain deficiencies
have been made —
63rd Bde 100, 64th Bde 60

[signature]

Major
SSO

26/9/15

Honey issued in lieu of Jam
($\frac{1}{2}$ allowance of Jam).

Iron Rations issued to adjust
certain deficiencies as follows:-

    62nd Bde   1100
    64th  "    100

Division moves this evening
    Supply Section fall for consumption
22nd  "  Coolness   "   "
21st  "  Supply Column empty.
Visited R.O. detached to get them
on same footing as rest of Divn.

Divn in area ARQUES - WITTES
    tonight

                      R. [signature]
                      Major
                      S.S.O.

21/9/15

Distributed from Supply Section
to units about 10 a.m.

Northumberland Fusiliers (P.) fed
by 64th Bde Group transferred
from 62nd Bde Group for
consumption on till further
notice.

Div³ in Area LAMBRES –
ROMBLY – NORRENT FONTES –
ST-HILLAIRE – LIÈRES – AMES –
ECQEDECQES – BOURECQ, tonight

R.A. rationed by me for 23rd (on their
return to Division)
Lorries returned today to
Supply Column

[signature]
Major
SSO.

22/9/15.

Division in area tonight as
follows - (including R.A.)
LESPESSES - LIÈRES - AMES -
FERFAY - AUCHEL - LOZINGHEM -
ALLOUAGNE - PONT DU
REVEILLON - BUSNETTES -
LECLEME - ~~LILLERS~~ Reg.
ECQEDECQUES -

Railhead changed to LILLERS

[signature]
Rangier
SSO.

23/9/15

Division in same position. Double rations of charge loaded on Supply Col. this evening for issue tomorrow 24th — This to be held as reserve & supplementary to Iron Rations. To be turned over daily in order that each man has a fresh ration on him.

R R— C. C—
Major
S.S.O.

24/9/15

Pea Soup loaded on Supply Column for issue tomorrow 25th. This to be treated in the same way as the cheese mentioned in yesterday's diary —

Rum loaded on Supply Col. for issue tomorrow night (25th) (200 gals were in Reserve on the Column already so I only required another 100 gals to complete the issue, this being obtained from B.S.O).

Division marches this evening arriving tomorrow morning in area on each side of BRUAY — NOEUX LES MINES road.

Supply Section Train Rolls for consumption 26/9/15

R. Rain  [signature]
Major
SSO

25/9/15

Prem loaded on Supply Column for issue tomorrow night to Division.

Division marched this evening westward taking up a position about MAZINIARBE.

Owing to no orders being given as to distribution from Train Supply Section this was not carried out, except by 63rd Bde Group who acted without orders. The actual distribution to units for consumption 26/9/15 was carried out early on 26/9/15.

No refilling took place today)

P.R... Capper
Major
SSO

26/9/15

Distribution carried out in early morning except in case of 64th Bde group who could not be found. Wagons returned still loaded to NOEUX LES MINES but later the Brigade was located & distribution carried out. The Officer i/c Supply Section 62nd Bde ~~Coy~~ handed over the Rations for this Brigade (Infantry & H.Q. only) to 45th Bde of 15th Divn in ~~error~~. Refilling was carried out as ~~most~~ empty wagons returned on BÉTHUNE – NOEUX LES MINES main road, wagons when filled ~~been~~ returned to Train H.Q. at latter place.

Rations ~~one day~~ were again sent out to 62nd Bde in afternoon, but 1st line Transport unable to deliver them. These rations were for consumption 27/9/15 but owing to casualties have been able to make the adjustment between the

26/9/15 (Cont-d).

~~troops so that there will be sufficient rations for all for 27/9/15. Distribution for 27/9/15 carried out this evening. Railhead today changed to FOUQUEREUIL. Supply column loaded up in early morning & dumped immediately afterwards (these supplies being for consumption 28th.)~~

Railhead today changed to FOUQUEREUIL. Supply column after dumping supplies on BÉTHUNE – NOEUX-LES MINES road which they should have dumped yesterday re-loaded at FOUQUEREUIL for consumption on 28th.

R.R. [signature]
Major
SSO

27/9/15.

Dumping from Supply Column carried out at 7 a.m.
Refilling at 8 a.m.
Distribution carried out in the afternoon for consumption tomorrow 28/9/15.
Supply Column reloaded* late in afternoon (rations for 29th) as the lorries have been evacuating wounded the whole morning.
Refilling point & Rail Head same.
Obtained 200 galls rum from R.S.O. Béthune to complete Divn for ~~today's~~ tomorrow's issue.

(* 5% Fresh Rations)
( remainder M & V ,, )

R.M. Aylmer.

[signature]
Major
SSO

28/9/15

Dump 7 a.m. } For consumption
Refilled 8 a.m. }
Reloaded at same Railhead for 29/9/15
consumption 30/9/15 (5% Fresh Rations)
Distributed in the afternoon —

(X. Remainder Pres'd M + Biscuit).

Division marches tonight back
in LILLERS area to refit.
(RE, D.AC, Pioneers, HQ Coy Train,
remaining behind)

Refilled today according to Normal
Grouping & will do so
tomorrow but owing to Division
being split up a regrouping
must take place & the
reloading of Supply Column
tomorrow will be based on
new Grouping (units enumerated
above forming No 1 Group &
62nd Bde Group taking over the
feeding of the remainder
of No 1 Group).

R Ren. Cox Cmdr
Troops in SSO

29/9/15

Dumped & refilled for whole Div.
as yesterday. - (.20)
R.A. Group lorries, who are
being detached from our Div'n
& attached to Guards Div'l
Supply Column were ordered to
reload at CHOCQUES, but
Groceries & Forage not being
available there had to
get these supplies from LILLERS
railhead, this being the
railhead today & until further
notice for remainder of our
Div'n.
Distribution to R.A. Group carried
out in afternoon for consumption.

30/9/15 -
R.A. Group now detached for
feeding to Guards Div -
Guards Div have Supply Column
empty at night & Supply section
Train full exactly the
opposite to our Div at present.
In order to bring R.A. Group
in line with them I ordered
Lieut Newton (S.O. Div Troops) &
Lieut Roberts (in charge Det'd Supply Col)

29/9/15 (Cont⁻ᵈ).
to refill twice tomorrow
(i.e. in early morning under
their own arrangements & in
afternoon at 1.30 p.m with
Guards Divⁿ).

Remainder of Divⁿ went by
Train to area WITTERNESSE -
LIETTRES - ESTREE BLANCHE -
LA TIRMAND - LIGNY LEZ AIRE
WESTREHEM - AUCHY AU BOIS -
RELY - LINGHEM.
1ˢᵗ line Transport became detached
from their units, result they
had no food for today's
consumption, in order to adjust
this Supply Column made detail
issues direct to units during
afternoon as Supply Sectⁿ own Train
(full) arrived in their Bde
areas so late in the dark -
Supplies issued by Column being
originally intended for consumption on 1/10/15.
⅟₁ as Supply Sectⁿ
½ Ration of Rum arrived at
Railhead for me being held
by R.S.O. as Reserve -
No Rum loaded on S.O. today

30/9/15

No refilling to take place today -
Units to eat today their
rations still on 1st Line
Transport originally intended
for consumption yesterday -
Supply Sections of Train
distributed today for consumption
tomorrow.
Column reloaded at LILLERS
at 10 a.m. rations for 2nd Oct.
½ Ration of Rum arrived at
Railhead being held by
R.S.O. for use in Reserve.
No Rum issued loaded on
Column today from Railhead.
Supply Officer Supply Column
obtained 10,000 Iron Rations +
200 Gals Rum today from
NOEUX LES MINES Station —
I had previously obtained
15,000 Iron Rations + 300 Gals
Rum from AIRE & BÉTHUNE
R.S.O. but yesterday these
were dumped at NOEUX LES
MINES Station —; the majority
has therefore been recovered
for issue when required

1/10/15

Division marched towards MORBECQUE to join 2nd Army. Prior to marching off refilled at 7 a.m. (Bde. refilling points) Supply Sections marching Coll. with rations for consumption tomorrow. Supply Column reloaded at LILLERS at 10 a.m. — (all passed rations as follows were) loaded on Supply Section wagons for units who had consumed theirs while in the trenches near LOOS, (the first line Transport being unable to distribute to their units)

  62nd Bde Group 2580
  63rd " " 1920
  64th " " 2540
        7040

Distributed to units today before dark.

      [signature]
      Major, DSO

2/10/15

Refilled at 8 a.m.
Dumping at 7 a.m.
Refilling point a divisional one
  by STEENBECQUE station.
Division marches towards
HAZEBROUCK with supply section
of Train full.
Reloaded at LILLERS about
11.30 a.m. (all fresh rations)
Distributed in daylight.

[signature]
Major
SSO

3/10/15

Dumped at 8 a.m.
Refilled 9 a.m.
Divisional refilling point on CAESTRE–
ROUGE CROIX road.
Division in area HONDEGHEM,
CAESTRE, STRAZEELE–HAZEBROUK.
Reloaded at new Railhead
HAZEBROUK GARAGE at 10 a.m.
Division now comes under
2nd Army & belongs to 2nd Corps.
Obtained 9 tons coal from
O.C. 2nd Corps Troops S.C. for distribution
to Brigades for washing men's
clothing & cooking purposes

R.H. Palmer
Major
SSO

4/10/15

Same arrangements as yesterday.
14 N.F (P) Batt⁰ arrived last
~~yesterday~~ night without
due notice being received
by me, they are rationed
up to and including to-day.
Arranged to draw their rations
for tomorrow's consumption
from CAESTRE Depot & delivered
to them by motor lorry direct.
Received 10 tons coal for Div⁰ from
O.C 2ⁿᵈ Corps Troops S.C. for
distribution to Brigades for
washing men's clothes & cooking
purposes.

R. R.
Major
SSO

5/10/15

Same arrangements as yesterday -
R.A. return today -
Loaded at Railhead on to
their lorries which came back
last night. Will feed
them for consumption 7/10/15
All fresh rations reloaded on
Supply Column today.
Distributed in morning to units

Major
SSO

6/10/15.

Dumping today same as yesterday except in case of R.A. group, their refilling point being S.W. of HONDEGHEM along the road running East to West just North of the words LES CISEAUX. —

344 re-inforcements arrived for 63rd Bde & 140 for 64th Bde. Sent out a lorry containing double these amounts of rations in each case (representing 2 days suppy) as the Dump refilling today had already taken place & the lorries were already loaded for refilling tomorrow.

Div HQ moved from HONDEGHEM to MERRIS late afternoon —

[signatures]

7/10/15

Refilled as yesterday but
grouping in case of 62nd Bde
& R.A. Groups altered as
follows –

R.A. Group.

95th Bde R.F.A.
96th    "    "
97th    "    "
D.A.C.
14th N. Fusiliers (P).
No 1 Coy Train.

62nd Bde Group.

| | |
|---|---|
| H.Q. 62nd Bde + | Div. H Q + No 1 Sec |
| No 2 Sec Signal Coy. | Signal Coy. |
| 4 Bns 62nd Bde. | Sanitary Sec |
| 97th Field Coy R.E. | C.R.E. |
| 63rd Field Amb | D.A.W. |
| No 2 Coy Train | Mob. Vet. Sec. |
| 94th Bde R.F.A. | Div Cyclists |
| H.Q. R.A. | S.I.H. (Div Cav.) |

Plan [signature]
Ag. dr SSO

8/10/15.

Refilled as yesterday except in case of R.A.
2 Brigades (95th & 96th) are moving up to PONT DE NIEPPE to join 50th Divn.
I ration these Bdes up to & including consumption 10th after which SSO 50th Div (who saw me today) feeds them.
Sent rations for Rt. ½ sections of Batteries who moved out yesterday to PONT DE NIEPPE by motor lorries, remainder refilled at LES CISEAUX as usual.
Det- 1st Northd Bde RFA (200 men & 200 horses) arrived today & require rationing by me from 10th.

R. de Poule
Major SSO

9/10/15

Refilled at PONT DE NIEPPE for 95th & 96th Bdes R.F.A., at LES CISEAUX for remainder of R.A. Group, at ROUGE CROIX for 62 + 63 Bde Groups, at a point on the small road South of FLETRE for 64th Bde Group, the Batt⁹ of this Bde having moved to MERRIS & BAILLEUL on their way up to the line. Regrouping of Div⁹ faun tomorrow is as follows —

### 62nd Bde Group.

| | |
|---|---|
| HQ 62nd Bde & 4 B⁹⁵ | Div HQ |
| No 2 Sec Signal Coy | No 1 Sec Signal Co |
| 9 63rd Field Amb | Sanitary Sec. |
| No 2 Coy Train | D.A.W. |
| 94th Bde R F A | Mob Vet Section |
| H. Q. R. A. | Div Cyclists |
| | S. I. H (Div Cav⁹) |

### 63rd Bde Group.

| | |
|---|---|
| HQ 63rd Bde & 4 B⁹⁵ | No 3 Coy Train |
| No 3 Sec Signal Coy | 65th Field Amb |
| 64th Field Amb | |

9/10/15 (Cont d).

### 64th Bde Group

HQ 64 Bde + 4 Bns  
No 4 Sec Signal Coy.  
HQ R.E.  
97th Field Coy R.E.  
98 " "  
126 " "  
14th Mxd Bn (P).  

} 3rd Bn  
} 21st Div  
} at  
} PONT  
} DE NIEPPE

### R.A. Group.

97th Bde R.F.A.  
D.A.C.  
No 1 Coy Train.  
Northumbrian Bde R.F.A. (now  
    concentrated from  
    50th Div).

The R.E. + 14th N.F. move tomorrow with 64th Bde up towards ARMENTIÈRES.

*[signed]*  
Major  
SSO

10/10/15

Refilled as before but
95th & 96th Bdes RFA feed
by 50th Div for consumption
tomorrow.
~~Rations for~~

RFA ?????
Major
SSO

11/10/15

Re Loading + Refilling as before.

[signatures]

12/10/15

Re-loading & refilling as before.
Re-inforcements arrived
& extra rations were
obtained for them.
½ A Battery 97th Bde RFA
& Reptation of their B.A.C. were
detached, fed for 13th by me,
Fed by 50th Div at PONT
DE NIEPPE tomorrow for
consumption 14th & until further
notice.

B.Ro. OgCare
Raig to SSO

13/10/15.

Refilling & Reloading as before.
Loaded at Railhead according
to New Grouping, 62nd Bde
having left to take over from
64th Bde (now attached to
50th Div). 64th Bde going to
25th Div =.

R.A. Group

As Before (Refilling point same).

62nd Bde Group.                    Refilling Point

HQ 62nd Bde + 4 Bns        ⎫  Near Church
No 2 Sec Signal Coy         ⎪       at
  HQ R.E.                   ⎬
97th Field Coy R.E.         ⎪  PONT DE
98th    "                   ⎪
126th   "                   ⎪   NIEPPE
14th North'd Fus (P).       ⎭

63rd Bde Group

HQ 63rd Bde + 4 Bns
No 3 Sec Signal Coy
63rd Field Amb

## 63rd Bde Group (Cont'd)

64th Field Ambulance ⎫
65th Field Ambulance ⎬ Refilling Point.
HQ & No 3 Coy: Train ⎪
94th Bde RFA ⎪
H.Q. R.A. ⎪ On
Div H.Q. ⎬ CAESTRE
HQ + No 1 Sec Signal Coy ⎪ –
Sanitary Section ⎪ ROUGECROIX
D.A.W. ⎬ road
Mob. Vet Y Section ⎪
Div Am Subs ⎪
S.I. It (Div Coy) ⎭

## 64th Bde Group

HQ 64th Bde + 4 Bns. ⎫ Refilling Point
No 4 Sec Signal Coy. ⎬ On BAILLEUL
 ⎪ – ARMENTIÈRES
 ⎪ main road
 ⎪ at a point
 ⎬ East of
 ⎪ crossing of
 ⎪ latter by
 ⎪ STEENWERCK –
 ⎪ NEUVE EGLISE
 ⎭ main Road.

14/10/15

Refilling etc as yesterday.
65th Field Ambulance added
to RA Group + taken off 63rd Bde
Group, otherwise grouping the
same.

[signature]

Personal
GSO

15/10/15

As yesterday.
Nothing unusual to record.

[signature]
Major
SSO

16/10/15
---

Railhead today changed to STEENWERCK. –

*[signature]*
Ramsay (?)
SSO

17/10/15

As yesterday.
1000 Iron Rations surplus
returned to CAESTRE
Depot.

[signature]
Major
SSO

18/10/15

Situation as regards Supplies.
"Normal" –
No change

BBR
Ramzi
Sgd

19/10/15

As yesterday.

20/10/15

Refilling point for R.A. Group changed from LES CISEAUX to road running EAST to WEST just south of the woods LE BREARDE (east of ST SYLVESTRE - HAZEBROUCK road)

BRa. GyPulo
Recy it
GHSD

21/10/15

Nothing unusual to report.
½ A, C + D Bty's 94th Bde +
½ B + C Bty's 97th Bde
move up to NIEPPE on
concentration of R.A. there.

R.L. Cayley
Major
CSO

22/10/15

Bde Am Cols of 94th & 97th Bdes R.F.A. move to NIEPPE.

[signature]
Major
SSO

23/10/15.

Bdes HQ's + remaining sections of Batteries of 94th + 97th Bdes move to NIEPPE.
This leaves B Battery 94th + D Battery 97th behind (A Battery 97th Bde having moved up previously (vide Diary 12/10/15).

R. Rait Kerr
Major
SSO

24/10/15

H.Q. 62.A. + 1 Sec D.C.C move to NIEPPE.
63rd Bde move up.
2 Bns 64th Bde move back —

R. Rain Copeland
Major
GSO

25/10/15

Remainder of D.A.C. move to NIEPPE. Move of Div'l Artillery now complete.
Refilled today according to new Grouping.

R.A. Group.

Hd Qrs R.A.
94th Bde RFA (less 1 Battery)
95th " " "
96th " " "
97th " " (less 1 Battery)

D.A.C.
~~16th (H) Bde RGA Hd Qrs.~~
~~2nd (H) Battery RGA~~
~~Mag - 14th " " "~~
~~11th " " "~~
~~Amm' Col (H) Bde RGA~~

Taken over from 50th Div'
{ 27th Anti-Aircraft Sec.
{ 14th " " "
{ 2nd " " Workshop
Belgian Gendarmes
No 1 Coy: 21st Div Train
45th Trench Mortar Battery.

Refilling Point by the T of

COURTE RUE ½ mile ~~N.E.~~
N.E. of NIEPPE.
(Ref Ordnance map 1/40,000 Sheet 36)

### 62nd Bde. Group.

As Before, refilling point same.

### 63rd Bde Group.

Hd Qrs 63rd Bde + 4 B^ry.
  No 3 Sec Signal Coy.
  No 3 Coy Train.
  Hd Qrs 64th Bde + 2 B^ry.
  No 4 Sec Signal Coy.
(H.Q. 16th (H) Bde R.F.A.
  14th (H) Battery R.F.A.
Taken  9th (H) " "
over  114th (H)
from
50th  Amm^n Col (H) Bde R.F.A.
Div

Refilling point just East of the road junction where main BAILLEUL - ARMENTIÈRES road joins NEUVE EGLISE road.

64th Bde Group.

2 Bns 64th Bde.
HQ & No 4 Coy Train.
63rd Field Ambulance
64th    "       "
65th    "       "
1 Section R E.
Salvage Coy
Grenade School
1 Battery 94th Bde R.F.A.
1   "     97th  "    "
Div HQ.
S. I. H. (Div Cavy)
Cyclist Coy
HQ & No 1 Sec Signal Coy.
Mobile Vet-y Section
Sanitary Section & D. A. W.

Refilling point on MERRIS-
OULTERSTEENE road
just east of where
road crosses stream.

26/10/15.

Refilling point of 63rd Bde Group changed to a point S.W of the B of BRUNE-GAYE North of -NIEPPE-
(B 10 a Ordnance map $\frac{1}{40,000}$ sheet 36).

From tomorrow the R.A, 62nd & 63rd Bde Groups have to be fed without using Supply column (i.e. loading up our wagons of Train Coys at Railhead in Bulk, dumping at refilling points & loading up again by units). In order not to loose 1 day's supply from the Railway the supply section of Train must sleep full (except 64th Bde Group) & Supply Col (except 64th Bde lorries) empty.
Refilled twice today (second time at 3.30 pm) in order to start this.

Shawe — After second
refilling the supply section
wagons of Base Group
returned hold to New
Train Coys.

P.R. [signature]
          Reay de
          S So.

War Diary
Oct. 1st – 31st 1915.

S.S.O.
21st Division.

27/10/15

Engaged a coal store for 3 advanced groups at PONT DE NIEPPE.
Established an Office for myself at NIEPPE.
The 3 full supply sections of Train distributed this morning 7 a.m., returning empty to railhead at Rail Head at 11 a.m.
After unloading Train wagons returned to Train Coys' Billets, watered & fed men & horses & went out to dumps in afternoon for refills.
After refilling full wagons returned to Train Coys.
64th Bde Group worked as before
(HQ & 2 Sections D.A.C. are at St JEAN CAPPEL & these are now to be fed by 64th Bde Group not by R.A. Group
42nd Trench Mortar Battery is added to R.A. Group

and fwd to Supply Officer today

Rear Admiral
Ranjit
SSO

28/10/15

Same arrangements as yesterday.

28th [crossed out] Trench Report as Battaria Red by 21st Divi. Attached to B.G. 2e Corps.

P.R. Carpano
Cap.tn
SSO

29/10/15

Supply Officers of 62nd, 63rd
+ R.A. Group refilled either
in or just outside their
camps.

R.Ra. [signature]
Norwich
SSO

30/10/15
As yesterday.

↑ the Balance being available for R.A. Group (detached) when required.

Blair Rae ~~~~
Rainy ??
S.S.O.

30/10/15

16th (H) Bde RFA
commence their march
to NUNCQUE.
Bde HQ & 1 Battery 12th (H) RFA
(the latter which I am not
yet feeding) move to
HAZEBROUCK.
Supplies for consumption 2nd sent
from Railhead to HAZEBROUCK
on a Battery cart.
Supplies for 1st on a Baggage
wagon.
Remaining Batteries of Bde
not marching till tomorrow
& fed as usual.

RBu. ReCall
Major
SSO.

12/
7153

21st Kuroiun

SSO. 23rd Arti: Gram
Vol I
Sep 1. 15.

Nov

War Diary
of
S.S.O.
21st Division.
Nov. 1st – 30th 1915.

S.23.B.

The Adjutant,
21st Div¹ Tr̲a̲i̲n̲

Herewith my Diary
for the period 1st – 30th Nov.
for transmission to the
proper quarter please.

[signature]

1.12.15   S.S.O. 21st Division   Major

1/11/15

Remainder of 16th (H) Bde
R.F.A. move to HAZEBROUCK
Lorries loaded up separately
for Btm at Rail Head
& sent to HAZEBROUCK for
consumption 3/11/15.
1st Canadian (H) Battery fed
by 63rd Bde Group for
first time (10 day's consumption)

[signature]
Major,
A.S.D. 21st Division

2/11/15

Lorries sent to LILLERS
with food for Heavy Bde
for consumption 4/11/15
(last date D feed them)
These lorries now taken on
by 3rd Army.

R.M. Cline
Major
AD 21st Division

3/11/15

H.Q 64th Bde. Red today
(day of consumption) by
S.O 64th Bde, having moved
from La CRECHE to
BAILLEUL, taken off 63rd
Bde Group.

Major
S.S.O 2nd Division

4/11/15

D Battery 97 Bde RFA
having reported to Ammunition
fed by R A Group for
today's consumption.
Struck off 64th Bde Group.

[signature]
Major
S.O 21st Division

5/11/15

42nd & 45th Trench Mortar Batteries taken over by 50th Div. & fed by them for today's consumption.

R. Shaw
T/O 21st Division

6/11/15

Sed 1st Monmouth Sr:ge Co: R.E
for today's consumption.
Attached to 62nd Bde Group

                                    R.R... Cap...
                                    _____
                                         Major
                                A.D 21st Division

7/11/15

Situation same as yesterday.
179 NCOs & men moved up
to ARMENTIERES today from
various Bdes of our Divn
forming a Sanitary Sec. These
from tomorrow will be fed
by 62nd Bde Supply Officer.

[signature]
Major
ADS 20th Division

8/11/15

31st Acute Aircraft Section struck off feeder strength of Divn - fed by our 4 Motors for lost times.

41 men & Horses of M.M.P. & S.T.H. 21st Div fed by 63rd Bde Group detached from 64th Bde Group

Detmt Sanl Sec 21st Div fed for today by 62nd Bde. So Grouping of Division is now as follows —

R.A Group..

H Q R A.
94th Bde RFA (Less B Battery).
95th   "      "
96th   "      "
97th   "
3rd Sec D A C.
H Q Coy A S C
14 AA Section
No 2 AA Workshop
Belgian Gendarmes
28th Trench Mortar Battery

8/11/15 (Cont_d).

62_nd Bde Group

H Q 62_nd Bde
 4 Bns.
Pioneer B_n (14_th North_d Fus).
 No 2 Coy ASC.
 CRE
 97_th Field Coy R.E (Less 1 Sec)
 98_th "    "    "  ( " " )
 126_th "   "    "
 No 1 Siege Train "
Det_n San_y Sec 21_st Div

63_rd Bde Group.

H Q 63_rd Bde.
 4 Bns.
 No 3 Coy ASC
 1_st Canadian (H) Battery R.S.A.
 14_th  D L I
 15_th  D L I
Det_n M M P 21_st Div.

64_th Bde Group.

H Q 64_th Bde
Div H Q.
Sanitary Section
D A C

8/11/15 (Cont'd).

1 Sec 97th Field Coy R.E.
Mobile Vet-y Section
Grenade School
Salvage Coy
No 4 Coy A.S.C.
S. T. H. (Div'l Ent'd Troops)
B Battery 94th Bde R.F.A.
Div'l Cyclists
HQ + No1 Sec Signal Coy.
63rd Field Amb.
64th   "    "
65th   "    "
   1 Sec 98th Field Coy R.E.
9th KOYLI
10th  "
D.A.C. (less 1 Sec).


S.S.O. 21st Division

9/11/15

B Battery 94th Bde R.F.A.
fired by R.A. group for
today's consumption, struck
off 64th Bde Group &
this Battery moved to
Armentières on 7th.

R.S. [signature]
S.O. 21st Division, Major

10/11/15.

63rd & 64th Bde (each less 1 Sec.)
fed for today's consumption
by S.O. 63rd Bde leaving
64th Bde Group.
They marched yesterday to
Armentières.

[signature]
A/Q W.
ADQ 21st Division

11/10/15
No change.

BR. Pearce

A.D, 21st Division

12/11/15

Mobile Vet Sec fed by 63rd Bde S.O. for today's consumption. The Remains Section of 63rd Field Amb + remaining section of 64th Field Amb fed by 63rd Bde S.O. for today. The above units moved to Armentières yesterday.

Div HQ + 64th Bde move to Armentières.

[signature]

S.O. 2nd Division
Major

13/11/15

S.T. Horse (Div'l M'td troops), D.A.C. (less 1 Sec) + 65th Field Amb. rationed for today's consumption by 50th Div. These units not having moved to Armentières with remainder of our Div.

Following units of 50th Div taken over for today's feeding by me & attached to groups shown against them.

50th Div R.E. H.Q.  
1st Field Coy R.E.  
2nd " " "  
7th " " "  
42nd Army Troops Coy R.E.  
R.E. Park.  } No 2 Group (62nd Bde)

23rd Trench Mortar Battery  
42nd " " "  
45th " " "  } No 1 Group (R.A. Group)

Mobile Vet Section fed for today by 64th Bde Group again.

51 Trench Mortar Battery fed by R.A. Group having just arrived from _____ J.S.O. 2?th Division

14/11/15

14 NF (Pioneers) Red/for today
by 63rd Bde S.O.
MMG from 63rd Bde Group to
64th Bde Group.
14th & 15th DLI from 63rd to
64th Bde Group
1st Canadian (H) Bty from 63rd
to RA Group
Anti Aircraft Sec & Workshop from
RA to 63rd Bde Group
Sanitary Sec to 64th Bde Group.
(Belgian Gendarmes not avail as 25th Div)
Grouping now as follows –

R.A. Group

Div RA.
94th Bde RFA
95th  "    "
96th  "    "
97th  "    "
No 3 Sec DAC.
1st Canadian (H) Bty.
28th Tr. Mortar Bty
51, 23, 42 & 45   "    "
No 1 Coy Train

14/X/15 (Cont'd).

## 62nd Bde Group.

HQ + 62nd Inf Bde.
21st Div R.E. HQ.
97th Field Coy R.E
98th     "      "
126th    "      "
50th Div R.E. HQ.
1 Field Coy R.E
2   "     "   "
7   "     "   "
42 Army Troops Coy R.E.
R.E. Park
R. Monmouth R.E.
No 2 Coy Train.

## 63rd Bde Group.

HQ + 63rd Inf Bde
63rd Field Coy.
64th    "     "
Pioneers 14th N.F.
14 AA Section
No 2 AA Workshop
No 3 Coy Train

14/11/15 (Cont'd)

64th Bde Group.

HQ + 64th Bde
Div HQ.
2 Signal Coy
Div Cyclists
Mob Vet Sec.
San Sec + D.A.W.
Grenade School
No 4 Coy Train
Px [?]
Div Salvage Coy.

[signature]

Major
S.S.O 21st Division

15/11/15

1st Lincoln Regts & 4th Middlesex Regt both arrived at Armentières last night. They are joining the Division & the 2nd East Yorks & 12th W. Yorks are leaving. Commenced feeding the 2 new Regts (from 3rd Div) for today's consumption. Refilled for them at Bailleul yesterday morning on their march to join us.
Am continuing to feed the 2 old Bns. up to & including consumption 16th. (They marched off this morning to join their new Division)
Refilled for the 2 old regiments for consumption tomorrow at 8 a.m. at PONT DE NIEPPE church.

ADC
S.S.O. 21st Division

16/11/15
No change.

[signature]
SO 21st Division

17/11/15

Nothing unusual to record.

Maj. C. Pearce
I.S.O. 2nd Division

18/11/15

Supply Column loaded this morning with rations they will hold as a reserve. The ordinary fresh rations taken from Pack Train - These are to be exchanged tomorrow morning at CAESTRE for Pres'd Rations -
Supply Section wagons distributed this morning but did not reload at Railhead -
Under this system wagons are empty at night and supplies are consumed the day after they are reloaded at Railhead not 2 days after.

Major
S.D. 21st Division

19/11/15

Reloaded at Rail Head on
G.S. Wagons at 8.45 a.m for
Ra + 62nd Bde Troops -
And at 9.15 a.m for 63rd +
64th Bde Troops. (Having taken
over the lines of 50th Div).

[signature]
Major
A.D 21st Division.

20/11/15

From today all Bread sacks have to be returned. I hand to the S.O. empty sacks for full sacks daily.

RSA.

I.A.O. 3rd Division

21/11/15

23rd Trench Mortar Battery rationed for today's consumption by SSO 50th Divn having left this district yesterday.

[signature]
SSO 21st Division

22/11/15

Nothing unusual to record.

[signature]
S.O. 2ⁿᵈ Division

23/11/15 — 26/11/15

Nothing unusual to record beyond arrival of 7th DLT Det.t which is rationed by me for consumption on 26th until further notice & attached to 63rd Bde Group.

[signature]
S.S.O 21st Division

27/11/15

14 D.L.I. leave 64th Bde on going to 6th Div
1st E. Yorks join from this Division
Commenced rationing the new Regiment from consumption 28th
Rationed the old Regiment today for consumption tomorrow for last time.

R. [signature]
S.S.O. 21st Division

28/11/15 - 30/11/15.

Nothing to report

[signature]
S.S.O. 21st Division Major

From 1/12/15 to 3/12/15

# WAR DIARY
## or
## INTELLIGENCE SUMMARY.
(Erase heading not required.)

Army Form C. 2118.

N.O. 21st Div

Instructions regarding War Diaries and Intelligence Summaries are contained in F.S. Regs., Part II. and the Staff Manual respectively. Title pages will be prepared in manuscript.

| Hour, Date, Place | Summary of Events and Information | Remarks and references to Appendices |
|---|---|---|
| 1/12/15 | Moved for Staff to 141 Rue Nationale PONT DE NIEPPE. Commenced cloth cutting for the Divisi[on] Hotel but have gone up to 3 prs were on 3 [?]. Turned over the Sagan, Salt & Charge Reserve on the Column | |
| 2/12/15 | Nothing to report | |
| 3/12/15 | No oils came up today as Pack Train owing to Staffing arrangements. Drew oils for whole Division from No 1 Field Supply Depot Baren | [signature] |

(73989) W4141—463. 400,000. 9/14. H.&J.Ltd. Forms/C. 2118/10.

# WAR DIARY
## or
## INTELLIGENCE SUMMARY.

Army Form C. 2118.

A.A.O. 21st Div.

| Hour, Date, Place | Summary of Events and Information | Remarks and references to Appendices |
|---|---|---|
| 4/12/15 | Same procedure today as regards oats. Issued oats from reserve on Supply Column replacing from the Granite. Obtained from No. 1 Rail Supply Depôt. Communication chaffs to Division. Communication above 50 tons coal from HOUPLINES. Officers left behind for a former Division. | |
| 5/12/15 | D Battery 97th Bde R.F.A move to join 2nd Canadian Divn. - Returned by me up to 4 including tomorrow's consumption. Loaded up their rations separately on Supply wagons at Rail Head. | |

# WAR DIARY
## or
## INTELLIGENCE SUMMARY.

Army Form C. 2118.

I/O 11th Div.

| Hour, Date, Place | Summary of Events and Information | Remarks and references to Appendices |
|---|---|---|
| 6/12/15 | Departure to 50th Div Area of CRE 50th Div, Nos 1, 2 & 7 Field Cos & R.E. Park. Our Reching 7th & 2nd Coy howitzers for consumption. 8th for lost time - Fed the remainder 10 days for consumption 7th for lost time. | |
| 7/12/15 - 8/12/15 | Nothing to report | |
| 9/12/15 | No 2 Mountain Battery leave this area. Our Reconnaissance duties in connection with this unit therefore cease | |
| 10/12/15 | 181 Tunnelling Coy. R.E. commences motoring item for consumption on hand. Attached to C.R.E. 6 1/2 Division herewith. | W.A.M. |

Army Form C. 2118.

No. 21st DW.

# WAR DIARY
## or
## INTELLIGENCE SUMMARY.
(Erase heading not required.)

Instructions regarding War Diaries and Intelligence Summaries are contained in F.S. Regs., Part II. and the Staff Manual respectively. Title pages will be prepared in manuscript.

| Hour, Date, Place | Summary of Events and Information | Remarks and references to Appendices |
|---|---|---|
| 11/12/15 | Nothing to report | |
| 12/12/15 | Turned over to the Charge to Sapper Column which became damaged over to the road. Capt W.S. Stuart reported futility as SSO from HQ Division. | |
| 13/12/15 - 14/12/15 | Nothing to report | |
| 15/12/15 | Changed our office to Chateau Crew | |
| 16/12/15 | A Battery 95th Bde RFA moves to CAESTRE - led by me to + for 17th often which bed for 50th Div | |

A.P.O. 21 Div.

Army Form C. 2118.

# WAR DIARY
## or
## INTELLIGENCE SUMMARY.
*(Erase heading not required.)*

Instructions regarding War Diaries and Intelligence Summaries are contained in F.S. Regs., Part II and the Staff Manual respectively. Title pages will be prepared in manuscript.

| Hour, Date, Place | Summary of Events and Information | Remarks and references to Appendices |
|---|---|---|
| 17/11/15 — 19/11/15 | Nothing to report | |
| 20/11/15 | 28th Trench Mortar Battery Red Bn 25th Bn for today's consumption. Found one gun & 10 + miscluding 19th Bn. | |
| 21/11/15 | C. Staff of Bde. Nothing to report | |
| 22/11/15 | C. Batt 96th Bde proceeded to NOOTE BOOM - arranged with 9th Bn to attach for rations as from 23rd. | |
| 23/11/15 | Lower Puddings (Kilt-pernen) drawn from Railhead for issue - to be exchanged on 25th. | |

W.A.

A.D.O 21 Div

**WAR DIARY**
or
**INTELLIGENCE SUMMARY**
(Erase heading not required.)

Army Form C. 2118.

| Hour, Date, Place | Summary of Events and Information | Remarks and references to Appendices |
|---|---|---|
| 24/12/15 | C.Batt. 95 Bde RFA moved to EECKE. Arranged that 9th Div. should feed unit as from 26th. (drawn 25th for consumpt. 26th.) | |
| * | Bangr.64 Inft Coal arrived - Saw Contractor M. Deloraque as to providing labour for discharging cargo into divisional jute packing (Filature) | |
| 25/12/15 | Nothing of importance - Enemy shelled Armentières heavily. | |
| 26/12/15 | Nothing of importance - Major R.W. Aylmer left div. for G.H.Q.T.S.C. | |
| 27/12/15 | N° 41 Anti-Aircraft Sec arrived. 63rd bde supply for feeding. Coal discharging from barges (277 tons for 2nd Corps) 21st div shares 70 tons. *Received on 24/12/15 | |
| 28/12/15 | A Batt 96 Bde RFA moved to MOOTE BOOM - transferred for feeding to 9th Div. "C" 96 returned to Div. from rest. | |

Weall

J.V.D. 21 Div.

Army Form C. 2118.

# WAR DIARY
## or
## INTELLIGENCE SUMMARY.
(Erase heading not required.)

Instructions regarding War Diaries and Intelligence Summaries are contained in F.S. Regs., Part II. and the Staff Manual respectively. Title pages will be prepared in manuscript.

| Hour, Date, Place | Summary of Events and Information | Remarks and references to Appendices |
|---|---|---|
| 2/11/15 | Nothing to report; completed discharge of Lord Barry N° 64. Total quantity taken out of her = 2497 tons. (21st Division Supply Column 1261 tons) (res. 21st Divl. Ammunition). | |
| 3/11/15 | Issued one day's supplies ordinary Column. (in reserve) | |

W.H.B. Hunt Capt.
S.S.O. 21 Divn.
3/11/15

Jan. 1st – 31st 1916.   No. 2nd Div.

Army Form C. 2118.

# WAR DIARY
## INTELLIGENCE SUMMARY.
*(Erase heading not required.)*

Instructions regarding War Diaries and Intelligence Summaries are contained in F. S. Regs., Part II. and the Staff Manual respectively. Title pages will be prepared in manuscript.

| Hour, Date, Place | Summary of Events and Information | Remarks and references to Appendices |
|---|---|---|
| 1/1/1916 | Nothing to report | |
| 2/1/1916 | No. 17 Anti-Aircraft Sec. joined Div. – relieved by 2nd Dvl. Trench Army 2nd (Consumption on 3rd) for first time. No Biscuit or Apple Train drawn from CAESTRE. Reported on bad quality of Hay lately, viz: – (Short) | |
| 3/1/16 | No. 41 Anti-Aircraft Sec. left Div. – for 3rd Army – Doullens – Returned upto & including consumption on 6th inst. | |
| 4/1/1916 | Nothing to report – | |
| 5/1/1916 | No. 14 A.A Section moved to STEENWERCK to join III rd Corps. Rationed up to & including consumption on 6th inst. | |
| 6/1/1916 | Nothing to report excepting C Batt. 95 Bde RFA returned from 9th Div. area – rest camp. A Batt. 96 Bde RFA also – | W.O.S. |

# WAR DIARY
## or
## INTELLIGENCE SUMMARY.
(Erase heading not required.)

Army Form C. 2118.

| Hour, Date, Place | Summary of Events and Information | Remarks and references to Appendices |
|---|---|---|
| 7/1/16 | A Batt & B.H.R.T.A. left Div. forced. at EECKE. B Batt & He R.T.A. left Div. Train at MOOTEBOOM (both places in 9th Div. area) | Contractors 10% Pres Wheat at R.H.P. unofficial supply available. |
| 8/1/16 | Nothing to report. | |
| 9/1/16 | Hay received at Railhead at rate of 6 lbs per horse. Forage Ration supplemented by issue of Chaff & Straw (Total 11lb) — Does Mr's Ration from CAESTRE — (none in train) to complete Meal Ration. | |
| 10/1/16 | 6 lbs Hay per horse rec'd from R.H'd — Supplemented forage rations tonight drawing 2lbs per horse (from reserve in supply Colt's), issue of Chaff & Straw in addition — | |
| 11/1/16 | 6 lbs of Hay per horse rec'd from R.H'd. — bal'ce of forage ration made up by issue of chaff & straw. | |

Mars

Army Form C. 2118.

# WAR DIARY
## or
## INTELLIGENCE SUMMARY.
(Erase heading not required.)

Instructions regarding War Diaries and Intelligence Summaries are contained in F.S. Regs., Part II. and the Staff Manual respectively. Title pages will be prepared in manuscript.

| Hour, Date, Place | Summary of Events and Information | Remarks and references to Appendices |
|---|---|---|
| 12/1/16. | 6 Bn. of Hay/s horse issued for R.H. Balance of horse ration made up of some of chaff & straw. | |
| 13/1/16. | 6 lbs of Hay/s horse issued for R.H. Ration supplemented by some of chaff & straw. New M.V. station open where up next station: ran a train from CAESTRE. | |
| 14/1/16. | Hay deficiency made up by issue of straw & chaff. Attended conference S.S.Os. at 2nd Army H.Q. | |
| 15/1/16 | Hay again deficient, arrangement made to continue chaff issue | |
| 16/1/16 | — " — | |
| 17/1/16 | "B" Batt. 96th Bde. returned. Hay deficient, chaff issued to complete ration. | |
| 18/1/16 | Hay deficient arrangements made to continue chaff in lieu. | |
| 19/1/16. | "B" Batt. 95th Bde. returned. Rice received in lieu of biscuit. Hay deficient, chaff issued in lieu. | [signature] |

Army Form C. 2118.

No 21 Divn

# WAR DIARY
## or
## INTELLIGENCE SUMMARY.
(Erase heading not required.)

Instructions regarding War Diaries and Intelligence Summaries are contained in F.S. Regs., Part II. and the Staff Manual respectively. Title pages will be prepared in manuscript.

| Hour, Date, Place | Summary of Events and Information | Remarks and references to Appendices |
|---|---|---|
| 20/1/16 | Hay as before. Staff moved to wake up in tin. des Vaux. | |
| 21/1/16 | — Ditto — Ditto — | |
| 22/1/16 | Ditto — Ditto — About 50% only of Pork Meat on train | |
| 23/1/16 | Ditto - Ditto - 6000lbs Pork Meat only for Div'n = 33 %. | |
| 24/1/16 | Ditto Ditto.. Aft 33 1/3 %. Freshmeat only Rec'd at R.H. | |
| 25/1/16 | Ditto Ditto - Fresh meat & bread 75% - | |
| 26/1/16 | Ditto Ditto - — " — | MODO |

Army Form C. 2118.

# WAR DIARY
## or
## INTELLIGENCE SUMMARY.
(Erase heading not required.)

| Hour, Date, Place | Summary of Events and Information | Remarks and references to Appendices |
|---|---|---|
| 27/1/16 | Hay 616 per horse contacted Received - Chaff + Straw to Mature + return to Park Meat + Bread. Normal percentage received - Requis.? 1,850 K Potatoes Steamwick Saft. | |
| 28/1/16 | Hay 6lb per horse at Railhead - Rat.n completed by issue of Chaff + Straw. Fresh Meat Rations 75%. | |
| 29/1/16 | — Ditto — Ditto — | |
| 30/1/16 | — Ditto — Ditto — | |
| 31/1/16 | — Ditto — Ditto — | |

Apl recd 29th 1916

Army Form C. 2118.

# WAR DIARY
## or
## INTELLIGENCE SUMMARY.
(Erase heading not required.)

I.O. 21st Div.

| Place | Hour, Date | Summary of Events and Information | Remarks and references to Appendices |
|---|---|---|---|
| PONT MEPPE | 1 Feby 1916 | 6lbs Hay recd from R.H.D. - Inag. ration made up by issue of chaff & straw - Meat Wheat 7/7lb | |
| | 2 Feby 1916 | Ditto - ditto - | |
| | 3 Feby 1916 | Hay 10lbs for Horses H.D., M.D. rations 6lbs - In the letter, chaff & straw to complete ration, for Horses H.D. chaff ration only. | |
| | 4 Feby 1916 | Ditto Ditto Ditto - Ditto - Half Company of 4th Labour Batt'n attd to Division from this date - returned by rail - | |
| | 5 Feb 1916 | 10 lbs Hay for Horses H.D. loaded at Railhead; other animals 6 lbs; shortage of bulk ration been received in lieu - | |
| | 6 Feb 1916 | 10 lbs Hay for H.D. & Horses. 6lbs for others recd at Railhead. No tadles for Rations of Wheat Biscuit - | Wall |

Army Form C. 2118.

HQ 21st Div

# WAR DIARY
## or
## INTELLIGENCE SUMMARY.

(Erase heading not required.)

Instructions regarding War Diaries and Intelligence Summaries are contained in F.S. Regs., Part II. and the Staff Manual respectively. Title pages will be prepared in manuscript.

| Hour, Date, Place | Summary of Events and Information | Remarks and references to Appendices |
|---|---|---|
| 7-2-1916 | Hay Ration 10.1b pm Horses MD. - 6lbs pm Other classes of Animals. Bread/Meat 75%. | |
| 8-2-1916 | Ditto - ditto - 100 Frenchmen drawn | |
| | from MAESTRE | |
| 9-2-1916 | — Ditto Ditto — Shortage of Rations Ration made up by additional quantity of bacon. | |
| 10-2-1916 | Hay ration 10lb pm Horses MD. - 6lb pm other classes of animals - Bread/Meat 75% - 1st Detachment of/ 9th Labour Bat'n. relieved by Pioneers from 25th Div. (125 men) | |
| 11-2-1916 | Hay ration for MD & Horse 10lb - for Other animals - 6lb - Bread/Meat 75%. | |
| 12-2-1916 | — ditto ditto — No 35 Anti-Aircraft Section joined div". these rations for first time - | M.A.L. |

# WAR DIARY
## or
## INTELLIGENCE SUMMARY.
(Erase heading not required.)

Army Form C. 2118.

HQ 21st Div

| Hour, Date, Place | Summary of Events and Information | Remarks and references to Appendices |
|---|---|---|
| 13/1/16 | St. Saken half rations returned to Division. Fresh Meat issued. Hay ration again 10 lbs per animal. Fresh Meat 75%. Prices 11,890 Rats P.Meat issued from Supply Column under Cops orders. Distribution to be made later at various Defences & Supplying Points. | |
| 14/1/16 | Hay ration 10 lbs per animal. Fresh Meat & Meat 75% | |
| 15/1/16 | Ditto — ditto — | |
| 16/1/16 | Ditto — ditto — Allocation of Reserve Rations for defensive localities as follows — | Quantity issued = 11,890 ₹ P.Meat & Biscuit. 2nd Inps G. 532/40/6  24/1/16 |
| |                P.Meat   Biscuit. | |
| | Salvage Coy =   832     871 | |
| | 62nd Bde     =   1,344    1,340 | |
| |                   100      100 | |
| |                 8,128    8,107 | |
| |                 1,600    1,608 | |
| | 63rd Bde     =   11,904   11,926 | |
| |                    100      100 | |
| |                 12,004   12,026 | |
| 19/1/16 | Hay ration 10 lbs per animal — Fresh Meat 75%. — 4th Afr. cav. Howimal deleted from ration issued to reserve supply Column. Total for deficiency thus caused by drawing 2 lbs per head on 11/1/16. | Walk |

# WAR DIARY
## or
## INTELLIGENCE SUMMARY.

(Erase heading not required.)

Army Form C. 2118.

A.D. 21st - Div 2.

| Hour, Date, Place | Summary of Events and Information | Remarks and references to Appendices |
|---|---|---|
| 18/1/16 | Hay ration normal - 10lb per animal - Meat/Bread 75% | |
| 19/1/16 | " | |
| 20/1/16 | " — 4th Hay reduced to supply, column broke up on proceed — opening convoy through drawing 14lb per head on 21/1/16 | |
| 21/1/16 | Normal conditions - Nothing to report - 7000 iron Rations drawn from Castre for defensive breaking of division. | |
| 22/1/16 — 23/1/16 | Pea Soup & Rum issued extensively to all troop units whole ration; → 5760 Pkest } returned by supply 3500 Biscuit } Col. to R.S.D. | Other units 1 pint of Rum & Plum Rum |
| 24/1/16 | " | " |
| 25/1/16 | — 75% Fresh Meat & Bread from 23rd | |

Wells

# WAR DIARY
## or
## INTELLIGENCE SUMMARY

(Erase heading not required.)

Army Form C. 2118.

No 21st Div.

| Hour, Date, Place | Summary of Events and Information | Remarks and references to Appendices |
|---|---|---|
| 26/1/16 | H.Q. for 1084 Arrivals returned to staff. Officers to take up Reserve of Hay (1 day) held - Leaving girths in all Perked. Fresh Meat & Bread 75%. Pea Soup & Rum as before. | |
| 27/1/16 | Fresh Meat & Bread 75%. Nothing to report. Pea Soup & Rum as before. | |
| 28/1/16 | — " — Pea Soup & Rum as before. | |
| 29/1/16 | Fresh Meat & Bread 75%. Pea Soup rotun. 1 ball men of Division Half Rum issue to Head Units. Half Rum issue to other heavy divs cancelled by A/Cpt. | |
| X | Of the 7000 Iron Rations drawn for defensive localities an allocation has been made as follows :— <br> 62nd Bde. 900 <br> 63rd Bde. 1800 <br> 64th Bde. 2480 <br> Total 5780 <br> thus leaving on hand 1820 = | |

M.A. Stuart
Capt.
G.S.O. 21st Div.

LAC SSO 21 DW Trans Vol 7

1916 MAR

## WAR DIARY
## INTELLIGENCE SUMMARY.

(Erase heading not required.)

Army Form C. 2118.

1/3/16 - 31/3/16

L.O. 21st Div —

| Hour, Date, Place | Summary of Events and Information | Remarks and references to Appendices |
|---|---|---|
| PONT NIEPPE | | |
| 1 March 1916 | Fresh Meat & Bread 75%. 1000 lb Rice shot & 120 lb Hay shot in train. 1 Turkey food raised to ANNEXE station for the first time. | |
| 2 March 1916 | Orders received from 2nd Army to issue 1 Extra Iron ration to all ranks. This is additional to the 2 drawn on 24/1/16. Much, distribution to be noted later. CAESTRE. every man in the division will be in possession of an extra iron ration. | 11,570 drawn from |
| 3 March 1916 | Nothing to report. | |
| 4 March 1916 | 62, 63, 64 & Machine Gun Corps joined division. Strength 446 men, 162 horses, rations drawn for first time. | |
| 5 March 1916 | Nothing to report | |
| 6 March 1916 | — " — | |
| 7 March | No. 19 + No 35 Anti aircraft sec. left division — Fresh Meat / Bread 70 %. Reserve/Coal 60 tons — | W.C.H. |

# WAR DIARY
## or
## INTELLIGENCE SUMMARY.

*(Erase heading not required.)*

Army Form C. 2118.

1 Co 21st Div.

Instructions regarding War Diaries and Intelligence Summaries are contained in F.S. Regs., Part II. and the Staff Manual respectively. Title pages will be prepared in manuscript.

| Hour, Date, Place | Summary of Events and Information | Remarks and references to Appendices |
|---|---|---|
| PONT MEPPE | | |
| 8/3/16 | No. 21 Anti-Aircraft Batty joined div & drew supplies for first time. Strength 9 Other- 182 Tunneling Co RE left division for III d Army - Visited DADOS 2nd Army H.Q. | |
| 9/3/16 | No. 1 Canadian Tram. S. Co. joined division & drew rations for first time - Strength 350 min. 51 French Motor Baty returned to their div. Fresh Meat & Bread 60% Issued rations to a group comprising following units :— 21st Div: Ammn Col — Refilling point H.Q. 2 South Irish Horse at METEREN. 65 Field Ambulance X 22 a 2·2 Sheet 27. | |
| 10/3/16 | Fresh Meat & Bread 60%. Strength of division 20,266 - Animals 5917 | |
| 11/3/16 | Fresh Meat & Bread 75% - Nothing special to report | |
| 12/3/16 | ditto | Nill |

Army Form C. 2118.

# WAR DIARY
## or
## INTELLIGENCE SUMMARY.
(Erase heading not required.)

S.J.O. 21st Division.

| Hour, Date, Place | Summary of Events and Information | Remarks and references to Appendices |
|---|---|---|
| PONT NIEPPE | | |
| 13/3/16 | Rgn Fresh Meat & Bread. Nothing Special to report. | |
| 14/3/16 | — " — — " — | 2nd Army Field Survey Unit strength 35 all ranks joined division & drew rations for first time. |
| 15/3/16 | Fresh Rations 70%. | |
| 16/3/16 | Fresh Rations 75%. Visited 17 Div Train & discussed arrangements for relief of 21st Div. & Supply matters. Also 21st Div. Supply Column. | |
| 17/3/16 | Fresh Rations 75%. Completed Supply arrangements for divisional move into Rest area | |
| 18/3/16 | Fresh Rhns 80%. Divisional Move into Rest Area commenced 1st D.I.J & 10 KOYLI + Attchd. 4 Coy Train moved to La-Crêche enroute for OUTTERSTEENE. | N.A.H. |

Army Form C. 2118.

# WAR DIARY
## or
## INTELLIGENCE SUMMARY.
*(Erase heading not required.)*

21st Div.

| Hour, Date, Place | Summary of Events and Information | Remarks and references to Appendices |
|---|---|---|
| 19/3/16 | Fresh Ratio 75%. | Divisional relief proceeds, 64th Bde employed. 4 Coy Tram moved to OUTTERSTENE. |
| 20/3/16 | Fresh Rations 80%. | " Half coy of dried Vegetables issued to Units. |
| 21/3/16 | Fresh Rations 75%. | " Special dried Vegetables drawn from Railhead. 3 Coy Tram moved to STRAZEELE. |
| 22/3/16 | Fresh Rations 80%. | " 4 Coy Tram moved to LA CRECHE. |
| 23/3/16 | Fresh Rations 80%. | " H.Q. Coy moved to PRADELLES. |
| 24/3/16 | Fresh Rations 75%. | " |
| STRAZEELE 25/3/16 | Fresh Rations 80%. | Divisional Relief completed. |

Army Form C. 2118.

# WAR DIARY
## or
## INTELLIGENCE SUMMARY.
(Erase heading not required.)

A.D.O. 1st Div.

Instructions regarding War Diaries and Intelligence Summaries are contained in F.S. Regs., Part II. and the Staff Manual respectively. Title pages will be prepared in manuscript.

| Hour, Date, Place | Summary of Events and Information | Remarks and references to Appendices |
|---|---|---|
| STRAZEELE 26/3/16 | 80% Fresh Rations - Orders received for division to join 4th Army - first entrainment to commence on March 30th at 9 a.m. - decided that CASSEL, BAILLEUL, & GODAERSVELDE be used for the purpose - | |
| 27/3/16 | 80% Free Rations - Proceeded to AMIENS to arrange supply details for division | |
| 28/3/16 | AT AMIENS - Capt Newton acting as A.D.O to Division in my absence. Visited proposed Corps area - | |
| 29/3/16 | AT AMIENS - Visited XIII Corps H.Q. | |
| 30/3/16 | AT AMIENS - Visited XIII Corps H.Q. + A.D.A.T. IV Army | |
| 31/3/16 | AT DAOURS. H.Q. of Train ; Division starts detraining from IInd Army area. Drew supplies from Railhead at MERICOURT L'ABBÉ for first issue. Brigades (Bns) as follows 2 bns 3 Co 4 Co H.Q.C. 1st to Corps } RAINNEVILLE RAMPONROT COISY BUSSY DAOURS. | |

(73969) W4141-463. 400,000. 9/14. H.&J.Ltd. Forms/C. 2118/10.

April 1st – 30th 1916.

Vol 8
L 16
Army Form C. 2118.

# WAR DIARY
## or
## INTELLIGENCE SUMMARY.
(Erase heading not required.)

G.S.O. 21st Div.

| Hour, Date, Place | Summary of Events and Information | Remarks and references to Appendices |
|---|---|---|
| DAOURS | | |
| 1/4/16 | Concentration of Division from IIIrd Army continues – Has pad of supplies from MÉRICOURT | |
| 2/4/16 | —"— —"— —"— Concentration of Division in XIII Corps now completed – Fresh Meat ration 75% – Strength of translated | |
| 3/4/16 | Fresh Meat ration 75% – heavy spells rain, prevai a lien of Fresh vegetables for 9th ration CCS also quantity of clarifying butter | |
| 4/4/16 | Fresh meat ration 75% – | "A" Batt. 94th Bde moved to Support lines & temply attached to 7th Div |
| 5/4/16 | Fresh meat 60% – Bread 75% – | |
| 6/4/16 | Fresh meat 60%, Bread 75% – Half of C/97 RFA moved to MÉAULTE | 1st Am Sub-park in LA NEUVILLE. 64th Bde moved from LA NEUVILLE |
| 7/4/16 | —"— —"— —"— 1% —"— | 63rd Bde moved from ALLONVILLE to BUIRE. 9th Bde Amm Col moved to VILLE |
| 8/4/16 | 62nd Bde moved from COISY etc to BONNAY area. DAOURS to VILLE. Hq RA | Divisional GRENADE School opened at LA NEUVILLE. |

Army Form C. 2118.

# WAR DIARY
## or
## INTELLIGENCE SUMMARY.

(Erase heading not required.)

S.Co. 34th Divn.

| Hour, Date, Place | Summary of Events and Information | Remarks and references to Appendices |
|---|---|---|
| JADOURS | | |
| 9/4/16 | Fresh meat 55%, Pres Meat 45%, Bread 75%. — Changed fresh meat for preserved. Bryate people — Preparing to drawing at Railhead by Horse Transport. | a. 63 - 164 & |
| 10/4/16 | Fresh Meat 60%, Pres. 40%. — Bread 75%. — Drew Rations from Railhead Pr.63 & 164 & Rles by Horse Transport — Other supper by Service. A/94 & R.F.A. returned to this 2 from 7th Divn. | |
| 11/4/16 | Fresh Meat 55%, Pres 45%. — Bread 75%. — | |
| 12/4/16 | — " — — " — 25% Rice issued in lieu of Biscuit. | |
| 13/4/16 | — " — — " — 3 oz Dried Fruit in lieu of Jam. 2 oz " " " " Dried Veg. | |
| 14/4/16 | — " — — " — Bread 60%, Biscuit 40% — | |
| 15/4/16 | Drew supplies by Horse Transport from Railhead at Henry MERCOURT for whole Divn. Fresh Meat 60%, preserved 40%. — Dried Fruit & Dried Vegetables issued (2 and 3). | |

Army Form C. 2118.

# WAR DIARY
## or
## INTELLIGENCE SUMMARY.
(Erase heading not required.)

No. 21st Div.

Instructions regarding War Diaries and Intelligence Summaries are contained in F.S. Regs., Part II. and the Staff Manual respectively. Title pages will be prepared in manuscript.

| Hour, Date, Place | Summary of Events and Information | Remarks and references to Appendices |
|---|---|---|
| DAOURS 16/4/16 | Change of Railhead to HEILLY. Men supplies for division by Horse Transport. Fresh Meat 60%, Pres. veg 70%, Bread 75% | |
| RIBEMONT 17/4/16 | MEAT Fresh Rations 60%, Bread 75% - Nothing of importance to note. | |
| 18/4/16 | Fresh Meat 70%, Pres. 20% - Meat 70%. | |
| 19/4/16 | Drew 10,860 Iron Rations for 64th & 63rd Bdes. remaining components of Ration drawn at R.H.& as usual. | Authority XIII Corps G/c 993. 10/4/16. In pursuance handing over Iron Ration a/c of Res. Park & those in the men. |
| 20/4/16 | Drew 11,000 Iron Rations for Div. Troops, Army, 62nd Bde, 63rd Bde, 64th Bde. Total quantity drawn = 19,020 lb = 21,860 - Troops concerned on the march replaced it by this issue. | Supply Column. The Iron Ration carried |
| 21/4/16 | Packhorses short of over 9000 rations of Meat & Biscuits - Obtained these from Corps CORBIE - otherwise nothing to report. Pres. Meat 69%, Biscuit 68%, Bread 16%, Rice 16%. | |
| 22/4/16 | Fresh Meat 70%, Bread 70% - Nothing special to report. | Maitl. |

(73989) W14141—463. 400,000. 9/14. H.&J.Ltd. Forms/C. 2118/10.

# WAR DIARY
## or
## INTELLIGENCE SUMMARY.
(Erase heading not required.)

Army Form C. 2118.

62nd Div.

| Hour, Date, Place | Summary of Events and Information | Remarks and references to Appendices |
|---|---|---|
| RIBEMONT | | |
| 23/4/16 | Fresh Meat 60%, Bread 75%. Nothing Special to report. | |
| 24/4/16 | — " — | — " — |
| 25/4/16 | Fresh Meat 65% Bread 75%. | |
| 26/4/16 | — " — | — " — |
| 27/4/16 | Fresh Meat 60% Bread 75%. | |
| 28/4/16 | — " — | Am. Bat. 9th t Bde moved to Buire att. 64th Bde & rch. |
| 29/4/16 | — " — | |
| 30/4/16 | — " — | Nothing Special to Report |

Allistis Pentin Cup?
Lt Col. CSO 21st Div.

May 1st – 31st 1916.

Army Form C. 2118.

# WAR DIARY
## INTELLIGENCE SUMMARY.
*(Erase heading not required.)*

S.S.O. 21st Divn.

| Hour, Date, Place | Summary of Events and Information | Remarks and references to Appendices |
|---|---|---|
| RIBEMONT 1/5/16. | B Coy. 17th N.F.s returned to 64th Bde. | |
| 2/5/16. | 1st twelve feet 3 63rd Bde. 104th & twelve & 8th Lincolns fed 62nd Bde. & C. 97th Bde fed 3rd 64th Bde moved to LA NEUVILLE 63rd Bde. moved to RIBEMONT. A.B.C.D. Bn Rfts 96 fed f 64 | |
| 3/5/16. | H.Q. 62nd Bn. Train moved to RUIRE. Unit at DOAURS train | |
| 4/5/16. | & 62nd Bde. | |
| 5/5/16. | Did Tmpts. Bde started camp at RUIRE. Train are R.A. & Divl Tmts units for 63rd & 64th Bde. | |
| 6/5/16. | nothing to report. | |
| 7/5/16. | H.Q. & Ambl. 96th fed 8 S.O. Divl Tmts. | |
| 8/5/16. | *5210 Tmts. Return shown for O/r Rgt. to the 1st place Oliveness. 1 Bn. 17th NF 1 fed f. 1 bn & twelve Rfts. 178th Twelve 16 fed 5 64th Bde. | (*constructing underneath of Priest + ground mats) caused by unusual parking of carts. |
| 9/5/16 | Visited XV Corps HQ. Bry Gen 2nd supply railway certain proposals for supplies in connection with defence trackite spots in the line – fresh rations received – Meat 60% Bread 80%. | M.L. |

Army Form C. 2118.

# WAR DIARY
## or
## INTELLIGENCE SUMMARY.
*(Erase heading not required.)*

A.A.O. 21st Div.

Instructions regarding War Diaries and Intelligence Summaries are contained in F. S. Regs., Part II. and the Staff Manual respectively. Title pages will be prepared in manuscript.

| Hour, Date, Place | Summary of Events and Information | Remarks and references to Appendices |
|---|---|---|
| RIBEMONT 10/5/16 | Nothing to report | |
| 11/5/16 12/5/16 | — " — | |
| 13/5/16 | Inspection 60%. N.T. 15%. Meat 75%. 64th Fd. relieved by 62nd. 10 Tons Potatoes drawn from F.S.D. at CORBIE'S authority DDS17 wire S1077 of 13/5/16 | |
| 14/5/16 | Fish Meat 50% - Pres: 20% - M.V. 30% - | |
| 15/5/16 | Anti Presentation 60%. Meat 75%. | |
| 16/5/16 | Fish Ration 60%. Meat 75%. Above 6 Coys of Attached from HERCOURT. N.L.L. | |
| 17/5/16 | — " — A/99 meat from AMIENS (64th Bde.) to DERNANCOURT (Div Troops Supply) | |
| 18/5/16 | 8/120 lbs Potatoes rec. from Railhead. | |
| 19/5/16 | — " — | hill |

Army Form C. 2118.

# WAR DIARY
## or
## INTELLIGENCE SUMMARY.
(Erase heading not required.)

A.D. 21st DIVISION

| Place | Hour, Date | Summary of Events and Information | Remarks and references to Appendices |
|---|---|---|---|
| RIBEMONT | | Promoted Temp Major Sarjate 11/5/16 | The Company of 6 Mules |
| | 19/5/16 | Fresh Rations 60%. 75% Meat. 10% Rice, 15% Biscuit. Oat fed by 6th Rideshop (40 pieces) this went. | |
| from DAOURS | 20/5/16 | Bread 75%. Fresh Rhin 70 60%. Full issue of Potatoes full supply (1939 lbs) Joined 3rd Troops front line 64 Mule pump at LANEUVILLE. Coto charroel Fuel Wood Pro rata. | "Whet 97 the RFFA Requested 8000 ft of grease |
| | 21/5/16 | Detachment of D.A.C. 103 Men & 172 E.D. Horses & Mules proceeded to ABBEVILLE. Fresh Rations 60%. Nothing on a Train. Drew 70 Salts from CORBIE Meat 25%. | Fresh meat all Mutton. Drew 70 Salts from CORBIE |
| | 22/5/16 | 63rd B.A. relieved by 64th. Fresh Rhin 60%. No butter on pack train. Meat 75%. Drew 2000 Pres't Ration, Milk, Butter, Eggs, Brandy from CORBIE for 63rd & 64th & 66th Field Amb. & Belliea a Reserve. Received 10 Ton Potatoes from 3 Pulot Supply Dept CANAPLES. | |
| | 23/5/16 | Usual preparations Fresh Rhin received. Also 15 potatoes for men. Drew 30000 Soda Tablets from CORBIE a divisional reserve. | Replacement all Mutton |
| | 24/5/16 | Nothing to report. No.1 remaining Sec of D.A.C. at DAOURS moved up to DERANCOURT 900 lbs Potatoes recd from pack train, also Bread Train in lieu of Jam. | Fresh Meat all Mutton |
| | 25/5/16 | Nothing to report | |
| | 26/5/16 | Fresh Rations 60%. Meat 75%. Potatoes full issue. Half frozen meat dry veg. No V. | Half frozen meat issued Potato |

(73989) W4141-463. 400,000. 9/14. H.&J.Ltd. Forms/C. 2118/10.

# WAR DIARY
## or
## INTELLIGENCE SUMMARY.
*(Erase heading not required.)*

Army Form C. 2118.

No. 2nd Division

| Hour, Date, Place | Summary of Events and Information | Remarks and references to Appendices |
|---|---|---|
| RIDEMONT 27/5/16 | Drew 10,000 Rbs of Onions from No 3 Field Supply Depot — CANAPLES — 9,900 lbs Potatoes drawn at Railhead — Usual proportion of fresh meat & bread. | |
| 28/5/16 | Fresh Meat 60%, Bread 75%. Substituting other half rations by 2 ozs M&V per man. | |
| 29/5/16 | Ditto — Ditto. Wing of 7th K.W.Kent at CORBIE relieved by Company 6th N.Staffs., B.Hd. of 18th Div. Substituted a bn. iron Group Pn rations | |
| 30/5/16 | Fresh Meat 60%, Bacon 20%. Balance made up by 2 ozs M&V per man. 9,864 lbs Potatoes rcd. from Railhead | |
| 31/5/16 | As on 30th. Potatoes 99.50 lbs received from Railhead. Usual proportions fresh meat & bread. | |

M. A. Hunt Maj.
S.S.O. 2nd Div.

June 1st – 30th 1916.

Army Form C. 2118.

A.O. 21st Division

# WAR DIARY
## INTELLIGENCE SUMMARY.
(Erase heading not required.)

Instructions regarding War Diaries and Intelligence Summaries are contained in F.S. Regs., Part II. and the Staff Manual respectively. Title pages will be prepared in manuscript.

| Hour, Date, Place | Summary of Events and Information | Remarks and references to Appendices |
|---|---|---|
| RIBEMONT | | |
| 1/6/1916 | Fresh Meat 60%. M&V 15%. Bread 75%. Potatoes 10.057 lb. | |
| 2/6/16 | – " – " – Port & Beans (in tins) 10%, Bread 75%. Party of 19th Cheshire Regt. issued 76 bones. | |
| | Rationed today for first time. | |
| 3/6/16 | Nothing to report. 60% Fresh Meat, 75% Bread | |
| 4/6/16 | 2190 lbs Dried Veg. recd from Railhead – Usual proportion of Fresh Meat issued. Turned over to fatigue party. Kept as reserve on Supply Column. | |
| | Bread 75% Fresh Meat 60% | |
| 5/6/16 | Units drawing rations for the first time – : RAILHEAD removed to MÉRICOURT – 34th + 38th Siege Batts. 112th & 2 Coys H.A.; 125th & 1730th Heavy Batts; 144th Siege Batt. – all attached to Divisional Troop Supply. | |
| 6/6/16 | Fresh Meat 60% Bread 75%. Strength of dusrn = 21316 men. Animals 5605. | |
| 7/6/16 | Fresh Meat 60% Bread 70% Dried Fruit 4031 lb. Potatoes 8560 lb. | |
| 8/6/16 | Usual percentage of Fresh Rations – 8600 lb Potatoes recd from Railhead | |

Army Form C. 2118.

A.S.C. 71st Div.

# WAR DIARY
or
## INTELLIGENCE SUMMARY.
(Erase heading not required.)

Instructions regarding War Diaries and Intelligence Summaries are contained in F. S. Regs., Part II and the Staff Manual respectively. Title pages will be prepared in manuscript.

| Hour, Date, Place | Summary of Events and Information | Remarks and references to Appendices |
|---|---|---|
| RIBEMONT 9/6/16 | Company of 7th Bedfords at Corbie relieved by 9th Suffolks of 71st Div. 18 MA - 24 KD & 26 Mules - drew rations from here for first time. 8332 lbs Potatoes issued from R.H.d | Strength 928 men horses |
| 10/6/16 | 12th Siege Batty RGA drew rations for the 1st time. 78th Bty RE  — " —  F Co, 2 Half Special RE  — " — (from 17th Div.) Usual proportion of Fresh meat & Bread. Drew 30,000 Toda Tablets from troops CURRIE as abnormal issue | |
| 11/6/16 | 7 Yorks Hames (17 Div Pioneers) 536 men drew rations for 1st time. 1st Canadian Hy Batty   — " —   35th Heavy Bath RGA   — " —   Fresh Mutton 60% issued 75%. — Potatoes 9,360 lbs - | Troops att: K 21 Divs. |
| 12/6/16 | Nothing to report | |
| 13/6/16 | Usual percentage of Fresh meat & Bread, potatoes 9762 lbs  — " —   — " —   potatoes 9960 lbs | |
| 14/6/16 | Dried fruit in lieu of Jam — " — Improved Iron Ration (P.Meat, Biscuit, Jam + Oxo) Placed in Reserve at Queens. Redoubt. (Div Dump) | [signature] |

Army Form C. 2118.

# WAR DIARY
## or
## INTELLIGENCE SUMMARY.
(Erase heading not required.)

Instructions regarding War Diaries and Intelligence Summaries are contained in F.S. Regs., Part II. and the Staff Manual respectively. Title pages will be prepared in manuscript.

F.P.O. 21st Div.

| Place | Hour, Date | Summary of Events and Information | Remarks and references to Appendices |
|---|---|---|---|
| KIRSENDON | 15/6/16 | Fresh meat 60%.  Bread 75%. - Potatoes 9760 lbs.  Rice 25%. - Left half of 1st Can. Hy Batt. & R.H.A. of 67th Siege Batt. returning for 1st time. - Feeding strength of division 24,540 men. Animals 6143 - | |
|  | 16/6/16 | Usual proportion of fresh meat & bread. Potatoes 9760 lbs. Men 24,764. Animals 6238. | |
|  | 17/6/16 | 51st Heavy Batty. R.G.A. arrived & drew rations for 1st time. Strength 165 men. Half of 67th Siege Batt. R.G.A arrived, strength not known at present. Usual proportion of fresh meat & bread. - Potatoes 10,000 lbs. | |
|  | 18/6/16 | 97th Siege Batt R.G.A. drew rations for 1st time. Strength 152 men - 3 days reserve rations drawn in by portion of all artillery, divisional and attached heavy & siege batteries. - | |
|  | 19/6/16 | 8/Suffolks, 14th Cheshire, 7th Borders, 78th Co R.E. returned to their divisions rations up to 20th inst - Usual proportion of fresh meat & bread. Potatoes 4,800 lbs. | |
|  | 20/6/16 | 12th Siege Batty. left divisional area being replaced by 97th Siege Batt. R.G.A. - Usual proportion of fresh meat & bread. - Potatoes 15,720 lbs. - 216 Army Troops Co R.E. drew rations for 1st time. | |
|  | 21/6/16 | Nothing to report. - 10,000 lbs potatoes received from railhead. - | |

(73989) W4141-463. 400,000. 9/14. H.&J.Ltd. Forms/C. 2118/10.

Army Form C. 2118.

# WAR DIARY
## or
## INTELLIGENCE SUMMARY.
(Erase heading not required.)

A.D. 21st Div

| Place | Hour, Date | Summary of Events and Information | Remarks and references to Appendices |
|---|---|---|---|
| RIBEMONT | 22/6/16 | All heavy siege batteries XV Corps N.A. left division for Corps Troops, their rations in consumption 23rd. Issued 9/10 of yesterday's Bread - Supply train send by Traffic Officer to NEUILLY in error. After delay train located supplies there. | |
| | 23/6/16 | Loaded at MÉRICOURT as usual. Issued a 9/10 Rum Ration of rats to all first line, field ambce. Reserve horses = 4895 in No. - 7th Yorks Manco (Pioneers) for returned to 17th div. rationed for consumption 24th. | |
| | 24/6/16 | Bombardment of enemy's line commenced at Noon. | |
| | 25/6/16 | " continued - Drew 6408 two places, 130 WO Horses from Corbie. | |
| | 26/6/16 | " " | Issued 3 days rations to all RE, Field Ambulance and Trench Mortars - Rum issued to Artillery, RE & Inf. Drew 300 gallons Rum from Corbie. |
| | 27/6/16 | " " | 2 days rations issued to 62nd Bde; to 2 Bn & M.G.C & 63rd & 64th Bdes. Drew 4062 Rtns from Supply Col. Reserve. |
| | 28/6/16 | " " | 2 days rations issued to Divl Troops front, all Artillery, 1 day to pay to all there except gr. Pde RFA. 133 G.S.T RE left division - Runtimes of Infy & Artillery, RE & Trench parties of Ambulance - Meats |
| Drew supplies from 2 am. PackTrain amended to 20% Bread & FreshMeat 80% Pres d Biscuit | | | |

Army Form C. 2118.

A.O. 91 Div

# WAR DIARY
or
## INTELLIGENCE SUMMARY.
(Erase heading not required.)

| Hour, Date, Place | Summary of Events and Information | Remarks and references to Appendices |
|---|---|---|
| RIBEMONT 29/6/16 | Draw from R.H? at 2 a.m. 1st Coy Aux Transport Co. drew rations for full train 90 men & 81 horses. Fresh Meat 30%. Pres. Meat 30%. Bis? 70%. Drew at Railhead by Supply Column. 2 days rations issued to R.E, Field Ambulance & French Motor Units. Rum issue as before. | |
| 30/6/16 | Drew at R.H. at 2 a.m. 80% Biscuit + P. Meat. Drew 2680 lb, Glasso 252 tins. Rum issue as before. Animals 57+20. Strength 21,389 | W.O.O.S.(?) wef 6/6 A.O. 21st Div |

Army Form C. 2118.

# WAR DIARY
## INTELLIGENCE SUMMARY.
(Erase heading not required.)

110  21st Div.

Instructions regarding War Diaries and Intelligence Summaries are contained in F.S. Regs., Part II. and the Staff Manual respectively. Title pages will be prepared in manuscript.

| Place | Hour, Date, Place | Summary of Events and Information | Remarks and references to Appendices |
|---|---|---|---|
| RIBEMONT | 1/7/16 | 21st Div (63rd Inf Bde) attacked enemy positions after intense artillery preparation. - Bombardment continued. Inf Bde Railhead at 2 a.m. - 80% Bread + Biscuit. 1334 lbs Potatoes. Rumours astopre. | |
| | 2/7/16 | Bombardment still continuing. Casualties incurred, the number of officers &c. (800 inf 63rd Bde 4200 in 63rd.) Bombardment shelling continue. Rumours made astopre. | |
| | 3/7/16 | Interview Bn complete rations. Number drawn - men = 15963 animals = 5377. 80% Field Bread + Biscuit. Rumours astopre. - Battle progressing - 21st Div. congratulated by Army Commander on its success. Estimated casualties 6500. lorries midnight. | |
| | 4/7/16 | Issued 1 a.m. - Drawn water a.s of ration ( artillery excepted) + moved to area round Allery air frame. Rations drawn 15983. - Train HQ at Picquigny. - Div HQ at BELLOY-SUR-SOMME. | |
| | 5/7/16 PICQUIGNY | Issued at 6 a.m. Railhead VIGNACOURT. Inf tsmt + trans 50%. Bread 50%. Biscuit on line of ???????. Troop Grps Satty HQ Coy at BUIRE-SUR-L'ANCRE + briefly attach to 115 Division. No ration issued at Vignacourt 12209. horses 1836. | |
| | 6/7/16 | Nothing to report. 36% Inf rsmt drawn. | |
| | 7/7/16 CAVILLON | Rations changed to Complete to Inf + SANS Inf rsmt 50% Bread 50% 63rd Bde + 3 Coy Transferred to 37th Div. 110th Bde + 2 Cy 37th Div Train transferred to 1st Div. Inf rsmt 85% Bread 100% obtained 2250 lbs Onions. | |
| | 8/7/16 | | |
| | 9/7/16 | Inf rsmt 95% Bread 100%. Exchanged 4500 lbs Potatoes wth DSTs without (issued to porton in front line.) W.M.A. | |

Army Form C. 2118.

# WAR DIARY
## or
## INTELLIGENCE SUMMARY.
(Erase heading not required.)

S.S.O  21st DIV.

| Hour, Date, Place | Summary of Events and Information | Remarks and references to Appendices |
|---|---|---|
| RIBEMONT | | |
| 10/7/16 | Dent. from EDGE HILL (DERNANCOURT) - Division moved up forward area. 110th Bde. to Meaulte, 62nd & 64th Bde. to MEAULTE aus VILLE - Time of loading 3 am | |
| 11/7/16 | Dernancourt - Great delay in loading - Field Must 20%, Present 80%. Hred 25% 170 rec'd for Bde - Time of loading 3 am | |
| 12/7/16 | Dernancourt. Most delay in loading - Drew drawn 22,989 animals 52.19. Field Must 85% Indented at 3 am Obtained 2,160 lbs Oats/a - Run drawn by all groups. Indented 15% - head 15% - | |
| 13/7/16 | Dernancourt - Field Rations 85%, head 15%. Run drawn by all groups. Indented 3 am | |
| 14/7/16 | ditto - ditto - ditto. Drew 7250 Iron Rations from CORBIE by place. Horses lost in recent operations & by drafts missing. Run drawn by all groups. 300 lb Oats/a obtained. | |
| 15/7/16 | ditto. Drew supplies at 2 am 20,815 men 5303 animals. Iron Meat Drawn 20%. 37 Iron Royal Fus all 3 for rations 620 men + 20 animals. "M Sec." Spa Batt. RE due return Stangth 76 men. | |
| 16/7/16 | Dernancourt. Field Rations 80% - Nothing to report | |
| 17/7/16 | - " - Issued rations to party of Dismounted Cavalry 125 men + 2 horses for first time. | |
| 18/7/16 | - " - Field Must 35% Pres? 65% - Absent 40% - Division withdrawn from Meline 62nd Bde to BUIRE, 64th BECOURT, 110 - TREUX & RIBEMONT. | hall |

# WAR DIARY
## or
## INTELLIGENCE SUMMARY.
(Erase heading not required.)

Army Form C. 2118.

S.S.O. 21st Div.

Instructions regarding War Diaries and Intelligence Summaries are contained in F.S. Regs., Part II. and the Staff Manual respectively. Title pages will be prepared in manuscript.

| Hour, Date, Place | Summary of Events and Information | Remarks and references to Appendices |
|---|---|---|
| RIBEMONT 19/7/16 | Nothing Report | |
| CAVILLON 20/7/16 | Division moved back to OISSY, AILLY-SUR-SOMME, CAVOY, &c - Divl Troops Group left at BVIRE | |
| 21/7/16 | Dreamsupplies at LONGPRE-TAXXI-LES-SAINTS CORPS | |
| 22/7/16 | -"- -"- -"- Examined supplies Installation Dumpdepot BVIRE & following tho 10.000 withdrawn from Instri Redoubt. Division moved to 3rd Army Area | |
| WAMIN. 23/7/16 | Draw Supplies from TINQUES. - Division reached 3rd Army Area & joined 6th Corps. - Divisional Artillery still in action & retained by H.Q. Coy at BVIRE-SUR-L'ANCRE. - Potatoes & Onions also received - Fresh Meat 85%, Bread 100%. | |
| 24/7/16 | TINQUES - Fresh Meat 60%, Bread 75% - dried Veg. following | |
| 25/7/16 | -"- Fresh Meat 70%, Bread 100% - Potatoes & Onions &c. | |
| 26/7/16 | -"- Fresh Meat 65%, Bread 85% - Potatoes 5912 lb, Onions 1860 lb | |
| 27/7/16 | -"- Fresh Meat 65%, Bread 75% - Potatoes 6797 lb | |

# WAR DIARY
## or
## INTELLIGENCE SUMMARY

Army Form C. 2118.

S.S.O. 21st Div.

(Erase heading not required.)

Instructions regarding War Diaries and Intelligence Summaries are contained in F.S. Regs., Part II. and the Staff Manual respectively. Title pages will be prepared in manuscript.

| Place | Hour, Date | Summary of Events and Information | Remarks and references to Appendices |
|---|---|---|---|
| MATTUN | 28/7/16 | TINCQUES:- 62nd & 110th Bde. marched up from recent billets & took up part of line handed over by 14th Div:- Fresh meat 55%- Bread 75%- Potatoes 5733 lbs. Drawn 19.20 lbs. | |
| Railhead TINCQUES | 29/7/16 | The following units themselves formed part new advance transfer from 14th Div:- <br> ✓ 235 G. A.T. Co R.E.    ⊙ 2nd West York.    ⊙ 23 Anti-Aircraft Batt.    ⊙ Tpn Major Area <br> ✓ P.P. Cable Sec.    ✓ 164 Training Co. R.E.    ⊙ 39   "   "    ⊙ Transport Millans <br> ⊙ 5th Inverness Fort.    ✓ 256   "   "    ✓ 144 A.T. Co R.E.    ⊙ 6th Corps Cyclists <br> ✓ New Zealand Tunny Co.    ✓ 1/2nd Glamorgan A.T. Co R.E.    ✓ D6gn Sec. 3rd Army Co <br> ✓ attached to 62nd Brigade <br> ⊙   "   "   110th   " <br> Fresh meat 60%- Bread 75%- Potatoes 6418 lbs.- <br> Index   H.Q.   I.D.   Cyts <br> 3000   106   60   6 | |
| TINCQUES AGNEZ-LES-DUISANS | 30/7/16 | TINCQUES:- Ration drawn 24,127 Animals 5399 Fresh meat 55%- Bread 65%- Potatoes 5731 lb. Drawn 1920 lb. Fourteenth Mortar batteries joined division. Strength 75 O.R.- Attached to 64th Bde. one about Rifle ratio strength. Division Troop Strgth (21st Artillery) Animals 8209. | |
| | 31/7/16 | Aubigny:- Railhead changed- Rations drawn 24,723. Ration area extreme + received ration- 14th Div artillery retained future time. Marched in from battle area on route 2804- Fresh meat 60%- Bread 75%- Potatoes 14090 lbs. Strength 3341 men Animals 2804. | |

A.A. Stewart
Maj. G.S.
S.I.O. 21st Div

Army Form C. 2118.

# WAR DIARY
## or
## INTELLIGENCE SUMMARY.
(Erase heading not required.)

S.S.O. 21st Div.

Instructions regarding War Diaries and Intelligence Summaries are contained in F.S. Regs., Part II and the Staff Manual respectively. Title pages will be prepared in manuscript.

| Hour, Date, Place | | Summary of Events and Information | Remarks and references to Appendices |
|---|---|---|---|
| AGNEZ-LES-DUISANS | Pickard Aubigny | | |
| 1/8/16 | | Mens rations w.t. 862, Annuals 6090 - Potatoes 10086 lbs, Onions 400 lbs - 62nd Div. Drawing Ration - their rations for first time - strength 91 men. | |
| 2/8/16 | | Fresh Meat 6090, Bread 7590 - Potatoes 10720 lbs, Onions 3600 lbs. | |
| 3/8/16 | | Fresh Meat 6090 - Bread 2590 - Pm. 1590 - Meat 7590 - Potatoes 11,200 lbs. | |
| 4/8/16 | | Unit parading of Fresh Meat & bread - Potatoes 6282 lbs, Onions 3360 lbs, Dried Veg. 1350 lbs - 14th Div. Artillery left this area & marched to join their division near DOULLENS - drawing Ham rations for the last time in 3rd | |
| 5/8/16 | | 320 Reinf. for 110th Bde - Fresh Meat 6090 - Pm. Mem. 2590 - Meat 7590 - Bread Veg 1340 lbs - Pickles 1340 lbs, Potatoes 4148 lbs. 9th Leicesters confirmed no Vegetable drawn for 3 weeks - This statement manifestly absurd Reported to Little & to 21st Div.? | |
| 6/8/16 | | Fresh Meat 6090 - P.M. 1090, Potatoes 30 90 - Meat 7590 - Dried Veg 480, Potatoes 2760 lbs. Onions 3720 lbs | |
| 7/8/16 | | Fresh Meat 6090 - Pres. 3590 - M.M. 1590 - Potatoes 3450 lbs, Dried Veg - 1160 lbs - | |
| 8/7/16 | | " Pork Meats 1590 - Potatoes 3960 lbs, Onions 3960 lbs, Dried Veg. 720 lbs - Lieut. 3rd Army Aux. Transpt Co interviewing Prefect Farm Men 55 - Horses 72 - | |

W.H.McIntyre Maj.
S.S.O. 21st Div.

# WAR DIARY
## or
## INTELLIGENCE SUMMARY.
*(Erase heading not required.)*

Army Form C. 2118.

D.A.D. 21st Div.

| Hour, Date, Place | Summary of Events and Information | Remarks and references to Appendices |
|---|---|---|
| AGNEZ-LES-DUISANS 9/8/16 | Jam+heat 60%- Meat 25%- Pork Beans 15%- Potato 75%- Bread 75%- Potato 350 lbs, Onions 4406 lbs, Dried Veg- 740 lbs. Meat 21144, Onions 5734. Transf: 11 Dr+ Cyclists from 110th Pol: to 64th Pol: Group - (3 Other Ranks, 1 item) R.Schuman of N.C. Inschne) | |
| 10/8/16 | Jam+heat 60%, Meat 15%, P.M 25%- Bread 75%- Potatoes 3859 lbs, Dried Veg - 1320 lbs | |
| 11/8/16 | Pack train did not arrive at Railhead owing to damage derailment. Obtained Supplies from emergency at Railhead 1 other Railhead - Fresh meat 25%- P.M 10%- P+V 50%- Pork Beans 33%, transp 100 men. Bread 40%- P.cent 60% | |
| 12/8/16 | Fresh meat 60%- P.heat 25%- P+V 15%- Meat 75%- Bread 15%- Beans 15%- Flour 15%- Potatoes 3859 lbs - Bread Veg. 1320 lbs. Feeding strength - Men 21323, Animals 5707 | |
| 13/8/16 | Fresh meat 60%- Preld 25%- Pork Beans fillings - Bread 75%- Issued own Rations in lieu subsisting present ration. Drew by Horse Transport for 64th Brigade + Potatoes 3640 lbs, Onions 3844 lbs. Dried Veg 960 lbs | |
| 14/8/16 | Usual percentage of Fresh meat + Bread - Potatoes 4410 lbs, Dried Veg - 1320 lbs. Issued Petroleum in ARRAS 300 Galls Petrol, 40 Galls Paraffin, 6 times Cotton - | |
| 15/8/16 | " " " " Potato 4790 lbs. Onions 456 lbs, Dried Veg. 1290 lbs.— Pork Beans fillings Issued Materials in ARRAS 40 Galls. Steam Cylinder Oil. | |
| 16/8/16 | Men 21518 Horse 1601. Fresh meat 30%- P.heat 15%- Meat 15%- Pork Beans 15%- Meat 75%- Potatoes 4190 lbs, Onions 4075 lbs, Dried Veg 970 lbs - Dried Fruit in lieu of Jam - | W.A.B. |

Army Form C. 2118.

# WAR DIARY
## or
## INTELLIGENCE SUMMARY.
(Erase heading not required.)

J.10.   37th Division.

| Place | Date | Hour | Summary of Events and Information | Remarks and references to Appendices |
|---|---|---|---|---|
| AGNEZ-LES-DUISANS | 17/8/16 | - | Fresh Meat 30% - P Meat 1370% - h.14 15% - P.h. 73% - Bread 60% - Potatoes 4011 lb, Dried Veg 1300 lb, Rice 20%. Received intimation that 37 Div. Artillery would be attached to this formation. Duty b Tpos Cpl b Wilchinks ARRAS. | |
| | 18/8/16 | | Fresh Meat 30% - Other immobiles arrived with addition of Pork/Beans - Potato 4460 & Onions 4460. 37th Div. Artillery & Supply Sec. of HQ Co Train drew rations for first time - Strength Men 3038 Animals 2761. Bread hastily demand for bread to 100 tons - | |
| | 19/8/16 | | Fresh Meat 12½% - h.14 15% - P.h. 15% - Bread 75% - Ham 20% - Potatoes 4144, Dried Veg 1500. Using h. feat Meat Frush. Heavy fall of rain at AUXEVILLE way. Small amount of fodment available - | |
| | 20/8/16 | | Fresh Meat 60% - Pork 25% - Pork/Beans 15% - Bread 75% - Potatoes 3360. Onions 2880 - Dried Veg 660 | |
| | 21/8/16 | | Fresh Meat 60%. h.14 15%. P.h. 25%. Beans 60% - Potatoes 3960 - Dried Veg 300 | |
| | 22/8/16 | | " Pork/Beans 15%. P.k.nt 25% - Meat 60% - Potatoes 3300, Onions 2965 - Dried Veg 300. | |
| | 23/8/16 | | " " " 3740 - 2964 - 300 | |
| | 24/8/16 | | " Pk.? Meat 25% h.14 15% " 3410 Dried Veg 1500 2. Glanangan R.E. transferred to } | |
| | | | 64th Def. force from 62 Div. | |

Army Form C. 2118.

# WAR DIARY
## or
## INTELLIGENCE SUMMARY.

(Erase heading not required.)

S.O.
21st Div.

| Place | Date | Hour | Summary of Events and Information | Remarks and references to Appendices |
|---|---|---|---|---|
| AGNEZ-LES-DUISANS | 23/8/16 | | Fresh Meat 60%, Pres. 25%- Pot: Meaw 15%- Bread 75%- Potato 15%- Meat 1/2ans 4400, Onion 4322, Dried Veg 1530 lb | |
| | 24/8/16 | | " " " " Flour 10% - Potato 10450 lb- | |
| | 27/8/16 | | " " " " Oat Meal " Potatoes 9103 lb, Onions 333 lb. | |
| | 28/8/16 | | " " " " Oat Meal " 817. Potato 11,015 lb. Lctr of 235th A.T.C RE left division + | |
| | 29/8/16 | | 2 fully Bt. Div. Strength 54 men. 13 Horses | |
| | 30/8/16 | | Usual proportion of Freshlation plus Pat Meanw. Potatoes 9112 lb. Onion 2717 lb. | |
| | 31/8/16 | | " " " " 15057 lb- Onion 2517 lb- stores Found in being Jam | |
| | | | " " " " 8992 lb- Onions 3456 lb- | |

W. Albert Major
S.O. 21st Div.

# WAR DIARY
## INTELLIGENCE SUMMARY

Army Form C. 2118.

A.D.O. 21st Division

| Place | Date | Hour | Summary of Events and Information | Remarks and references to Appendices |
|---|---|---|---|---|
| AGNEZ LES DUISANS | 1916 1 Sept | | Fresh Meat 60%. Bread 75%. Potatoes + Onions - 6th Corps Cyclists. | |
| | 2 " | | " - 11th Divl Cyclists} drew supplies for last time - Transfer to 6th Corps Troops | |
| | 3 " | | 1 in 160 38th Div & Arranged transfer of Q.Q. Cattle here, 189 Cattle etc, 144 Oct. CoRE, 184 CoRE, 258 CoRE, New Zealand Tunnl Co, 62 A Rolls, 3rd Inntry Co RE, Transport Matl M32, 233 ATT. RE, 5th Intinsly Bdr, Party 22nd Hotel Yorks, 39 A&SCoth, Town Major Arras, 37th Divl Artillery & 288 Co ASC, 7 Kite Balloon Sec, 2 Hannigan Pl, 3 lorry aux HT Co; all new supplies for last time to day from 21st Div. Total 6700 Men and 3000 Animals. Rations changed to TINCQUES. Fresh Meat 50%, Pork Beans 16%, Oxo + Peas 20%, Bread 70% - Potatoes 680lbs Onions 2248lbs. | |
| | 4 " | | Fresh Meat 66%, O.Ph. 26%, M.H. 15%, Bread 75%. - Onions 2223lbs. - Hartelecover Remains affild to SSO 21st Div | 110th Berhincourt 64th Vilers, Sire Sitten |
| | | | Biscuits, - Oat tins, Steam Coal tins, Oats tins, Charcoal tins. - | |
| WAMIN | 5 " | | 21st Div milk exception of Pioneers + Artillery relieved by 35th Divn - Railhead TINCQUES. { Div Troops - Maistretlle 62 Bde. Sombrin } | |
| | 6 " | | Usual percentage of Fresh Meat & Bread. Rice 25%. Potatoes 8600 lbs Onions 2222 lbs. | |
| | 7 " | | Undertook packing of Iron ration of oats issued to 1st line of 62nd Bde in IV Army area - | |
| | 8 " | | " | |
| | 9 " | | 14th R.F.(Pioneers) moved from Arras to Villers-Sir-Simon & attached to 64th Bde. Ammunition. moved to locality around | |
| | 10 " | | ETREE-WAMIN - Usual percentage of Fresh Rations plus 25% Flour - Drew 185 Portions for 1st line & 60 for 64th Bde. Fresh Meat 65%, Bread 80% - Divisional Artillery (less 97th Bde) moved to locality of WAMIN. from Hauteville - | |

W.R.S.

# WAR DIARY
## or
## INTELLIGENCE SUMMARY.

Army Form C. 2118.

S.S.O. 21st Divn.

(Erase heading not required)

| Place | Date | Hour | Summary of Events and Information | Remarks and references to Appendices |
|---|---|---|---|---|
| WAMIN. | 11/9/16 | | XIII Corps wired that 12000 Oxo Cubes had been ordered on pack train from Base - Also enquired what quantity of Rum should be held in reserve - Replied 188 Gallons - Issue off by Army Commander on requisition from Medical Officers being obtained - | |
| | 12/9/16 | | Left WAMIN for 4th Army - Joined XV Corps - Division concentrated around LONGPRÉCOURT | |
| BUIRE | 13/9/16 | | Railhead EDGE-HILL (Dernancourt) 30% Fresh Meat, 30% Bread - sent to CORBIE for Rum - | |
| | 14/9/16 | | " " " Rum issue to fighting troops | |
| | 15/9/16 | | " " " " | |
| | 16/9/16 | | " " 30% Fresh Meat 50% Bread, Rum Issue as above | Stew 17th Jan - Ration for 110th Div. |
| FRICOURT | 17/9/16 | | " 64th Div to Trenches - | " " |
| | | | " 62nd " " " | |
| | | | ALBERT - New scheme of feeding instituted - Main line has cleared Contalmaison Interlink Motor Lorries Convoy to proceed to MONTAUBAN - Billets alongside railway - Dumbarnyo Mametz to Guillemont and attack - 2/3 Heavy Gunners eighty troops. Deposits 1814 tons & 26 lorries - Altogether 51.H Stores, 1 ASC Ray two 655 Lb's & 30 horses, 112 28 cwt. lorries. New rations proposed here on Heavy Attacks to Divisn - Planes 176 Truck to 110th Div - 76 tons of M.T. Lorries to transport refused here | |
| | 18/9/16 | | HUBERT - Fresh Meat 30% Pres? 70% - Meat 4.6. - Potatoes Onions - 9.9 am - Cheese ration reduced from 3 oz to 2½ oz. Received 1 Caterpillar in billets in Sodium grade ¾ fleece short. Twenty of fourth Tank the not this, by Austerity justification. 2/3 Heavy Gun to follow Heavy See: M.G. Corps (Armoured Cars "Tanks") 3 of have returned perfect him - Party of 1st. Lanes Fus - 105 have returned to perfect him - Unable prestus | |
| | 19/9/16 | | Effect prev? Ration (30% Meat + 45% Bread) 1 hr Lerries addition moved in here of these return Lectins 2nd Reserve Park 81 Rev. & 60 Lorries new rations perfect him. Full three of Rum to Division directly for Mechcheril to CORBIE for. Rum, Tea Sugar Jam Salt - hour of Meat & picked at Track - | |

# WAR DIARY or INTELLIGENCE SUMMARY.

Army Form C. 2118.

N° O. 21st Division.

| Place | Date | Hour | Summary of Events and Information | Remarks and references to Appendices |
|---|---|---|---|---|
| FRICOURT | 24/9/16 | | Fresh Meat 30%, Pres.? 70%; Bread 50%. Biscuit issued in lieu of flour. Rations of Rum issued to all ranks. Obtained 400 lbs Anti-Frostbite Grease from CORBIE, issued 100 lb to each pump. Had to send pump Hd to seek to CORBIE for Tea, Sugar, Salt. There are 7 men on each train. Lost 6 Carboys (N° 8 F.S. Depot) for Tea, Sugar, Salt. 30% Fresh Meat. 40% Bread. Drew 320 Iron Rations from N° 8 F.S.D. | |
| | 25/9/16 | | 100 Fr bi³ Pkts. 220 fr 110 lb. Time of loading 3 a.m. Transferred 37th Regt. Rns. 12 d. persons, 20 t. Rns. Pack, 15 Carps Salvage Coy, 675th Corps Troops Supply Col; Issued 70% Fresh Meat Flours (30% & 50% respectively) whilst operation in progress. 25 800 Iron Rations issued to 110th Bde. Full Rum issue to all ranks. | |
| | 26/9/16 | | 280 Iron Rations for Divl Troops (95th & 96th R.F.A.) & 6 lbs. Hessian was drawn from N° 8 F.S.D. Centre. 30% Fresh Meat, 40% Bread a/c. Notified that 2 qr Potatoes only will in future form Ration on 1st. Fresh Meat 30%. Preserves 70%. 50% Bread. Potatoes 12.10 lb. Onions 2534 lbs. Issued 2/3 issue Rum to all ranks. Gallino glasses issued to Groups. 2/3 issue of Rum. | |
| | 27/9/16 | | Nothing to report. 6 oz. of Vegetables only issued per man. Usual proportion of P. Meat Present. Drew 250 Galls Rum for Brigade 2/3 issue of Rum. | |
| | 28/9/16 | | Time of loading at Railhead (ALBERT) 2 a.m. " " " 6 oz Vegetables iss? per man. Drew 250 Galls. Rum from CAMPLES. 30% Fresh. 70% Pres? meat. 50% Bread. 2/3 issue of Rum. & 9 carryalls received per train. Pres? Meat 85%. Fresh 15%. Meat 60%. Vegetables 6 oz per man. 2/3 issue Rum. | |
| | 29/9/16 | | " 65% " 35% " 60% 6½ q. of Fresh Vegetables by per man. Full issue Rum. Loaded Supplies at Railhead by H.T. (the 3 brigades contain of the trains making double journey to clear out troops from supplies. Time of loading 2.30 a.m. Railhead ALBERT. | |

M.A.S.

# WAR DIARY or INTELLIGENCE SUMMARY

**Army Form C. 2118.**
S.S.O. 21st DIVN.

| Place | Date | Hour | Summary of Events and Information | Remarks and references to Appendices |
|---|---|---|---|---|
| FRICOURT CHATEAU | 30/9/16 | | Trains still loading at ALBERT 2 a.m. Usual proportion of field supplies received. 64th Bde moved to BUIRE. 62nd Bde also moved out of the line. 110th remains in. Issue of Rum & Rations. | |

Wallnut Major
P.P.O. 21st Division

Army Form C. 2118.

Vol 5  M.D. 21st Div —

# WAR DIARY
# or
# INTELLIGENCE SUMMARY.

(Erase heading not required.)

Instructions regarding War Diaries and Intelligence Summaries are contained in F.S. Regs., Part II. and the Staff Manual respectively. Title pages will be prepared in manuscript.

| Place | Date | Hour | Summary of Events and Information | Remarks and references to Appendices |
|---|---|---|---|---|
| FRICOURT | 1/10/16 | | Railhead ALBERT — drew supplies at 2 a.m. (Mustertime). 30% Railhead 70% Pack? 50% Bread — Followed Rum — Followed — Hot tea served out of time, division relieved by 12th Div. Transferred S.I. Horse 28 men — orgs horses & HQ Corps (O Coy) Tanks. 31 men to supply officer 35th Bde will come return on 2nd inst to march — | |
| | 2/10/16 | | Railhead ALBERT. Drew supplies at 2 a.m. 35% Pack 65% Pack? Pack? Meat, Vegetables 64 or lb — Dried 40 lb. | |
| ST. SAUVEUR | 3/10/16 | | 62nd & 64th Brigades moved to Xth Corps Area West of AMIENS South of the Somme. Railhead at VIGNACOURT Billeted at ST. SAUVEUR. Rail head 25% — Pack head 75% — Potatoes 3140 lb — Artillery still in Action. — | |
| AILLY-LE-HAUT-CLOCHER. | 4/10/16 | | Moved to AILLY-LE-HAUT-CLOCHER. Railhead VIGNACOURT. — Artillery still in Action. HQ Coy. left behind at BECORDEL. Railhead 20%, Pack 80%. — Fresh Vegetables 4,500 lb. — Dried 40 lb. 2½ gs of sugar issued to sweet milk drawn — Lt Grant R.O. 110th Bde returned to base depot HAVRE. | |
| | 5/10/16 | | Rail head 30%, Pack? 55% — Pack 15% — Fullcrane of bread. Drew Dried Veg issued also. Obtained 5 tons loaf from S.S.O. 4th Canadian Div. 2½ oz Sugar drawn in pieces Milk was also drawn from RMF. Feeding strength 12,308 men. 21,570 Animals — But Artillery still in action HQ Co. at BECORDEL | |
| | 6/10/16 | | Nothing to report. | |
| | 7/10/16 | | Left Ailly-le-Haut-Clocher for NOEUX-LES-MINES attached to Divn 6 1st Army. | |
| NOEUX LES MINES | 8/10/16 | | Railed D.A.S.T. 1st Army — 62nd Bde concentrated around MARLES. 64th MBde at ALLOUAGNE | |

# WAR DIARY or INTELLIGENCE SUMMARY

Army Form C. 2118.

N.O. 21st Div.

| Place | Date | Hour | Summary of Events and Information | Remarks and references to Appendices |
|---|---|---|---|---|
| MEAUX LES MINES | 8/10/16 Contd | | 110th R.A. arrived FOUQUIÈRES. No supplies drawn from Railhead to div. returned up to frg.t Railhead BÉTHUNE. A/t Div. Suppy. Col. assigned to div. 14 loaders only given. 60% Fresh Meat 70% Bread. 6 oz. vegetables. Dumped supplies at LAPUGNOY (Gr. Bks.), 64th near HAUT RIEUX, and 110th Bde. on MEAUX-BETHUNE Rd. Drew 10 Tons Coal from Base / BRUAY. | |
| | 9/10/16 | | 533rd Batt. R.F.A. arrived from England & drew rations before attached to Div. Strength 170 men & 195 L.D. Horses. 60% Fresh Meat 77% bread, Pot. & Beans 100% - 436 O.R. Reg drawn from R.S.D. 62nd, 110th Bdes. refilled on main road 300 yds. S of FOUQUIÈRES - 64th Bde on road near HAUT RIEUX. All three brigades refilled on BETHUNE-HESDIGNEUL Road - 110th Brigades on night of 10th. Exps. Pack. Reg. recd. from R.S.D. | |
| | 10/10/16 | | 60% Fresh meat, 80% Bread, 100% Pot. & Beans, Rice 20% - Greates purchased 5.50s 60% Fresh meat, M/P 39%. Bread 77%. Potatoes 145% only, viz. - Purchases of freshly matured S.O.S. to supplement ration issue. 8th Div. transport killed was pull'd from him on 14th - Application made thru I.Corps to save Rum twice weekly. 0.60 Lead only horse - Taken on Renche. Orders to run Steam boat from BaseaneltilleCanal. | |
| | 11/10/16 | | Div. H.Q moved to SAILLY-LABOURSE. Train H.Q. at NOEUX. Rations for Divl. school at TERFAY & detach: 63rd F. Ant. at AUCHEL. | |
| | 12/10/16 | | 8th Div. Suppy Col. ordered to relieve 110th Bde. 8th Div. Suppy. Col. delivers divisional ration Maintenance pack 20000 rations - Detach at Bethune by 40th Step- | |
| FOUQUIÈRES | 14/10/16 | | Last train. Usual % of fresh rations received. Rations for Div. School & Field Amb. red. by Lorry to Terfay & Auchel. | had |

# WAR DIARY / INTELLIGENCE SUMMARY

Army Form C. 2118.

A.D. 21st Division

**Place:** FOUQUIÈRES

### 15/10/16

Drew supplies from Béthune by Horse Transport. 6th Supply Col loaded. Replaced 21st Div - milk supplies to be purchased locally by the army. Fresh vegetables not allowed for by Base in packing train - issued of fresh meat & bread. Despatched lorry to Fosses with rations for Divl School & to ACHIET for party of 63rd Fus. Wire ore from 6th Div. Issued 31 Trotobe & 24 Trus Charcoal, also 164 galls Rum, 7 4/5 Candles, Glycerine & other supplies. Rationed 6th Div Troops for 1½ days - Strength Men 4800 Animals 3160.

### 16/10/16

Took over from 32nd Div. Coal 15 Tons. Coke 1½ Tons. Charcoal 2 Tons. 2 yds Bacon received in lieu of Butter. Issued rations to 140 Heavy Batty R.G.A. - Men 370, H.D. 201, L.D. 32. Supplied only time. Tot Tonn Supply Units from 32 Div received rations for first time ~ 257 Tonn. G.H.Q. 635 (Signals) K.O Tunn Co R.E. 656 ellranh - t (H.D. 3 L.D Horses) 10 H.D. Horses } Tonn Major Annequin 85 men } No 1 Arm. Train 52 men } H.Q. 26th Heavy Artillery Group 24 men } Anti-Aircraft Unit 35 men. 140th Heavy Batty R.G.A. 312 men., 200 Hd 34 F.D draw rations for first week, time they Issued 9/10 of fresh meat & bread. Ration Strength of Division including 8th Divnl Artillery fring = 19,118 Men 5835 Animals. Lorry to Fosses as usual. Nothing exceptional occurred - A.C. Train went on leave for 10 days to London.

### 17/10/16

Pack Train arrived with 90 Pats. Drew Rats for 21 Div & 8th Div Troops from Barges Béthune.

### 18/10/16

Men & Tms Coal from 1 Corps Troops S.C. 60% Fresh Meat, 70% Bread.

### 19/10/16

Fresh meat 60% Bread 75% 39% Potatoes 23% vegs drawn. Hay drawn from Barges, BÉTHUNE. Drew & tm Coal from 1 Corps Troops S.C. Issued Rum to the three brigades -

M.A.L.

Army Form C. 2118.

# WAR DIARY
## or
## INTELLIGENCE SUMMARY.
(Erase heading not required.)

A.D. 21st Division

| Place | Date | Hour | Summary of Events and Information | Remarks and references to Appendices |
|---|---|---|---|---|
| BOUQUIÈRES LES-BETHUNE | 20/10/16 | | Richment 55%. Bread 75%. 6 oz Vegetables per man. Arles & two cookes from 1st Corps Troops - to two Field Works from 6 T.S. Dept. 21st Div Artillery drew rations from reinforcements 22nd - arrival in HARNES-LES-MINES area - Drew Hay from Bangro BETHUNE. Ready issued to the three brigades. | |
| | 21/10/16 | | Interim supplies for Divl Troops from three brigades themselves have met with remainder drawn as per supply letter. Rations proportions arrangements from 8th Divn - 1st Army R.E. Workshops; M.T. less 4th Res Park; 253 Tunnying Co R.E.; 197 Land Drainage Co R.E.; 18th Divn Salvage Co. 60% Freshmeat 75% Bread, 6 oz Potatoes drawn per man. Issued ration to three brigades | |
| | 22/10/16 | | 68% Freshmeat, 80% Bread 5 oz Potatoes per man this with alloc of M.T. sent up made trip return trip to three bgdes. Sent to Bangros for rations of oats. Drew 6 tons cord from Bangros & two from M. Corps Troops Sup. | |
| | 23/10/16 | | Drew 10 tons field bread from N°6 F.S.D. 60% Freshmeat 75% Bread 3½ oz Potatoes plus M.V = 6 oz Vegetables. Straw from Aartha - sent to Range Bethune for Rum. Beans & tinned from Bruay Mines - | |
| | 24/10/16 | | 53% Freshmeat Bread 65% - 6 oz Vegetables drawn - Sent to Range for Rum - 333 Patty transport from 110th Bde sample & Divl Troops Sup. | |
| | 25/10/16 | | Normal Cheese ration of 3 oz resumed - 3 cwt Chestnuts sent up from base to experiment with. Supplied 2 oz of Rice = 4 oz of Potato. Issues made to 1 batt of each brigade & 63/64 Field amb for trial. | |

Hall

Army Form C. 2118.

# WAR DIARY
## or
## INTELLIGENCE SUMMARY.
(Erase heading not required.)

D.D.D. 21st Division

| Place | Date | Hour | Summary of Events and Information | Remarks and references to Appendices |
|---|---|---|---|---|
| Fouquières | 26/10/16 | | Fresh meat 60%. Bread 75% - Sup. vegetables drawn from Pott? including about 15% M.V. Drew Pats 7 Hay from Ranges - 180 Funny Co. R.E. left Army area. Drew an addit? days rations 5SD. 10 LD. Horses - | |
| | 27/10/16 | | Fresh meat 67%. Bread 62%. Veg. 69% per man. Drew Petrol, Pres? meat from Ranges BETHUNE. | |
| | 28/10/16 | | " 66%. " 83%. " 6? " - , Drew Sugar, Jam, Pots Hay from Ranges BETHUNE - | |
| | 29/10/16 | | " 65%. " 80%. " 8? " - , Drew Pats, Hay, Tea, Sugar, Jam from Ranges BETHUNE - | |
| | | | Anti-Aircraft Unit drew rations blank time arrangm to IV Army. Drew & two wood from BARLIN. | |
| | 30/10/16 | | Fresh meat 65%. Bread 7%. 6 oz Pot. + Onions. Drew Jam, Milk, Biscuit, Pres? meat from Ranges. | |
| | 31/10/16 | | " " 60%. " 75%. 2 oz bacon 5/16. 8 tin of Pork & beans issued to complete therein - 1 oz cheese 29/ VDS. | |
| | | | Iomt up to complete ration, 6 oz Vegetables also. Anti-Aircraft Unit drew rations blank have adjustment to 4 - | |
| | | | Army. Drew groceries & Petrol from Range BETHUNE | |

Mal Stuart Major
D.D.O. 21st Div.

# WAR DIARY or INTELLIGENCE SUMMARY

Army Form C. 2118.

N.n  
21st Div.  
J.O.  
Oct-5  
Vol 76

| Place | Date | Hour | Summary of Events and Information | Remarks and references to Appendices |
|---|---|---|---|---|
| FOUQUIÈRES | 1/11/16 | | Fresh Meat 61%, Bread 75%. Bacon ration 2ozs remainder replaced by 5/16 of a tin of Pork & Beans per man. ½ oz Cheese. 2oz Vegetable to complete ration. – Boy Vegetables drawn – Drew Hay, Oats, Jam, Milk, Peas Meat, Biscuit from Bayes BÉTHUNE. | |
| | 2/11/16 | | Fresh Meat & Bread – 60% & 75% respectively – 4ozs Potatoes. ½ oz Cheese, Bacon as usual. Drew Forage, Milk, Jam, Biscuit, Peas, Meat from Bayes, also Petrol & Oil. | |
| | 3/11/16 | | Ditto – Ditto – | |
| | 4/11/16 | | | Started |
| | | | Fresh Meat 54%, Bread 68%, 4oz Potatoes. Drew P. Meat, Biscuit, Sugar, Milk, Oils etc from Bayes. Béthune. Chaff Cutting Plant at SAINS-LAROUSSE – 3 machines working. Drew 13 tons straw from Purchase Board. Arrangements for supply of Yeasted Cake weekly. Purchased 15 tons in BÉTHUNE – 3 tons in FILLERS. | |
| | 5/11/16 | | Fresh Meat 65%, Bread 80% Potatoes with Bacon Ys = 4oz. Hay 6lbs only. Draw from Bayes 10 Tons wood. | |
| | 6/11/16 | | " 60%  " 75%  Pots Pasys = 4oz Veg | |
| | 7/11/16 | | " 60%  " 75%  Pots 6oz Sardines Pulse drawn each day 1½ oz Cheese | |
| | 8/11/16 | | " 45%  " 75%  Pots 6oz H2O Cheese Coal from Bruay 20 Tons 3rd Australian Tunnellers to rations to be drawn on 9th to 19th ozs | |
| | 9/11/16 | | " 45%  " 73%  Pots 5oz. 1 oz Bacon in lieu of 1½ Butter Cheese 1½ oz, 2 oz Veg in lieu Coal from Bruay 10 Tons | |
| | 10/11/16 | | " 45%  Bread 73 60% Bacon 4th Pot. Half ration drawn only in consequence of introduction of RCO for D.S.& T. ration drafted at AUCHEL taken over from 63rd Div Aurker by 6th Div 2oz Butter 2oz Veg in lieu of 1½oz Cheese. A Bus ration | |
| | 11/11/16 | | " 46% Bread 76% Veg 6oz. 1.5 Bacon in lieu of 1 oz Butter. Children at work of 6 men to 7 oz tea = 1½ oz cheese per man. 20 Ton Coal from Bruay | |

Army Form C. 2118.

# WAR DIARY
## or
## INTELLIGENCE SUMMARY.
*(Erase heading not required.)*

D.D.O. 21st Divn.

| Place | Date | Hour | Summary of Events and Information | Remarks and references to Appendices |
|---|---|---|---|---|
| FOUQUIÈRES | 12/11/16 | | Frzn Meat 60%. Bread 76%. Veal Loaf and Potatoes issued in lieu of cheese | |
| | 13/11/16 | | " 61% " 75% " 10% of Bacon in lieu of 10% Butter. 20 Tins of Lard from Bray. | |
| | 14/11/16 | | Frzn Meat 62%. " 78%. 20 Tins of Lard drawn from Bray Junc. | |
| | 15/11/16 | | " 61% " 79% | |
| | 16/11/16 | | Instead of 1 lb 1 of Tinned Cake = Hz 3 oz Frzn Meat 61%. Bread 79%. Full issue ration drawn. 20 Tons Lard drawn ec Bray. | |
| | 17/11/16 | | Frzn Meat 5-8½%. Bread 75%. 20 Tons Lard drawn ec Bray. Buns | |
| | 18/11/16 | | " 60% " 75% Unusual Lordies authorised moved wave to men in Trenches every night except when Rum Supply of Oxo was issued. | |
| | 19/11/16 | | Frzn Meat 61%. Bread 75%. 10% of Dried fruit issued in lieu of 4 oz of Potatoes | |
| | 20/11/16 | | Frzn Meat 60%. Bread 75%. 10% of Dried fruit issued in lieu of 4 oz of Potatoes. 0.8. 10% of Butter un-available. Milk issued in lieu of 2 oz Bacon. 20 Tons of Lard drawn from Bray Junc. | |

Army Form C. 2118.

# WAR DIARY
## or
## INTELLIGENCE SUMMARY.
*(Erase heading not required.)*

S.S.O. 21st Divn.

| Place | Date | Hour | Summary of Events and Information | Remarks and references to Appendices |
|---|---|---|---|---|
| FOUQUIÈRES | 21/11/16 | | 7.ozs Meat 5.8%. Bread 7.2%. 1 oz of Dried Fruit issued in lieu of 2 ozs of Bacon. Men's sand in lieu of 2 ozs of Bacon. And 6 ozs of Oats pr. horse issued from Retherd; 9 lbs pr. H.S. and 4 lbs pr L.S. made up for 4th Res. Pr. to D.D.S & T. intimates that a weeks reserve of Corn should be accounted for. | |
| | 22/11/16 | | 7.ozs Meat 6.0%. Bread 7.5%. 4 ozs of Potatoes drawn at Retherd. M.V's in lieu of 2 ozs Bacon. 16 lbs pr. H.S. and 10 lbs pr L.S. Oats drawn at Retherd. 16 Trs of Bard. | |
| | 23/11/16 | | 7.ozs Meat 6.1%. Bread 7.5-%. 1 oz of Bacon issued in lieu of 1.9 Potatoes. 16 Trs of food drawn from Lillers. | |
| | 24/11/16 | | Fresh Meat 6.1%. Bread 7.5%. 4 oz of Potatoes. 16 Tons of coal from Pernes. | |
| | 25/11/16 | | " 5.6%. " 7.4%. 4oz " | |
| | 26/11/16 | | " 6.1%. " 7.5%. No Potatoes rec'd — 8lbs Hay Potatoes. | |
| | 27/11/16 | | " 6.2%. " 7.5%. 2oz Potatoes. | |
| | 28/11/16 | | " 6.2%. " 7.5%. 1oz Potatoes. 1oz Dried Fruits in lieu of Bacon — 2ozs Bacon per man. | |
| | 29/11/16 | | Ration made up by 2ozs Fresh Meat in lieu. Freshmeat 6.0%, Bread 7.5%, 4oz Potatoes, to return Bacon balance M.V; iss'd to 4th Res Pk moved to 4th Army. | |
| | 30/11/16 | | No freshmeat drawn. 6.0% Pres. 4.0% M.V. Bread 7.6%. 4oz & 2oz Potatoes drawn for 60% & 40% — 2oz Bacon balance drawn in M.V. | |

Turned over to A.D.S. of Divisional Troops Group Forage — (days reserve ration)

M.A.S. Sturt Major
S.S.O. 21st Divn.

# WAR DIARY / INTELLIGENCE SUMMARY

Army Form C. 2118.

**Dec 1st – 31st 1916**

21st Division

| Place | Date | Hour | Summary of Events and Information | Remarks and references to Appendices |
|---|---|---|---|---|
| Fouquières | 1/12/16 | | No Meadow Flour; all flour rec'd with exception of 700 lbs Rice; Party of Salt Fish Flour 25 men length at'd to R.E. New ration issued time from 6th Div group. No Bacon received. Fresh Meat 75%, Bread Veg in lieu of potatoes. Mule cover issued time from Shaftesbury Ave at Fouquières. (B^3. 6v & 110th Bdes) | |
| | 2/12/16 | | Fresh Meat 75%, Bread 63%, Veg. Potatoes, Issue of Bacon & Cheese. Turned over portion of Ord. Troops rats supplied. | |
| | 3/12/16 | | " " 100% " Issue who did not get hvy. | |
| | 4/12/16 | | " 73% " 100% " 2og Potatoes & 2og Fresh did men not receiving 24 hr Ration. BRUAY MINES closed. | Bruay mines closed |
| | 5/12/16 | | " 61% " 87% " 2.og Potatoes 1og Dried Fruit. | |
| | 6/12/16 | | " 62% " 72% " Potatoes 1og. Onions 1og, 1og Dried Fruit. Turned over portion of Ord. Tps rats a supply Column. | |
| | 7/12/16 | | " 60% " 79% " 2og Vegetables per man, a dist to Men + RE's. 1st issue on rest billets. | |
| | 8/12/16 | | " 60% " 75% " " " " " Shortage of MRO | |
| | 9/12/16 | | " " " " No Vegetables rec'd – 2nd time O.P? Sent to Berges for 3000 lbs Hay (short on Train) R&O | Shortage |
| | 10/12/16 | | " 61% " 77% " " ; Shortage MRO , all vegetables purchased locally | |
| | 11/12/16 | | " 60% " 79% " " " " " " | |
| | 12/12/16 | | " 61% " 75½% " All vegetables purchased locally | |
| | 13/12/16 | | Fresh Meat & Bread as usual – 197 Stnd Drainage C.R.E. transferred to 6th Div. three supplies at least time. | |
| | 14/12/16 | | " " " No Vegetables rec? | |

W.A.S. Short Major
S.S.O. 21st Div.

# WAR DIARY
## or
## INTELLIGENCE SUMMARY

Army Form C. 2118.

D.D. 21st Div.

| Place | Date | Hour | Summary of Events and Information | Remarks and references to Appendices |
|---|---|---|---|---|
| Auquise | 15/10/16 | | Fresh meat & bread as normal. No vegetables tea. | |
| | 16/10/16 | | " 2 oz Potatoes ie? from Railhead. Changed Railhead to MOEUX-LES-MINES. area | |
| | | | Supplies at 9.45 am. | |
| | 17/10/16 | | Nothing to report excepting that 1 oz Potatoes iss? from base (Havre) | |
| | 18/10/16 | | Nothing to report. Usual proportion of fresh meat & bread, no vegetables. Started trucking charcoal bits. Only 30% Fresh meat packed at base. No vegetables. 110th Bde cause out of the line & proceed to marched to AVCHEL, RAIMBERT & area. - No 3 Co Train to AVCHEL. | |
| | 19/10/16 | | 30% Fresh Meat only; other supplies as usual. | |
| | 20/10/16 | | 30% " " 3 oz Vegetables drawn from Railhead. | |
| | 21/10/16 | | 60% " " Nothing particular to note. | |
| | 22/10/16 | | " " 4 oz Vegetables. Nothing particular to note. | |
| | 23/10/16 | | " " 4 oz Cheese. Perman drawn from Railhead. 4 oz Vegetables also. | |
| | 24/10/16 | | " " 4 oz Vegetables. 1½ oz Cheese. 2 oz Potatoes in lieu of other half. - Drew 4500 lbs. Hay from 47 S.D. | |
| | | | Shortage of Paraffin. only 20 galls available. Sent both its units to half deficiency. | |
| | 25/10/16 | | Usual proportion of fresh meat & bread, 4 oz Vegetables drawn from Railway. Extra case of Cavalry drawn | |
| | 26/10/16 | | Nothing special of note. | |
| | 27/10/16 | | 12" Bde moved into MAROC-LES-MINES - LAPUGNOY & area. No. 2 Coy Train to CHOCQUES. | |

wah

Army Form C. 2118.

# WAR DIARY
## or
## INTELLIGENCE SUMMARY.
(Erase heading not required.)

S.C.O. 21st Division

| Place | Date | Hour | Summary of Events and Information | Remarks and references to Appendices |
|---|---|---|---|---|
| FOUVIÈRES | 28/12/16 | | 64th Bde. moved from Trenches to FOUVIÈRES, FOUENCOURT, MOEUX-LES-MINES area - 6 lbs of Hay only received from Railhead - Balance of ration made up by chaff & mealcake - usual proportion of fresh meat issued - Cancelled extra cheesed fruit base. | |
| | 29/12/16 | | Nothing to report | |
| | 30/12/16 | | No Pickles, Butter, or Flour available at Railhead. 700 Vegetables drawn - Usual props Red Meat Meat. | |
| | 31/12/16 | | Candles not drawn from Railhead as supply available - Drew 570 lbs from U.F.D. | |

M E Elliot Major
A.D.O 21st Divn.

# WAR DIARY or INTELLIGENCE SUMMARY

Army Form C. 2118.

ADS 21st Div.

| Place | Date | Hour | Summary of Events and Information | Remarks and references to Appendices |
|---|---|---|---|---|
| OUVRIÈRES | 1/11/17 | | 50% Fresh meat, 73% bread. 20% Onions drawn from Railhead. No Butter or pickles available. | |
| | 2/11/17 | | Total meat at Railhead preserved meat issued. No vegetables drawn from Railhead. | |
| | 3/11/17 | | Received 60%, Bread 75%. No Vegetables drawn from R.M.T. Transport 4 N.F. to 6.2 M.L. from dept at | |
| | 4/11/17 | | " " " But Troops refilled at HURIONVILLE | |
| | 5/11/17 | | Ammunition Troops refilled at BURBURE. Other groups as usual. 30% Fresh Meat 75% Bread. | |
| | 6/11/17 | | Nothing to report excepting that only 25% Fresh Meat received. | |
| | 7/11/17 | | 8th Bty received from Base Fresh meat 25% Bread 75%. Vegetables nil | |
| | 8/11/17 | | Fresh Meat 25%, Bread 50%, Biscuit 50%. 2% Onions rec'd from base. | |
| | 9/11/17 | | " 95% 20% Onions for men received | |
| | 10/11/17 | | " " 20% " " " " | |
| | 11/11/17 | | Nothing unusual to record. 20% Onions | |
| | 12/11/17 | | 6 Bttys out of action. Frozen meat received at R.M.T. 15% Pork & Beans 85% Pres'd Meat. Meat 75% - 6 bttys only came up. | |
| | 13/11/17 | | 30% Potatoes. 20% Onions rec'd from base. 30% Frozen Meat. No Cheese. 20% Currants. MTV in lieu of Bacon. Train did not arrive at Railhead until 5.30 p.m. L.D. 10 lbs. | |
| | 17/11/17 | | Lack of oats reduced - HD = Nils. 60% Frozen Meat + 6 oz Vegetables | |
| | 18/11/17 | | Rats reduced to 13 lbs H.D. Horses 1½ lbs for L.D. 60% Fresh Meat + usual proportion of Bread 6 oz Vegetables | |
| | | | Lt Col Munro went on leave to England | M.A.S. |

# WAR DIARY
## or
## INTELLIGENCE SUMMARY.
(Erase heading not required.)

Army Form C. 2118.

No. A.10    21st Division

| Place | Date | Hour | Summary of Events and Information | Remarks and references to Appendices |
|---|---|---|---|---|
| HOUTKERQUE | 25/1/17 | | Inspected 67% Bread 75% - 6 ozs vegetables red purchase. Clgw & Dlgw baths returned bus Attols after having been att to 20th Div. Reorganised - Working part of 190 men | |
| | 26/1/17 | | Off 4th N.F. returned to Units from depôt on support line — Fresh Meat 61% Bread 71% ,, 6 ozs veg. | |
| | 27/1/17 | | " 60% " 6 ozs " 4½ ozs Veg. 2 ozs Dried Fruits | |
| | 28/1/17 | | " 60% " 60% " 4 ozs Potatoes 2 ozs " — others allotted not received Mt returned — | |
| | 29/1/17 | | | |
| | 24/1/17 | | Readjustment of rations 1 lb per man — Hay increased to 6 lbs per animal — 4 ozs Potatoes | |
| | 25/1/17 | | " 1 lb per man - | |
| | 26/1/17 | | " 80% " 6 ozs Dried Vegs. 1 oz Potatoes, 4½ ozs Chestnuts - Horseman 6 lb Oats returned | |
| | | | from Divl School — | |
| | | | 62nd Bde & Artillery moved to 2nd Army area — Six Reserve supplies from 8th D.S. | |
| | | | 110th Bde 64th Bde " " " " " Issued 14 days | |
| | 27/1/17 | | Rations (first) to parties left behind from Units proceeding above to | |
| | | | Railhead PROVEN- División concentrated around WORMHOUDT, HERZEELE, HOUTKERQUE and | |
| WORMHOUDT | 28/1/17 | | WINNEZEELE - 30% Freshmeat (75% to Freust. Drafts on addit of days trage to all | |
| | 30/1/17 | | Supps from M2 F.S.D & Railhead (Precaution against then). 21st T.M. Bde returned to the Division | |
| | | | from TERDEGHEM. Rations for Divis. 6,711 O 1114 L.D&L. Strength 200 O.R. | |
| | | | M Albert Vey | |
| | | | SSO 21 Divn | |

**WAR DIARY**
or
**INTELLIGENCE SUMMARY.**

Army Form C. 2118.

ADS 21st Divn.

| Place | Date | Hour | Summary of Events and Information | Remarks and references to Appendices |
|---|---|---|---|---|
| WORMHOUDT | 30/1/17 | | Drew supplies from PROVEN. All reserved Rations to issue 1 days food rations being held in supply Col- Drew 1 extra days forage for the Drivers & held in reserve. Partially obtained from Railhead CAESTRE M.2. F.S.B. & Railhead HAZEBROUCK. Obtained 20 tons Coal from R.M.F. | |

W.A.Stuart Major
ADS 21st Divn.

**Army Form C. 2118.**

Initials [signature]

January 1st – 31st 1917

# WAR DIARY
## or
## INTELLIGENCE SUMMARY.

(Erase heading not required.)

ADO 31st Divn.

Instructions regarding War Diaries and Intelligence Summaries are contained in F.S. Regs., Part II. and the Staff Manual respectively. Title pages will be prepared in manuscript.

| Place | Date | Hour | Summary of Events and Information | Remarks and references to Appendices |
|---|---|---|---|---|
| OUDIZEELE | 1/1/17 | | 50% Beef lost, 25% to troops. Eggs & lines drawn from ration. Without. No Butter at all this week. | |
| | 2/1/17 | | Total meat at Railhead reserved. Meat issued – Vegetables drawn from Railhead. | |
| | 3/1/17 | | Railhead 60% troops 75%. No Vegetables drawn from R.H. – Transferred 14 NF to 62 Div. Transferred | |
| | 4/1/17 | | " " But Troops refilled at HONDEGHEM. 30% Rail Head 75% Mead. | |
| | 5/1/17 | | Armament Troops refilled at BIRBURE. Other Units to be issued. 30% Rail Head 75% mead. | |
| | 6/1/17 | | Nothing to report except HH only 25% Rest Rest received. | |
| | 7/1/17 | | 8 lorries received from Base. Railhead 25%. Bread 75%. Vegetables Nil | |
| | 8/1/17 | | Railhead 40%. Mead 50%. Bread 50%. 25% Onions also furnished. | |
| | 9/1/17 | | " 75% 25% Onions for men received. | |
| | 10/1/17 | | Nothing unusual to record. 25% Onions. | |
| | 11/1/17 | | 6 lorries returned to depot | |
| | 12/1/17 | | No Forage heads received at R.H.H. 40% Pork & Beans 85% Pres & Meat. Meat 75%. 6 lorries only came up. | |
| | 13/1/17 | | 25% Onions. 25% Onions rec'd from Ind. | |
| | 14/1/17 | | Train did not arrive at Railhead until 5.30 p.m. 30% Frozen Meat, No Cheese. Vegetables, MO in lieu of Bacon | |
| | 15/1/17 | | Pack of Mule reduced. HD = N th LD 20 th. 60% Improvement & usual Proportions drawn. | |
| | 16/1/17 | | Mts reduced to 13 th HD Horses 1/2 th for LD. 6 lbs Vegts &c. | |

[signature] H.A.R.

# WAR DIARY / INTELLIGENCE SUMMARY

Army Form C. 2118.

A10   21st Division

| Place | Date | Hour | Summary of Events and Information | Remarks and references to Appendices |
|---|---|---|---|---|
| FOUQUEREUIL | 24/11/17 | | Inspected 6½% Bread 7½% - 6% vegetables and potatoes - 0/94 + 0/94 trks returned treat tablets after having been aff. to 2nd Div - temporarily. Working part of 90 men | |
| | 25/11/17 | | 0/94 N.F. returned to unit from Leffey on support line - | |
| | 26/11/17 | | " " " " Bread 7½% B.gn reg. | |
| | 27/11/17 | | " 65% " 70% 4½ gr. veg. 5 oz. dried fruits | |
| | 28/11/17 | | " 60% " " 60% " 4 oz. potatoes kilos " - potatoes should not exceed 11½ ozs ration - | |
| | 29/11/17 | | " " " - Provisioned at rate of 116 per man - | |
| | 29/11/17 | | " " " - 116 per man - They increased to 116 per animal - 4 oz. potatoes - | |
| | 26/11/17 | | " 65% " 80% - 5 ozs Dried veg. 1 oz. potatoes. 1444 lbs chestnuts - Horses fed by Dke returned from Divl School - | |
| | 29/11/17 | | 1st Bde + Artillery moved to 2nd Army area - Pre-Reserve Supplies turn 5th Div - | Issued 14 days |
| WORMHOUDT | 29/11/17 | | 110th Bde + 64th Bde " " " " | " " |
|  | | | Return (prov.d) to parties left behind from Units Guarding stores | |
|  | | | Railhead PROVEN - Division Concentrated around WORMHOUDT, HERZEELE, HOUTKERQUE, and |  |
|  | 30/11/17 | | WINNEZEELE - 30% F.S.D. + 30% Reserve Ptr Pd. Ord. Otter an additional day transport to | |
|  | | | Troops from Nos 2 F.S.D. + Railhead Ypres, carting general stores. 21st T.M. coke returned to the Division | |
|  | | | | Strength 200 O.R. |
|  | | | | H.Q. Mkt Thy |
|  | | | | SSO 21 Div |

Army Form C. 2118.

# WAR DIARY
## INTELLIGENCE SUMMARY.
*(Erase heading not required.)*

ADO 21st Divn.

| Place | Date | Hour | Summary of Events and Information | Remarks and references to Appendices |
|---|---|---|---|---|
| WORMHOUDT | 30/11/17 | | Drew Supplies from PROVEN. All reserved Rations to receive 1 days pud rations being held in supply Col. Drew 1 extra days forage for H.Q. Bruns & refilled in reserve. Partially obtained from Railhead, CASSEL M2 7 SN, & Railhead HAZEBROUCK. Obtained 20 Tons Coal from R.R. <br><br> M.A.Elliot Major <br> ADO 21st Divn | ADO 21st Divn. |

S.S.O. 21st Division
DAD S + T Divn

# WAR DIARY
or
# INTELLIGENCE SUMMARY
(Erase heading not required.)

| Places | Date | Hour | Summary of Events and Information | Remarks and references to Appendices |
|---|---|---|---|---|
| WORMHOUDT | 1/4/17 | | Railhead PROVEN. Drew supplies from Pack Train, Transhipped by lorry to Meters Enage Railway at PROVEN. Refilled at Railhead as follows: — Divl Tps HERZEELE, 64th Bde WORMHOUDT, and 110th Bde HOUTKERQUE. 62nd Bde drew supplies by M.T. direct from R.H.d. 21st Trench Mortar Bde arrived in WORMHOUDT from FERFAY with no rations. Issued 200 ration rifle meat meal. 30% Fresh Meat 75% Bread. Loading of Meter Guage not completed until 7pm Refilling delayed partly. | |
| | 2/4/17 | | | |
| | 3/4/17 4/4/17 | | Nothing special to record. Reported that refilling very late owing to late train arrivals. Drew 2000 men 1400 Horse Rations for reserve in Supply Col — making 2 day's reserve of supplies held there of 20,000 men + 5700 animals. Late arrival of supply train from Base, refilling very late in consequence. 30% Fresh Meat, 75% Bread. 75% Fresh Meat. | |
| | 5/4/17 | | 80% Fresh Meat, 100% Bread. Bomb dropped at Railhead by hostile plane. 3 killed + 7 wounded. 62nd Vegetables recd. 39th Divl Sply drew rations for first time from 64th M/port, 34 men. | |
| | 6/4/17 | | 21st Trench Mortar Bde transferred from 64th Bde group to Divl Troops — Strength 186. 12 O.R. 75% Fresh Meat, 100% Bread, 6 ozs Veg. | |
| | 7/4/17 | | 75% Fresh Meat, 100% Bread, 6 ozs Vegetables — 21st Divl Wing Le returned from M'long area. | WLU |

Army Form C. 2118.

# WAR DIARY
## or
## INTELLIGENCE SUMMARY.
(Erase heading not required.)

J.J.O. 21st Div -

| Place | Date | Hour | Summary of Events and Information | Remarks and references to Appendices |
|---|---|---|---|---|
| WORMHOUDT | 8/1/17 | | 70% Fresh bread, 100% bread. 6 ozs Vegetables. | |
| | 9/1/17 | | " " " 10% Dried Fruits - | |
| | 10/1/17 | | supply in hand to whole of division. No Dried Fruits. | |
| | 11/1/17 | | No forage arrived at Railhead, so moved away the days Reserve supply in hand to whole of division. No grain arrived on Train. Refilled by Rlw twice. No forage arrived at Railhead. No forage arrived at railhead, so moved the second days reserve to hand to units of division. 64th Fld marched at 6.30 am to HAZEBROUCK en route for I Army. | |
| | 12/1/17 | | HQ Co & Artillery units marched from HERZEELE and to I Army Area - Refilled at HAZEBROUCK | |
| BETHUNE | 13/1/17 | | 64th Fld Amb concentrated around BETHUNE. N°4 Co Train at ANVEZIN. Drew supplies from BETHUNE for 64th Fld & Div Tps - 64th Fld went into billets in relief of brigade of 6th Div | |
| | | | Drew supplies for 110th - 64th & Div'l Troops | |
| | | | " " " - " - " 110th Fld went into huts in relief of brigade of 6th Div | |
| NOEUX | 14/1/17 | | Drew supplies by Horse Transport from 64th & 110th Fld Ambs. Rest for 62nd Div Train. Took over the following units from 6th Div - drew supplies for 1st time for same 14th - 1 Army Rd Workshop, No 1 Army Dec: 9th Rd Park, | |
| | 15/1/17 | | 251 Tunn Co RE, 253 Tunn Co RE, 170 Tunn Co RE, 197 Land Drainage Co RE, 3rd Army F.A. Pde. The 38 AFA Pde, 21st Div Amb Details, attd 764th Fld Amb forp: the 170, 251, 253 Co RE & 197 Co RE, 1st - 2 Co to | |
| | 16/1/17 | | 9th Rd Park add to the Pde. 62nd Bde arrived in area from II Army. | |

Army Form C. 2118.

No 21 Div—

# WAR DIARY
## or
## INTELLIGENCE SUMMARY.
(Erase heading not required.)

| Place | Date | Hour | Summary of Events and Information | Remarks and references to Appendices |
|---|---|---|---|---|
| NOEUX | 17/1/17 | | Drew supplies for 64th, 110th & Div. Tps hy H.T. & for 62nd by lorries. Full Hay/oats ration received. Oats 13 lbs. H.T. quits for other classes of animals. Fresh meat 60%. Bread 75%. Replied at 8 am. drew from RHQ at 12-15 pm. Train H.R. moved from BETHUNE to NOEUX; arrived at 1/6th Div. | |
| | 18/1/17 | | 2 9/0 drew 3 up dried veg issued per man. Rum/pickles/candles drawn. 60% fresh meat & 75% bread. ½ | |
| | 19/1/17 | | 2nd Squadron machine guns arrived from 1st Cavalry Div. 101 men. 4 H.D. Rations drawn for consumption 20th. by 62 Bde R.F. pump. Usual preparation of fresh ornament. Full allotment ration drawn. Bathing particulars attached. | |
| | 20/1/17 | | " | |
| | 21/1/17 | | " | |
| | 22/1/17 | | Authority issued from DDSUT to obtain extra forage from Army Purchase B°, up to S16 ff 17 ad W76h 2. Fresh Meat 30 lb. until further notice. D.D.S.T. S.1642. 2.1.17 | |
| | 23/1/17 | | " | |
| | 24/1/17 | | Nothing particular to record | |
| | 25/1/17 | | " | |
| | 26/1/17 | | " | |

Army Form C. 2118.

# WAR DIARY
## or
## INTELLIGENCE SUMMARY.

(Erase heading not required.)

S.S.O. 21st Div

Instructions regarding War Diaries and Intelligence Summaries are contained in F. S. Regs., Part II. and the Staff Manual respectively. Title pages will be prepared in manuscript.

| Place | Date | Hour | Summary of Events and Information | Remarks and references to Appendices |
|---|---|---|---|---|
| | 27/2/17 28/2/17 | | 30,000 Soda Tablet drawn to be held in reserve. Nothing further to report. | |

[signature]

2353 Wt W2544/1454 700,000 5/15 D. D. & L. A.D.S.S./Forms/C. 2118.

# WAR DIARY

**Dubbcah**

Army Form C. 2118.

## INTELLIGENCE SUMMARY

MO M.T. Div.

| Place | Date | Hour | Summary of Events and Information | Remarks and references to Appendices |
|---|---|---|---|---|
| HONDTHOULST | 1/4/17 | | Railhead PROVEN. Drew supplies from Pack train. Transhipped by lorry to Motor Lorry Railway at PROVEN - trafficked at Railhead as follows - Dual Tps IRELEEK, 6 yrd Div HONDTHOULST, 2nd Div Pole HOUTKERQUE. 62nd Bde drew supplies by M.T. direct from R.H. 21st Tren.h Mortar Bde arrived in HONDTHOULST from TERFAY with no rations. Issued 200 Rations that night. 37% Fresh Meat 75% Bread. Loading of motor lorries not completed until 7 p.m. Supply delayed badly. | |
| | 2/4/17 | | | |
| | 3/4/17 | | Railway opened to new depot. Report that refilling vehicles ony to take train arrivals. Over 2000 men 1400 horse Ration for reserve supply. Col. Dalby today recommended supplies held there of 20,000 men + 5000 animals - Late arrival of supply train from Base - refilling very late in consequence - 30% Fresh Meat 75% Fresh Bread - other commodities as usual. | |
| | 4/4/17 | | | |
| | 5/4/17 | | 80% Fresh Meat, 100% Bread. Bomb dropped at Railhead by hostile plane - 3 killed + 7 wounded. | |
| | 6/4/17 | | 62 gd Regulation red - 3rd Div Hy. Ammunition Park from 64th Div from 64th Div front 34 men F.D. 21st Trench Mortar Bde transferred from 64th Div front to Dual Troops - Strength 186 - 1180 F.D. 75% Fresh Meat, 100% Bread. bags veg - | |
| | 7/4/17 | | 75% Fresh Meat, 100% Bread, 6 gd Nipplates - 2 H.O.W. tehnicals returned from M.W. rep mn - | |

MLM

# WAR DIARY / INTELLIGENCE SUMMARY

Army Form C. 2118.

T.P.O. 21st Div.

| Place | Date | Hour | Summary of Events and Information | Remarks and references to Appendices |
|---|---|---|---|---|
| ERMITOUDT | 8/4/17 | | 75% detrained, 100% horsed, 6 yards Vegetables. | |
| | 9/4/17 | | — | |
| | 10/4/17 | | In Divl. Reserve. | |
| | 11/4/17 | | Advance arrived at Rackhead so issued enough for days Reserve. | |
| | | | Supply in hand to strength of Division. No gun arrived on Train. Refilled 64th Fd Tunnl. 62nd Fd Ambce, 73rd Fd Amb. Advance arrived at Railhead. Services returned kays reserve issued to units of Division. 64th Fd Amb marched at 8.30 am to HAZEBROUCK en route for I Army | |
| | 12/4/17 | | 143 Co & Artillery units marched from HERTZEELE area to I Army area. Refilled at HAZEBROUCK | |
| BETHUNE | 13/4/17 | | 64th Fd Amb concentrated around BETHUNE. No 4 Co Train at ANNEZIN - Drew supplies from BETHUNE for 64th F.A. 1 Divl. Tps. 110th Fd Amb went into line in relief of 6th Dvn | |
| | | | Drew supplies for 110th Fd & 62nd Bde Troops. | |
| NOEUX | 14/4/17 | | — — — 110th Bde went into line in relief of Brigade of 6th Dvn. | |
| | 15/4/17 | | — — — | |
| | 16/4/17 | | Drew supplies by Motor Transport for 64th, 110th Bdes, Divl Tps, 62nd Bde Tps. Took over the following units from 6th Div. Divisional Supplies for same 19th. 1 Army Workshops, No 1 Mt Sec. 9th Res. Park, 251 Tunn Co RE, 183 Tunn Co RE, 170 Tunn Co RE, 38th Army F.A. Bde, 147 Corps Railway Co RE, 38 AFA Bde, 21st Div Arty details, 465 Bty - 4th Arty Bde Army, 110 Bde 183 Co RE & 147th RE, 142 Sec. 9th Res. Park all to the 6th Bde, 62nd Bde arrived in area from II Army | |

2353  Wt. W2544/1454  700,000  5/15  D, D & L  A.D.S.S./Forms/C. 2118.

# WAR DIARY

## INTELLIGENCE SUMMARY

Army Form C. 2118.

A.D. 31 Div.

| Place | Date | Hour | Summary of Events and Information | Remarks and references to Appendices |
|---|---|---|---|---|
| NOEUX | 17/1/17 | | Drew supplies for 94th - 110th & 3rd Tps by H.T. & for 62nd by lorries - Full vegetable ration received. Oats 13 lbs per gun to other classes of animals. Jack rent 637 Pere 757. Refilled at 8am directs from R.I.P. at 12-15 pm - Train H.Q. moved from BETHUNE to GIVEUX & ditto of 16th Div. | |
| | 18/1/17 | | 2 pontoons & m.g. dried Mg. issued per man - Bulletproof tanks drawn - 6 of Jack rent & 7 of Pere rent. ¾ | |
| | 19/1/17 | | 2nd Squadron Machine Guns arrived from 1st Cavalry Div - 101 men & 4 h.d. Returns drawn to consumption 20 th by 62nd ambulance & 2 Bde.p ost - Several inspection of bread equipment. Mill vegetable ration drawn - | |
| | 20/1/17 21/1/17 | | Nothing particular to record | |
| | 22/1/17 | | Authority rec'd from D.D.S.T. to obtain extra bags from Army Purchase Bd. offr - Ship H.Q. received 7 h.d. | |
| | 23/1/17 | | Next 30 lbs until further notice as with D.D.S.T S/1842 dated 22-1-17 | |
| | 24/1/17 | | Nothing particular to record | |
| | 25/1/17 | | | |
| | 26/1/17 | | | |

# WAR DIARY

## INTELLIGENCE SUMMARY

Army Form C. 2118.

S.S.O. 21st Div

| Place | Date | Hour | Summary of Events and Information | Remarks and references to Appendices |
|---|---|---|---|---|
| | 27.2.17 | | 30,000 Sudu Tablets drawn to be dealt in reserve. | |
| | 28.2.17 | | Nothing to hand to report. | |

Macintosh

# WAR DIARY
## or
## INTELLIGENCE SUMMARY.

Army Form C. 2118.

S.S.O. 21st Div.

| Place | Date | Hour | Summary of Events and Information | Remarks and references to Appendices |
|---|---|---|---|---|
| | March 1917 | | | |
| | 1. | | Genl'd to 1st Bde hqrs by hqrs of BUSNES | |
| | 2. | | 1 6 2nd Bde hqrs, infield at BUSNES | |
| | 3. | | Arrangts drawn in view of that very 5th return. | |
| | 4. | | Arrangmt drawn for 6th Div. 1st Air R.E. Coy. to relieve 9th Bde. Parts 197 tons, R.E. 2/1 Transport tons 2:53 Tank tons 2:1170 | |
| | | | ½ Transport tons. | |
| | 5. | | Railhead BETHUNE. 6y of ALKBrigs handed to 3 armys; other drawn | |
| | | | Horse Ts. 24th Batt 38th Army  +   2 A.T. Bde drawn to 24th Div. | |
| | 6. | | Railhead BETHUNE " " | |
| | 7. | | " " 24th Batt 38th Army field Bde returned by 24th Div. | |
| | 8. | | " " moved to LILLERS while division loaded by M.T. Did Tank. | |
| | | | 1st field at OTH'm, 6r & Div of BUSNES. 64 at ROBECQ, 110 at NOEUX LES MINES. | |
| | | | Sum 2 8th. H.Q. 38th A.F.A. Bde D.B.B & A.C returned by 24th Div. | |
| | 9. | | A"38 Bde by 6th Div. and 72 mt Bde by 5th Div . 110th Bde rel'd 6th Div. | |
| | 10. | | Railhead LILLERS, division began march and arrived as much | |
| | | | Fred a possible. | |

hMM

# WAR DIARY or INTELLIGENCE SUMMARY.

Army Form C. 2118.

S.S.O 21st Div.

| Place | Date | Hour | Summary of Events and Information | Remarks and references to Appendices |
|---|---|---|---|---|
| | March 1917 | | | |
| | 11. | | Relieved Bryan. | |
| | 12. | | Drew rations for 1st Tpt MT, 62nd and 64th Bde Synk & ran trans. Sadie down in lieu of infantry Tpt. P.M. 62nd and 64th Bde Synks drew from ROUQUEMAISON. 1st Tpt drew from PREVENT. | |
| | 13. | | 62nd and 64th Bde Synks drew from ROUQUEMAISON. 1st Tpt drew from LIGNY. 64th Bde drew fm 2 H.T. Echn Refromed all the Synks. Stated aby Tpt finished cleary and 1st Tpt drew by horse transport " " " fm the Synk. | |
| | 15. | | | |
| | 16. | | 30% Rest Meat. 6½ op Veg (potatoes + onions) 75% Bread. LEO returned from 10 days specl leave. | |
| | 18 | | Half Batt. 1st Yorks moved to FOSSEUX enroute to DAINVILLE for work in tramways there - 21st French Motor Bde moved to ARRAS - attached to 30th Div. Rations as from 19th (145th Bde RFA) hoped next. [All MT ration (reduced to 150 M+V) drawn fm Jagutin y Bread - Half Bt: 1st Yorks Moved Synds B: moved from 7th Corps area to FOSSEUX & att. to 14 Div fm supplies - Rail supplies for that Bt: to DAINVILLE by lorry | |

Army Form C. 2118.

# WARE DIARY
## or
## INTELLIGENCE SUMMARY.
(Erase heading not required.)

Ab 21st Div

| Place | Date | Hour | Summary of Events and Information | Remarks and references to Appendices |
|---|---|---|---|---|
| LUCHEUX | March 20th | | BOUQUEMAISON Ref. Notified meal at Richbent - all Ref. | |
| | 21st | | " " | |
| | 22. | | 60% Reapplant drawn. 1 Serjeant det Co 494 all ranks. Kindom det Co 440 men att to Div. | |
| | | | Serration - Drew from Railhead Head returns to DOULLENS. | |
| | 23. | | 9th Bde, Det DAC, Thistle reached St Pol in march homefrom II Army. Supplies drawn from | |
| | | | RSO St POL (in these units) - 64th Mtr moved to POMMERA & GRESNATS. | |
| | 24th | | 9th Bde RFA, Thistle rejoined Division from 1st Army. Drew supplies 62 Bde from SAULTY. | |
| | 25th | | 2nd and 62nd Bde marched to found area. 2Co. Train to KIENVILLERS | |
| | 27th | | 110 Bde. to Trenches - 95th Bde R.FA. marched to found area. HR Co to ADINFER | |
| | 28th | | Drew Supplies for HR group from Bouquemaison. 4th 62 Bde y 64 Bdes from SAULTY. | |
| | | | No 3 Coy Train of 110th Bde marched from I Army area to rejoin division - | animals 76 |
| | | | Handed over the attached labour + tobacanits to 56th Div. Rations- Strength 3900 | |
| | 29th | | Took over 291 Bde R.F.A. + there unto 1749 men 845 Horses- | |
| | 30th | | " " " Drew supplies from Bouquemaison for Div Troops + 110th Bde; from SAULTY for 62nd + 64th Bdes - | |
| | 31st | | " " " from GOUY | |

# WAR DIARY or INTELLIGENCE SUMMARY

Army Form C. 2118.

S.S.O. 21st Div

**1917**

| Place | Date | Hour | Summary of Events and Information | Remarks and references to Appendices |
|---|---|---|---|---|
| BAVINCOURT | April 1st | | Railhead BEAUMETZ forward division - Train from Base arrived 4 p.m., loaded supplies at Thun. roads very bad owing to traffic - motor lorries making transport difficulties very great - | |
| | 2nd | | loaded supplies by H.T. for 62nd Div. - K190th Isdes 7 lorries for Div Tpt. Train did not arrive at railhead until 8 a.m. 3rd. great disorganisation of supply services in consequence coupled with indifferent goods. Rifled late in the evening. Pollution of oats downfall artillery horses. | |
| | 3rd | | Orders to dump 19416 Iron Rations from SAULTY / Indivision - transport arranged by S.M.T.O. 7th Corps. Supplies dumped at ADINFER. - Full Div ration drawn fr Artillery horses. | |
| | 4th | | 32nd Railhead drawn from Railhead - 60 % - friend - Lifts/5min rate. New supplies of Tp.m. | |
| PUMMIERS | 5th | | Railroads still responsible for difficulties of transport - shortage of lorries - Unable to have supplies forwarded to Div through 9 addnl. lorries of St.G. Div being attached to 62nd Div. - Troop train of BEAUMETZ 1990 × 20 Iron Rations 1370 × 50 oats. | |
| | 6th | | 21st Div drew 31,000 Iron Rations + 8400 lbs oats from their store. 56th Div. drew 7,200 Iron Rations & balance of oats remaining at BEAUMETZ Store, total left on hand 12m Iron Rations gradually being drawn by NCO i/chard of 56th Div Train. Distribum fr. Br. | |
| | 7th | | Indivision from Beaumetz store to 56th Div. 130. 21st Div leaving 700 Iron Rations in our net. 57. Headcheat 139th Arind. M. tc. forwarded 24 rd rations - Orops. moved fruit load to DOULLENS fr. rail - Road generally 7 Coles M. Ogoody 9 p.m. 21st Div. | |

W.M. Westroper
S.E.O 21st Div.

Army Form C. 2118.

# WAR DIARY
## or
## INTELLIGENCE SUMMARY.
(Erase heading not required.)

Instructions regarding War Diaries and Intelligence Summaries are contained in F. S. Regs., Part II. and the Staff Manual respectively. Title pages will be prepared in manuscript.

| Place | Date | Hour | Summary of Events and Information | Remarks and references to Appendices |
|---|---|---|---|---|
| | April | | | |
| OHMIERS | 8th | | 2 days' rations issued to whole Division & 1 from Sd Ration feed dumps. 2 1/5 galls. Rum drawn from Corps reserve. Rum issue to troops. Weather very cold. | |
| | 9th | | " " | " |
| | 10th | | " " | " |
| | 11th | | " " | " |
| | 12th | | 1 out ration of Army ration. No drawing from Railhead. Still cold | |
| ADINFER WOOD | 13th | | Railhead changed to BOISLEUX. Supply train arrived early, drew supplies by Train bearers, no man arrived on train. Transferred several units to 7 Corps Troops - 58th Div. Arty & Other Troops received orders to report new division. Preparations drawn. No supply train arrived at Railhead - drew on 1 day's reserve held in Supply Col. & refused (2 d/m of units). 1 Preserved Rations drawn. | |
| | 14th | | Supplies dumped at 1 p.m. Supplies held in reserve - proceeded to ACHIET-LE-GRAND to load again - loaded supplies for 181 Tun. Co. RE, 338 Road Construction Co RE, 132 A.T. Co RE, for first time. No petroleum wheat arrived, all preserved rations - | |
| | 15th | | loaded at WARLINCOURT, all preserved rations - Division which in the line by 33rd Divn. Pres. Rations. Preserved Rations, Men in line & Reserve. | |
| | 16th | | " " | |
| | 17th | | Loaded supplies for Divl Troops Group at WARLINCOURT. 62, 64 & 110 Bdes at BOISLEUX - all preserved rations - Men in heavy bacon. On arrival at WARLINCOURT was informed by R.O. that supplies should have been drawn for whole division at BOISLEUX - 3rd Army Q. 19th Corps Cavalry (Northumbd. H'rs) transferred to 33rd Divn. Endeavd to draw on part of Corps Q. 1 Now balance of forage deficit to be drawn from WARLINCOURT, also rum. | |

# WAR DIARY or INTELLIGENCE SUMMARY

Army Form C. 2118.

S.S.O. 21st Div.

| Place | Date | Hour | Summary of Events and Information | Remarks and references to Appendices |
|---|---|---|---|---|
| ADINFER WOOD | April 18th | | Loaded all Groups at BOISLEUX by M.T. Shortage of supplies there, drew 7,000 rations from SAVLTY. 70% Fresh Meat recd., instead but Biscuit. Not in lieu of Bacon, tho in lieu of Vegetables. Issued the shortages from ACHIET drawn from BOISLEUX to the 62nd but 110th Bdes. 11th Lancers(P) drew supplies for 1st time from Div. Transport. Run issued | |
| | 19th | | Drew supplies from railhead by Train Wagons for all Groups. 50% Fresh Meat, 75% Bread, 100% Potatoes. 1% of Oranges, 20g figs in lieu of Onions. M.H. 4 ozs.; 1 oz Pickles. Drew from SAVLTY 49,00 lbs Hay. 800 rations delivered on supply train at BOISLEUX — Run drawn from divisions from Corps dump in ARRAS & kept on supply Column. — Run issued to brigades & full issue to Artillery | |
| | 20th | | Fresh Meat 60%, Bread 100%, 4 oz Potatoes, M.V. 4 oz; 8 oz Minced Cake drawn = Figs in lieu of Onions — Rum full issue. Sent to Savlty for 1500 rations 10 galls whale oil 10 Masks D. Lp. 160 hurricane lamps; 170 lb Candles. | |
| | 21st | | Fresh Meat normal proportions, no hay arrived sent to SAVLTY for 41,790 lb Hay. 11th sent Lances(P) rationed for last time by S.O. Div. Tho. previous to returning to 30th Div. — Drew supplies from Railhead 2 groups by Lorries & by 14th Bde. Horse Transport. | |
| | 22nd | | Loaded at R.M.S. Lorries for B/21/10th. Due tho 70th Bde by H.T. 60% Fresh Meat, full issue of Bread, 11% of Potatoes. Onions, 1 ration Bacon & ration M.V. to make up — 11% of Potatoes. | |
| | 23rd | | 110th Bde. moved from BOISLEUX to BOIRY — 62nd Bde. to BEAUREVILLE — Hd.Qrs. Train moved to HAMELINCOURT N° 3 c. to BOIRY-ST-RICTRUDE — | WMcL. |

**Army Form C. 2118.**

# WAR DIARY
or
## INTELLIGENCE SUMMARY.
(Erase heading not required.)

ADS 21st Divn

| Place | Date | Hour | Summary of Events and Information | Remarks and references to Appendices |
|---|---|---|---|---|
| ADINFER WOOD | 24th | | Rather shelled by high velocity gun - no damage done. Drew 2500 lb frozen Rabbits in part of meat issue. 90% Rest meat. Overissue from Park Distribution - dues have gone to division. Rumour received a forward following to Artillery & one to Brigade. Motor Train moved from BEAUMETZ to BEAUREVILLE. Obtained an increase in proportion of Candles from 240 to 7 cases x 7 Ms daily - hens run for division. | |
| | 25th | | Drew Rations and Milked for 150th & 11th Rde Marshal; 7th A.A.B.th, 235 A.T.C. R.E. 'M' Sec. Sph G. R.E., & VII Corps Mule Column, 18th Middlesex, 'B' Sqd 33rd Dac 19th Cattle & RE. Tortoise 3063 & 861 animals. All transferred from 33rd Divn. Freshmeat 60% Bread & Rice (trades) fullissue. Obtained authority from 7th Corps & 223rd of 25th to destroy 150 lb Mutton & 468 lb Rabbits damaged by frost & chemical extinguishers when hills on along at 8th Supply Col. Camp on 24th. The chickens the duty proved by OC Supply Col. | |
| HAMELINCOURT | 26th | | Forwarded full dump from SEO 33 Divn - 15 Tons Coke, 7 Tons Charcoal, 6 Tons Wood. Train A139 moved to HAMELINCOURT, bn # 1110th R. 8 to trenches, 63 in relief of 33rd Divn. 60% Rest Meat. | |
| | 27th | | 75% Meat. Rations shop also - Received 18 Tons (oat) from HARDINGCOURT & ARRAS. Supply Train arrived at 11 am - 18th Middlesex (Pioneer) rejoined 33 Divn. 33rd Divn Salvage Coys divisn Empty, Demobilized infant Tim - 106 Men & Animals - Took over a Petrol dump of 33rd Divn. at BOISIEUX station - Coke 7 tons charcoal 3 tons wood 6 tons - Normal percentage of flesh meat frozen Hyp. chickens, Rabbit also rurus. | |

MMM

Army Form C. 2118.

ADS 21st Div.

# WAR DIARY
## or
## INTELLIGENCE SUMMARY.
(Erase heading not required.)

| Place | Date | Hour | Summary of Events and Information | Remarks and references to Appendices |
|---|---|---|---|---|
| | April | | | |
| MMEUINCOURT | 28th | | Enemy shelled locality for third night in succession. No casualties. Whizzbangs appear to have been used at intervals from 9.30 pm to 4 am. Drew supplies of RFC by Horse Transport. 50% rations and bread. Chestnut Horses drawn to - Remounts division. | |
| | 30th | | No Supply Train arrived at Railhead. Drew the 1(extra) days reserve dumped at Supply Coy Camp. Learned same. Hostile shelling around BOISIEUX station. No damage done. | |

W. A. Stuart Major
SSO 21st Div.

Army Form C. 2118.

# WAR DIARY
## or
## INTELLIGENCE SUMMARY.
(Erase heading not required.)

L.L.O 21st Divn

| Place | Date | Hour | Summary of Events and Information | Remarks and references to Appendices |
|---|---|---|---|---|
| | 1917 | | | |
| MELINCOURT | May 1st | | Resumed drawing supplies from BOISLEUX-AU-MONT. 40% Fresh Meat +70% Bread Which included 2 oz Rice & fresh head ration. Cheese ration awarded to 2 oz daily. | |
| | 2nd | | 40% Fresh Meat +70% Bread with 2 oz Rice added. Run Ration. Undrinken 2010 Men's Rations. Taking this quantity off Reserve & supply Col which leaves a balance of 800 there in reserve. | |
| | 3rd | | Fresh meat about 35% Bread 65%. Although supplies loz Rice. Cabbage grown quantity of Kale & fell near MOYENVILLE and opened at 6 pm troops. No troops in village. Received agreement. | |
| | 4th | | Transferred to Cotelar 33 DAC & 33 Divn Trains to 33 Divn for consumption 7.. Fresh head Meat train purchased about 50%. Dried Veg & Figs drawn & 2 oz potatoes. Made arrangements some Kale the division always find being found in Knightland with no meat. Kale toward | |
| | 6th | | 40% Fresh Meat +33% Bread, Figs & Potatoes. Kale round, also Lime Juice | |
| | 9th | | by the Kale carts out of plain. 62+110 - received in -. 50% Fresh Meat +80% Bread. | |
| | 10th | | Full issue of Lime juice obtained, fresh & sour about 50%. Fresh Veg. had Dried Veg drawn | |
| | 11th | | to the moment. BELLACOURT own Train by Road also. Transferred 336 R.E. +TAT.C.P.S. 570 Men + 61 Animals, 132 A.T.C R.E. 290 Men 63 Animals & 187 Train to R.E. 524 Men & Horses to 33rd Divn for consumption to the night. Took over details of 33rd Divn & PERLES +73rd Env NERS. 36 Men & attached to 110th R.H.Amp for consumption 15th. Drew 60% Fresh Meat + Bread, 30% Potato 3 oz Onions & Dried Veg from RMB. | |

MWW

# WAR DIARY or INTELLIGENCE SUMMARY

Army Form C. 2118.

ADO 21st Divn.

| Place | Date | Hour | Summary of Events and Information | Remarks and references to Appendices |
|---|---|---|---|---|
| ADINFER WOOD | May 12th | — | Division moved into Corps Reserve, Divl H.Q. Train H.Q. moved from HAMELINCOURT to ADINFER WOOD). No 1 Coy Train at A.S.C. 3 E. (54°). Artillery still in action. No 2 Coy S & T. o. g. (54°). No 3 Coy W 30. a. g. r. (57°). H4 Coy R 31 a. 8. 8. (56°). Respective brigades concentrated around the area. Arranged that time Jume should be drawn three times weekly from Railhead for the division — 50% fresh bread & 50% bread drawn from Railhead. The dates & kind of fire amount of bread supp¹ for consumption so did not draw them. H.Q. left for encampment in hands of R.S.O., BOISLEUX. | |
|  | 14th | — | Sent to ARRAS for 2273 lb Bacon, 910 lb Cheese, 2706 lb Oats, 360 lb Chloride Lime (for 21 Divn.) (Burial party). Train shut loaded in that consignment. 50% fresh bread Rosp Bread including ray. rations Rationed Town Major BIENVILLERS (included 33rd Dnl. details about 27 men). Reported some 110th Brigade front. | |
|  | 16th | — | Sent to coal from BOISLEUX. Supply Train arrived deficient of certain commodities, also 50 Tons of coal from BOISLEUX. Sent KARCAS for 26.000 lbs HAY. CHEESE 960 lb., Bacon 1224 lb., Tea 160 lb. Arrange supplies of fresh Meat & Bread. | |
|  | 13th | — | XIX Corps Cavalry (Mothuen? Hrs B. Sqn²) left m Corps Area for I.T.P.O. Area — 110 men & 114 horses. Sent kit. | |
|  | 17th | — | Issued Supplies for first time to Town Major BERLES-AU-BOIS 13 men, Town Major BAILLEULVAL 444 men for first time. Supplies for BERLES sent by 110th Isle Supply Offr. Shoes for BAILLEULVAL by | |

By the S.O. Lu

half

# WAR DIARY
## or
## INTELLIGENCE SUMMARY.

Army Form C. 2118.

S.P.O  21st Divn.

| Place | Date | Hour | Summary of Events and Information | Remarks and references to Appendices |
|---|---|---|---|---|
| RIDINGER WOOD | May 18th | | Sent to ARRAS for 2,300 lb Hay, 42,600 lb Oats; Supply Train being defrosted - 50% Fresh Bread/Meat - Onions Dried Fruits - | |
| | 20th | | Sent to ARRAS for Tea 90 lb, Sugar 1200 lb, Biscuit 700 lb, P.Meat 1652 Rtns, M+V 2692 Rtns, + 700 tins M+V in lieu of Bacon. Obtained 6 Tons Steam Coal for Forden Machines (Div. Hdy) | |
| | 21st | | Drew 10 Tons Pressed Cake from Railhead, distributed this in due proportion to all Groups. | |
| | 22nd | | Sent to ARRAS for 10,000 lb Hay 1/26, 100 lb Oats. Potatoes drawn 4 oz per man. | |
| | 23rd | | 15th Army F.A. Bde drew rations ? last time from unit 25th. Transferred to 19th Corps en route for IInd Army. Strength men 10t6. Animals 969 (including 28 HD). | |
| | 25th | | Drew 15 Tons Coal from ARRAS - Arrangements made to ration 2 French Troops working inland at HENDECOURT Concerned. Rations undertaken. Usual % of Fresh Bread/Meat; Orange, Potatoes + Onions drawn - | |
| | 26th | | 21st Employed C. arrived from Peace - Strength 100 men 1 officer. Fresh rations from 27th. the Party is inducted to replace bodies at present sent by Units to Train Company. Ten officers were decipred out. 6.9% Fresh Meat & Bread; Onions, Potatoes & Orange drawn from Railhead. | |
| | 28th | | Other 12,000 pieces of Clearing Gun from SAVIETY (authorised by DDST 3rd Army) Released as Supply Co. to be issued subsequently to Infantry Brigades - 50% Fresh Meat & Bread; 2 oz Onions 3 oz Potatoes - | MSW |

# WAR DIARY
## or
## INTELLIGENCE SUMMARY.

Army Form C. 2118.

S.S.O. 21st Division

| Place | Date | Hour | Summary of Events and Information | Remarks and references to Appendices |
|---|---|---|---|---|
| ADINFER WOOD | May 29th | | About 50% Field Bread Ovens drawn from Railhead, full Repleate ration (including equivt of Bread) drawn with less 33rd Div. to take over certain units from 1 on consumption. 19 June Tal cookhand one Town Major in back area at present in 21st Div ration strength. | |
| | 30th | | (Transferred) 338 R.E. Carts. Coll: B busmen 158 horses, 132 A.T. Carts. 236 men 436 horses, 181 Turn Co R.E. 524 men + 8 horses from 33rd Div. to more 31st Rang't Rantii one Town Major HENDECOURT 2 O.R. Town Major BERLES 19 lain Town Major BAILLEULVAL 44 o.r., Town Major BIENVILLERS 33 O.R. for consumption 2nd June all to 33rd Division. 30% Regimental adjnt and A.P. at Railhead, other supplies as usual. 60% Impersed & 70% Bread + Race. Other components of the ration as usual. Trans. H.Q. remained in Div. Reserve; HAMELINCOURT on relief of 33rd Div. by 21st Div., by 10 a.m. 110th Regt. remained in Div. Reserve; | |
| HAMELINCOURT 31st | | | 69th Field Amb. transferred for ration purpose to 33rd Div. strength 363 men + 52 Horses for consumption 2 June onwards. | |

W.R. Kent Major

S.S.O. 21st Div.

Army Form C. 2118.

# WAR DIARY
## or
## INTELLIGENCE SUMMARY.
(Erase heading not required.)

June 1st – 30th 1917.

A.D.O. 21st Division

| Place | Date | Hour | Summary of Events and Information | Remarks and references to Appendices |
|---|---|---|---|---|
| AMPLAINCOURT | 1st | | Obtained 400 tins of solidified paraffin. Issued 150 tins to 64th Bde & 250 to 62nd Bde. Camp kettles to replace lost part of the front. 60% Fresh Meat & 70% Bread. ⅓ up Potatoes. | |
| | 2nd | | 255 Reinforcements arrived from Reinforcement Depot – 24 for 62nd Bde, 74 for 64th Bde & 147 for 110th Bde. Reinforcements await orders to rejoin Railhead. SS 90 Fresh Meat 60%, Bread 70%, Potatoes ⅓ ration. | |
| | 3rd | | 1st Supply Column Co. moved from ADINFER to BOIRY ST. RICTRUDE & informed S.O. 62 Bde they were during rations from 7th Corps Troops. SS 90 Fresh Meat 60%, Bread 60%, Potatoes ⅓ ration (50 again all) drawn. Transferred C.R.E., 21st Div. H.Q., 4 P.M. from 62nd Bde tempt. to Div. Troops for same time. | |
| | 4th | | Drew 1170 tins solidified paraffin from ARRAS. Issued 250 tins to 64th Bde & 150 to 62nd Bde. Draws 15 galls "C" disinfectant solution from 3rd Army tps supply Column. Issued equally between 62 and 64th Bde about 50% Meat, 60% Bread received. Check of rations estimated at 4 trs served at Railhead of about 10% for fresh rations. Meat disrupted - This was distributed among Bde Tps, 62 and 64th Bde. | |
| | 6th | | 100% Bread. SS 90 Fresh Meat, full vegetable ration & potatoes & onions drawn. Issued 5 galls "C" disinfectant fluid to 62 & 15 to 64th Bde, also 2000 solid tablets to each Bde. | |
| | 8th | | Issued 340 tins Solidified Paraffin to 110th Bde. Sent out 15 cwt cart to Lallee & BOYELLES – Drew 20 tons Coal from ARRAS. Sent 2 days rations to LA BAZEQUE Farm for 96 officers & men proceeding on leave to IIIrd Army, numerous Rest camps at BOULOGNE. Issued 17.02 iron Rations drawn from R.H. to division as follows – Div. Tps 80, 62nd Bde 400, 110th Bde 400, 64th Bde 300. Indents for coal not required week 9th. | |
| | | | BOISLEUX – Railhead shelled by Hostile Artillery – 15 killed & 25 wounded J. horses delayed. Clearing Yard by 11.00 pm. | |

Army Form C. 2118.

# WAR DIARY
## or
## INTELLIGENCE SUMMARY.
*(Erase heading not required.)*

SS.O 21st Divn

| Place | Date | Hour | Summary of Events and Information | Remarks and references to Appendices |
|---|---|---|---|---|
| MAEURCOURT | June 9th | | O.C. Train England 10 days leave. Assumed command in his absence. Including a proportion of Rice for meal - 56% Frozen meat. 70% Bread. Sardines 1oz per man. Full Vegetable Ration drawn including Dried Veg. | |
| | 10th | | 55% Fresh meat, 70% Bread, Rice for meal, Sardines 1oz per man - 40oz Potatoes, 2oz Onions - Party of 4th Divl. Artillery bq men 112th Horse arrived & to be attached to D.A.C. for consumption 13th inst. | |
| | 11th | | 60% Frozen meat, 80% Bread - 5oz Onions & Potatoes. | |
| | 12th | | Shortage of suits to hand - 100% Bread. 60% Frozen meat - Send supply of hay to party of 4th Divl Arty. 1 bay wire t.river animals Walter Green Vegetable. could be obtained if send supplies not plentiful at present AMIENS & Ecancham prices excessive - 40% Importment 90% bread - 5oz Vegetables - Sent 1 Ton Oats to 62nd Bde. Bath opening at MOYENNVILLE. | |
| | 13th | | | |
| | 14th | | 60% Meat Frozen - 80% Bread including 2oz Oatmeal 02oz Rice - 64zVegtbls potatoes & Onions. 235 Army Troops Coy R.E. moved from Divisional area without notice leaving ration consumption 16th Advised. Hostile shelling at Observation Balloon vicinity of No 1 Co. Train from 6.30 to 7.30 pm - No damage or casualty. | |
| | 15th | | Nothing to record except that Supply Train arrived with no biscuit or frozen meat. Obtained these from SAULTY. Enemy fired 3 shells into HAMELINCOURT at about 4.30 pm - 2 were duds - No damage. | |
| | 16th | | Hostile shelling of locality from 1.30 am to 4.30 am. No damage done. Sent to SAULTY for Frozen meat for division - none drawing in Park Train. Fresh Meat 60%. Bread 80%. Sent to field quantity of Flour & Oatmeal. | |
| | 17th | | D.H.Q. 65 Tons Coal from ARRAS. Dumped at 64th Bde Refilling Pont. Sent to BELLE EGLISE for present meat (70%) A.5834 Wt.W.4973/M687. 7:30,000 8/16 D.D.&I.Ltd. Forms/C2118/13C(p/s) | |

# WAR DIARY or INTELLIGENCE SUMMARY

Army Form C. 2118.

N.O. 21st Divn.

| Place | Date | Hour | Summary of Events and Information | Remarks and references to Appendices |
|---|---|---|---|---|
| HAMELINCOURT | 18th | | 64th Fd. Amb moved to RASSEUX & BRETONCOURT area. 2 Coy Train to BELLACOURT. Rifled Rds Pompier BELLACOURT returned 6 Tons Coal these. | |
| | 19th | | Transferred to 33rd Divn. 338 Road Const W.R. 580 men, 38 animals; 161 Tun Coy R.E. 334 men 18 animals; 132 A.T. Coy R.E. 457 men + 55 animals; 235 A.T. Coy R.E. 165 men and 58 animals; 7 Coy Works Labour 80 men; 8 Cattle Sec" R.E. 38 men + 28 animals; Parks 4 Divn Arty 69 men + 134 animals – all for 64th Fd. Ade moved frontal trenches + support to POMMIER area. Divn was 20th demonstration 21st. 64th Ade moved frontal trenches + support to POMMIER area. Divn Supplies rail-railed from 62nd Ade by M.T. Took over the undermentioned units from 33rd Divn. Consumption 21st - Town Major Staff - BERLES AU-BOIS - BIENVILLERS 64 men. 1 L.D.; HENDECOURT 2 men; BAILLEULVAL 40 men; 64th Field Ambulance 450 men + 52 animals. | |
| ADINFER WOOD | 20th | | 110th Ade moved to BLAIREVILLE area. Drew supplies from Railhead to 62nd + 64th Ades. Lorries 62nd dump at BELLACOURT; 64th POMMIER CHURCH. Sent 3 Tons coal to 64th Ade dump. Train R.E. moved to ADINFER WOOD as relief of dump by 33rd Divn. | |
| | 21st | | 30% Fresh Meat. 90% Fresh Bread. 7 oz Vegetables including dried. | |
| | 22nd | | Sent 6 Tons coal to 2 Coy Train at BELLACOURT. 3 Tons Wood to 4 Coy Train at POMMIER. 30% Fresh Meat. 90% Bread. 5 oz Veg. Returned. Sent to BELLE EGLISE for some biscuits. Sent 3 Tons Coal to POMMIER for 64th Ade. | |
| | 23rd | | Nothing to report except Bread + Meat remained at same percentage as previously. – M.W. | |

# WAR DIARY
## or
## INTELLIGENCE SUMMARY.
(Erase heading not required.)

Army Form C. 2118.

S.S.D. 21st Division

| Place | Date | Hour | Summary of Events and Information | Remarks and references to Appendices |
|---|---|---|---|---|
| BIMPER WOOD | June 24th | | Reinforcements arrived - 62nd Bde 71 men; 64th Bde 56 men; 110th Bde 117 men - Thursday's rations drawn & issued to these parties - Divisional Rest Camp party of 68 men proceeded to VALERY-SUR-SOMME - Sent rations to "B" Hutments AT BAZEQUE farm [unclear] by lorry - 30% frozen Meat, 90% Bread, 4 oz Potatoes and Dried Veg - dried fruits also - 20% fresh meat; other supplies arrived - obtained 11 sacks of flour & distributed them over numerous [unclear]. | |
| | 25th 26th 27th | | " " | |
| | 28th | | Sent to ACHIET-LE-GRAND for 40 tons Rice - to BAPAUME for 600 tb Bread - | |
| | 29th | | 64th Bde moves up to forward area from POMMIER. 60% Bacon & meat, 95% bread, 6 oz vegetables drawn - 62nd & 63rd Bde moved to FEUILLE - M'Vay to BOIRY-ST-RICTRUDE. 60% Frozen Meat, 90% Bread, 5 oz vegetables - 8 oz potatoes - | |
| | 30th | | Transfer from 33rd Divn :- Transport Column 79 men; "Cable sec'n" RE 39 men; 28 Horses; 132 A.T.Co RE 495 men & 69 animals; No.1 Sec. 27 Res. Park 47 men & 33 animals; Infantry 4th Divn Artillery 106 men & 176 animals - all in Divisional Troops Group ; 338 Road Construction Co RE 608 men & 35 animals m 62nd Bde group; and 181 Tunn. Co RE 576 men and 10 animals in 64th Bde - 110th Bde to MOYENVILLE from BRIMREVILLE Area. | |

W.A.E.Elliot Major
S.S.O. 21st Divn.

**Army Form C. 2118.**

# WAR DIARY
## or
## INTELLIGENCE SUMMARY.
(Erase heading not required.)

No. 21st Divn

| Place | Date | Hour | Summary of Events and Information | Remarks and references to Appendices |
|---|---|---|---|---|
| HAMELINCOURT | July 1st | | Divn. HQ. moved from Adinfer to MOYENVILLE – Train HQ to HAMELINCOURT. 62% Fresh Meat. 86% Bread. Issued 2 tins Solidified Paraffin to biv. file & 5 to 64th — | |
| | 3rd | | 37th Pontoon Park drew supplies from 110th F.A. for first time. Strength 120 men & 136 animals. 2 days rations issued to adjust. 60% Fresh Meat. 90% Bread. No potatoes & onions drawn. "9" Cakes". Left areas for 1st Army – 2 days supplies issued – Strength 38 other ranks 428 horses. | |
| | 4th | | Shortage at Railhead as follows. Sent to SAVOY for 97% lb. Bacon. 15% ration Pro. Meat. 72 lb. Candles. 20 lb. Carbide. 30% only Horse Meat sent up — other supplies normal — Drew 16 tins Coal from VII Corps dump. Issued 350 tins Solidified Paraffin to 110th Bde. | |
| | 5th | | Sent to SAVOY and ACHIET-LE-GRAND for following deficiencies – Pres. Meat 467× rats, Petrol 288 galls. Lub. Oil 55 galls. Grease 10 lb., M.R.O. 30 galls, Carbide 10 lb. W.P.Oil 20 galls. Creosote 30 galls. from 95 lb. — Issued 350 tiny specified Paraffin to 110 Pdr. – 250 tins to 64th Bde. | |
| | 6th | | Sent to SAVOY for 300 galls Petrol. 30 galls. Lub. Oil. 55 galls M.B.O. 35 galls CRESOLI. 55 lb Carbide. 35 galls. W.P.Oil. 10 galls. Petr. S.F. and 58 9/s Pres. Meat. (3712 Rations). Drew 10 tins Solidified Paraffin from RSO. | |
| | 7th | | Fresh Meat 18%. Bread 90%. Potatoes 60%. Sent to ACHIET-LE-GRAND for 4035 rations of Pres. Meat. | |
| | 8th | | Commenced to substitute 1 lb. oats per animal. New to ACHIET-LE-GRAND for 4352 rations of Pres. Meat. Fresh Meat 28%. Bread 90%. Potato 5 9/s. C. | |
| | | | 6 TREATS for 40 lb. Grease, 1 30 galls. W.P.Oil., to SAVOY for 30 galls. M.B.O. 55 galls CRESOLI. ' 10 lb. Carbide. Replaced tribes deficient Tobacco issued to 7th Leicesters by minimum Quantity – by H. Pdr. received | |
| | 9th | | Sent to ACHIET-LE-GRAND for 71 9/s. P. Meat, deficiency of train – Fresh Meat 60%, Bread 90%. Potato 30 lb. Defective Tobacco issued to 64th Bde. – | N.A.A. |

# WAR DIARY or INTELLIGENCE SUMMARY

Army Form C. 2118.

S.S.O 21st Division

| Place | Date | Hour | Summary of Events and Information | Remarks and references to Appendices |
|---|---|---|---|---|
| HANGINCOURT | JULY 10th | | Two cases of Biscuits found to be mouldy unfit for issue were replaced at Railhead respectively by Divl Troops transpt & 110th Bde. the cases have no tin canister. 60% Important, 90% of Bread, 50% Bacon of the above 50% made up by M.M.F. Sings Potatoes, Pork & Beans. | |
| | 11th | | Ration Regt. 290 N.C.O. men., him. 60% hops meat, 90% Bread, 5% of Potatoes. Amst 12 Tons Cut to 48th Div. 12 Tons to 50th Div. from Corps Dump - Sent a supply officer to KAMIENS to enquire price of fresh vegetables. | |
| | 13th | | Frozen meat 60%, Potatoes & Onions 2 op. each, Bread 67%. Drew 9 Tons Coal for Division from Railhead Issued 2 Tons Coal to 50th Div. from VII Corps Dump. Sent to ARRAS for 78 cp Pres. Meat. | |
| | 14th | | 1st Corps Water Cols. left area returning to their H.Q. took when up to the 16th. Sent to ARRAS for 58 cp | |
| | 15th | | Pres. Meat. Usual proportions of Fresh Meat, Bread & Vegetables. | |
| | 17th | | Drew 1500 Tons Mineral Paraffin from Railhead retained in supply Column 237th Machine Gun Coy arrived & was attached to Division strength 187 W.W. & 55 O.D. Arrivals. Vegetables for supplies to Divisional Troops first issue on 18th. | |
| | 19th | | Sundays on Train as follows - Sugar 3120 lb. Cheese 2150 lb. Pres Meat 3904 rations obtained from other R.H. Ds distributed over division - Transferred 63rd Field Amb from 110th to 62nd Bde, & 64th F.A. from 62nd to 110th Bde. | |
| | 20th | | Returned 2105 lb of Dripping to Railhead - proportion as follows Divl Troops 165 lb, Supply Cols 66 lb, 62nd Bde 511 lb, 110th Bde 846 lb, & 64th Bde 517 lb. Sent a supply officer to ACHEUX Rd area to look for fresh vegetables. Returned 2105 lb Dripping to Railhead for same - Received 736 75 from E.F.C Chandeleur | |
| | 21st | | to Draag 21st Div on no report of this Army. [signature] | |

Army Form C. 2118.

# WAR DIARY
## or
## INTELLIGENCE SUMMARY.
*(Erase heading not required.)*

SS.O. 21st Divn.

Instructions regarding War Diaries and Intelligence Summaries are contained in F.S. Regs., Part II. and the Staff Manual respectively. Title pages will be prepared in manuscript.

| Place | Date | Hour | Summary of Events and Information | Remarks and references to Appendices |
|---|---|---|---|---|
| HANGINCOURT | July 23rd | | Nothing to report except that issue of 200 tons of Solidified Paraffin issued to 62nd & 110th Bde. | |
| | 24th | | Visit Transport Asst. from Training. Relief Wakefield visited Army area Railhead to Train. - Showed him system of supply in the field. Lt. Jones Remounts Riding horses of 62nd & 110th Bde to 7th Corps Authority. - 120 returns in all. - Issued 400 tons Solidified Paraffin to 62nd & 110th Bde. | |
| | 26th | | Returned 17,743 lbs of Supply to Railhead Intransmission to Base. - Obtained receipt for 610 to 05 cent. from RSO Railhead named RFC Freds hauled next draft to Divn. | |
| | 27th | | 30% Supplied 100% Meat drawn from RSO. - issued 400 tons Solidified Paraffin to 62nd & 110th Bde. Sent supply of fresh Brd Tempo to DOULLENS to purchase vegetables for Division. 2 3 ton lorries. 1 Crossley tender sent. - 5000 kilos of Turnips obtained & distributed via various points. | |
| | 28th | | Drew 12,500 rgs Solidified Paraffin from Railhead. Issued 400 say ton to 62 & 110th Bde. - Meat proportion of Fresh, meat, bread vegetables. | |
| | 29th | | Notified of arrival of 133 reinforcements from Depot. - | |
| | 30th | | Drew Iron Rations for AAPAS as follows :- Brd Tp 880 , 62nd Bde 1740 , 110th Bde 1740 , 116th Mo Bty , & 64th Bde 900. issued 30% turnover in minimum strength. Withdrawals gradually made at Railhead. - No Fresh meat issued. Preserved men. Meat proportions of their equivalents. | |
| | 31st | | all preserved meat. balance of fresh in train. | |

Lt 8.34 (T) W. APARHS 5000 P. 8/16 WC, SSS Ld W/Aesp, 13 short in Train. All preserved meat, balance of fresh
M.L.O.Stewart Major
SSO 21 Divn

Army Form C. 2118.

S.S.O 21st Divn

# WAR DIARY
## or
## INTELLIGENCE SUMMARY.
*(Erase heading not required.)*

| Place | Date | Hour | Summary of Events and Information | Remarks and references to Appendices |
|---|---|---|---|---|
| HAMELINCOURT | 1917 Aug 1st | | All preserved meat drawn from R.H.P. Full head ration. 60% Vegetables - asked Army to renew requirements of other rations on Section 7. | |
| | 2nd | | 30% Fresh meat. 100% meat. 16 ozs Vegetables. Drawn from R.H.P. Sent S.O. Divl Troops down to DOULLENS to purchase fresh vegetables for Division. Returned 1032. lb Dripping to Railhead. Received cash voucher from R.S.O. for 361. 2d which forwarded to D.A.P.S. | |
| | 3rd | | Cashed vouchers at EFC Paid out more to remove mess uniforms :- Bn Troops 20-c-; 62nd Bde 90 fr; 64th Bde 53 fr; 110th Bde 196 fr being the amounts earned by each grp in respect of dripping returned to France for period ended 2nd August. (Returns made each Thursday). 60% Fresh meat drawn from Railhead. | |
| | 4th | | Sent S.O. Divl Troops to AMIENS to purchase 300 kilos Cabbages. Purchase made included Cabbages 1900 kilos Carrots 1500 kilos - all distributed & divisional troops- | |
| | 5th | | Obtained 6 Tons Coal from Railhead & Dumps on Div'l fuel dump. 21st Divn Reinforced Depot joined division from LE SOUICH. Strength 110 men. Drew rations for first time. | |
| | 6th | | Drew 4 Tons Coal from Div Cps dump. Tom Major St LEGER transferred from VII Divn. | |
| | 7th | | Party of 6th Canadian Railway Troops strength 90 men transferred to 21 Divn from 3rd Army. Drew rations for them. Transferred 63rd Field Amb. from 62nd Bde to 64th group on removal to ERVILLERS. | |

Army Form C. 2118.

S.S.O. 21st Divn.

# WAR DIARY or INTELLIGENCE SUMMARY.

(Erase heading not required.)

| Place | Date | Hour | Summary of Events and Information | Remarks and references to Appendices |
|---|---|---|---|---|
| HAMELINCOURT | July 8th | | Returned 2310 lbs Tripe to Railhead. Army unfit for consumption. Average prices: Queen's Regt. pound ration from 12th Divn - 883 men & 55 animals. Drew supplies from first new order 62nd Bde Group. 181 Tunn. B.A.S. left Divan area en route to 17th Corps & letters to 30th Divn. | 3rd/4th Bon R.I.R. for |
| | 10th | | Drew 2 bulls from Railhead 50. Two ½ tonnes & 37 by N.T. Issued as per "Appollo" Run to 64 Bde and 3/- pulls for 110th Bde. Presided over Board of Officers at BOISIEUX to Cadavres Reclam: supplies found unfit for consumption. Approval application of Supply Head & Read etc. Purchased 3000 Kilos Oil Cabbage at AMIENS for delivery on 14th inst. 3000 for delivery on 21st | |
| | 11th | | Tom Major ST. LEGER (43 men) drew rations for first time from Divl Troop dump. 100% Frozen Meat at Frozen Meat issued to 64th Bde HQ. Movement to TERVILLIERS. quantity Fresh Meat - Divisional Concert party attached to 64th Bde HQ. | |
| | 12th | | Paid out Supplying money as follows :- Div Tps 106.30 ; 62nd Bde 90.00 ; 110th Bde 204.00 ; 64th Brigade 162 francs - Supply total 23 f.r.; total 515.25. | |
| | 14th | | Handed over at Railhead to S.D.I.- Div 24,000 lbs Cake & 6000 lbs Charcoal - Purchased | |
| MOYENVILLE | | | 3000 Kilos Cabbage in AMIENS - Train H.Q. moved from HAMELINCOURT to MOYENVILLE. | |
| | 16th | | Returned 2511 lbs of Dripping to Railhead - Divl Troops 1114 lbs ; 62nd Bde 754 lbs ; 110th Bde 1025 lbs ; 64th Bde 648 lbs. | |
| | 17th | | Paid out Supplying money as follows :- Div Trpt 39f.90 cd ; 62nd Bde 266f. 45c ; 110th Bde 359f. ; 64th Bde 226f.70c | |

Army Form C. 2118.

# WAR DIARY
## or
## INTELLIGENCE SUMMARY.
(Erase heading not required.)

S.S.O 21st Divn

| Place | Date | Hour | Summary of Events and Information | Remarks and references to Appendices |
|---|---|---|---|---|
| MONENVILLE | August 1917 | | | |
| | 19 | | Received approx. 4000 lbs of straw in lieu of Ptls at Railhead. | |
| | 20 | | Bread 93 lb. Meat 62 lb. 4 days ration of Potatoes & Onions. | |
| | | 6.15 | Tons of food drawn by lorry from Railhead. Made purchases of vegetables in Amiens to complete ration. | |
| | 22 | 7.5.0 | Bread. 46 lb Frozen Meat drawn | |
| | 23 | 6.7.2 | " 54 lb " | |
| | 24 | | Approved 3rd Divn Pack and Baggage & Supply Train & Reserve to Diff Train Supply from 110th Fd Ambce S.A.D.O.S. 3rd Divisn, M.T.O.d. Supply transferred to 64th Bde drawn from 110th Bde. | |
| | 25 | | 64th Fd Amb arrd. <9.8> Fd Ambce R.E. transferred to 64th Bde from 63rd 110th Fd Amb transfd to 63rd Fd Amb from 64th Bde Fd Amb. 110th Bde. Reserve days supplies unloaded at 110th Bde supplied from reserve days supplies and loaded at Railhead. 8 lorries sent drifted at BEAUFORT in the afternoon. The g't drew full forage ration. 176 of straw drawn in lieu of hay. | |

Army Form C. 2118.

# WAR DIARY
## or
## INTELLIGENCE SUMMARY.
(Erase heading not required.)

S.S.O. 21st Div.

| Place | Date | Hour | Summary of Events and Information | Remarks and references to Appendices |
|---|---|---|---|---|
| MOYENVILLE | 26th 1917 | | W. Dbe. Divion drew full forage ration in accordance with 6th Bn Of/235/1/24.8.17. | |
| " | 27th | | All undivisional units transferred to 3rd Tn.Sp.Coy. 62nd = 110th & 64th all drew 2 days. 110th Bde dumped in the afternoon with the transferred from 3rd Tn.Sp to 62nd Bde. C.R.A transferred to 64th Bde. 227 M.G.Coy. transferred from 3rd Tn.Sp to 64th Bde. 10 H.Q. M.M.P. & O.R.E. transferred to 64th Bde. Gave from 3rd Div. Inf. Handed over Amd. Review to S.S.O. 16th Div. M.I. Tnsp. Bnd. 62d Tn. Left the road to Chocard 7½ tn. Paid out ammo received for Division. 3rd Tn.Sp 79th Poc. 62 = 171.65 fr. 110th Bde. 188.65 fr. 64th Bde 261.10 fr. Supp. Rel. 59.50 f. Railhead for 110th = " 62nd = " and 64th Bde Agnez-les-Doisans. | |
| AGNEZ-LES DOISANS | 28th | | (3rd Tn.Sp drew a report from BOISIEUX AUTHONT O nos 3317) 62d = 64 = Bde. drew by these transport and spread on DOISANS. Supp. Return dispatched supplies drawn for 27th for 62nd, 64th Bde. Prime Tn.Sp Bnd drawn 0.3 tn ammo to east end | |

# WAR DIARY
## INTELLIGENCE SUMMARY

Army Form C. 2118.

S.S.O. 21st Divn

| Place | Date 1917 | Hour | Summary of Events and Information | Remarks and references to Appendices |
|---|---|---|---|---|
| AGNEZ-LES-DUISANS | Aug 29th | | 2 lbs 3 oz Stew drawn in lieu of 3 oz Hay, Fr. & veg. packed for the three days by S.O. 64th Bde. New Tms of bread drawn from Railhead. Arranged that S.O. 110th Bde kept the supplies dumped with him in the afternoon and issued to comp'n 21st Div supplies dumped in the 30th. | |
| | 30th | | 240 Men of R.E. Field Coys/am (97th & 98th) went into 13th Divnl Area with stores to 1st Army. Wired SSO. 13th Divn to instruct the new coms n with camp'n 21st Div. New Tms of bread drawn from Railhead. | |
| | 31st | | New of Field Coys/am cancelled. Men Trans't bread drawn fr Rlhm. 62nd Bde. 245 lbs. 110th Bde Rlhead. S/lft. returned to supplies. SUPP del. 103 lbs. 233 lb. 64th Bde. 409 lb. SUPP del. 103 lbs. | |

Major ADA SO
Presso 21 Divn

Army Form C. 2118.

S.S.O. 21 Div

# WAR DIARY
## INTELLIGENCE SUMMARY.
(Erase heading not required.)

| Place | Date | Hour | Summary of Events and Information | Remarks and references to Appendices |
|---|---|---|---|---|
| AVESNE LE-COMTE | Septr 1917 1. | | Nothing to report. Moved office to AVESNE-LE-COMTE. | |
| | 2. | | Diem and convoy to Divnl. and Front out to following. 62nd Bde 85 tons, 110th Bde. 82 tons, 64th Bde. 143 tons supply tot. 36 t. | |
| | 3 | | Resumed duty, return from leave to U.K. Nothing to report. Meninl. | |
| | 4 | | Drew 20 Tons Coal from BOISLEUX; No.3 Coy Train moved from BEAUFORT to LATTRE ST. QUENTIN, refilled 110th Bde. there. 3 qr Potatoes drawn from Rght. Purchased 300 tons baln of cabbage crcurots in ACHICOURT. | |
| | 5th | | Headquarters of No.1 Coy moved to AUBIGNY en route for II Army. | |
| | 6th | | Authority obtained from DDSIT. to have 300 lbs straw for blds & Qr. December her sleeping nature floors. Shows obtained an certificate of ROMS from Dump. Purchase Boars at ETREE WAMIN. 97th, 98th, 126th, 6 NF tH Bn RE, 14th Bn NF (Pioneer) entrained for II nd Army, lorries entraining supplies previous 7th. sent to 39th Divl Train No.2 Coy— 93, 94th, 95th Bdes R.F.A, 21st Trench Mortar Bde, DAC also entrained for II nd Army area. Lorries will supply previous 7th. sent by road. | |
| | 7th | | Supply officer Divisional Troops R.O. proceeded to new area. Drew 10 Tons Coal from ARRAS. Had train E/110th Bde to remounts to Divl dump. | |

WAA

# WAR DIARY or INTELLIGENCE SUMMARY

Army Form C. 2118.

S.S.O. 21st Divn.

1917

| Place | Date | Hour | Summary of Events and Information | Remarks and references to Appendices |
|---|---|---|---|---|
| AVESNES LE-COMTE | September 8th | | Returned 2385 lbs of Dripping to Railhead. as follows :- 8 Supply Bdn 37 lbs ; 62nd Bde 828 lbs ; 110th Bde 592 lbs ; 64th Bde 928 lbs. Money paid out as follows - 62nd Bde 289.80 110 Bde 207.55, 64 Bde 324.80 francs. DADS Third Army authorized issue of 2,000 lbs Straw for billets of Leicester Regt. taken from III Army dump at ETREE-WAMIN. Drew 10 Tons Coal from ARRAS. Sent S.O. but Bde to ACHICOURT to purchase vegetables for division - 4,500 Kilos purchased | |
| | 9th | | Drew Sims meat & bread from Canadian Factory, Mess BRAMINCOURT and issued to 110th Bde - DADS 10 Tons Coal from ARRAS. 75 Reinforcements arrived for division. 65 men from 62nd bn., 110th 237 - Medicine from Companies proceeded to II Army area on 8th - rationed up to + including 9th inst. Present 20% | |
| | 10th | | Drew 3 Tons Coal from ARRAS for 110th Bde. - No fresh meat received from Base 60% Present 20% in Arr Ten% in Sundries 100% tinned - Purchased 6000 kilos fresh vegetables at ACHICOURT. (Cottage, Turnips, Carrots) 60% Fresh | |
| | 11th | | Drew 2 Tons Coal for 110th Bde from ARRAS and sent to No. 3 Coy Train by lorry. Meal & 90% Bread arrived from Base, also ration of Potatoes & onions | |
| | 12th | | Sent to ARRAS for 6000 lbs Oats & 6 Tons Coal. Fresh meat & bread arrived normal issue drew 400 population french brigade from Tenderloin Committees. Iron biscuit tea & sugar. | |
| | 13th | | Drew 9 Tons Coal from ARRAS ; advance parties of 62nd bn. & 110th Bdes moved by rail to II Army area - Rationed up to + including 16th inst. | |
| | 14th | | Drew 9000 lbs Oats from BERNIETZ issue of 6 tons Coal for conveyance to II Army area, half ration Bacon only drawn | |

Army Form C. 2118.

# WAR DIARY
## or
## INTELLIGENCE SUMMARY.
(Erase heading not required.)

SS O 21st Divn

| Place | Date | Hour | Summary of Events and Information | Remarks and references to Appendices |
|---|---|---|---|---|
| NESMES | Sept 15th | | Proceeded to II Army area & arranged supplying points for Divl troops. Divn posted to XI Corps. | |
| LE COMTE | 16th | | Drew supplies by MT from CAESTRE at 10 a.m. 1 Coy Train RENINGHELST, > Co. Train BORRE, 3 Coy Train near CAESTRE, 4 Co. Train near KOORTEN LOOP. Brought up by Lorries 9 Coys up Coal from sidings for 62nd, 64th & 110th Brigade troops. | |
| CAESTRE | 17th | | Whole of 21st Division concealed in & around CAESTRE, BORRE, HONDIGHEM; Artillery in action. Headquarters at RENINGHELST where No 1 Coy Train is camped. Nos 2, 3 & 4 Coy Train in 62nd, 110th & 64th Brigade area. Drew supplies from Railhead & whole division by M.T. 1 Section 63rd F.Amb. 125 men + 10 animals moved to M10 b.7.5 & work over HOSPICE from 140th Field Amb. (41st Divn). Took over Fuel Dump up 7th Divn at MORBECQUE as follows - Coal 56 Tons, Coke 6 Tons, Charcoal 4½ Tons. Draw 21½ Tons Coal from Railhead, distribution as follows - Divl Tps Pumps 6 Tons, 110th Bde 6 Tons, 62nd Bde 6 Tons, 43/4 Tons each - | |
| | 18th | | Loaded at Railhead by Horse Transport for 62nd, 64th & 110th Bdes, Hy M.T. for Divl Troop Supp. Wood percentage of fresh meat & vegetables. Sent S.O. 64th Bde to HAZEBROUCK to purchase green vegetables for division. 100 OR arrived for 3rd/4th Queens, 79 OR for 9th K.O.Y.L.I. & 78 for 10 - K.O.Y.L.I. | |
| | 19th | | Purchased £20 of Carrots for Division in HAZEBROUCK which ton. distributed from lorry today to every H.V. Quarantory. 13" a note 48 OR arrived for 9th K.O.Y.L.I. | |
| | 20th | | 100 Reinforcements arrived for 6th Leicesters & 90 OR for 7 - Leicesters. Otherwise nothing to record. Lorries with supplies for 8/10 & 1st Lincolns moved forward area, transferred unit to S.O. Divl Trs Sp & every loaded at Railhead accordingly. | |

# WAR DIARY or INTELLIGENCE SUMMARY

Army Form C. 2118.

21st Division

| Place | Date | Hour | Summary of Events and Information | Remarks and references to Appendices |
|---|---|---|---|---|
| CAESTRE | 21st | | Drew 35,000 lb. ratn. Hay from Railhead to complete forage ration issued at rate of 11 lb. per HR. 11 lb. per I.D. horse. Demn/3100 lb. Oats from No. 2 Field Supply Depot - No oats Issue up Railhead | |
| | 22nd | | Railhead changed to BAILLEUL. Loaded Div. Sup. Col. Hay & Oats by lorry. 1110 lb. Rations drawn by Horse Transport. Fresh meat only 30%. Bread 65%. Potatoes drawn 50%. Bns 27 Tomtd from R.A.P. | |
| METEREN | 23rd | | Loaded Railhead at 7.30 am by M.T. 30% fresh meat. 65% bread. Its op vegetables. Division moved into RERTHEN area. 62nd Bde around LE ROUKLOSHILLE; 64 Bde THEUS HOOK, 110th Bde FONTAINE HOUCK. Refilled 62nd Bde at X3.c.5.2, 64th Bde R.25.b.3.7. 110th Bde at X4.a.b.6. (Sheet 27) - 15000 lb coke & charcoal drawn from Railhead & rd to camp of No.1 Coy Train at Q.35.c.7.b (Sheet 28). Issued Rum to Artillery 1st Inniskis on X Corp Authority. Hauled own fuel Sump at MORBECQUE to SSO 1st Australian Divn. Obtained receipt for Coal 36 Tons, Coke 6 tons. Charcoal 42 tons. Issued Rum to Artillery 1st Inniskis & West Kent. Cashed Voucher for 399 Francs at E.F.C. HAZEBROUCK in payment for briquettes returned. 40% Bread 65% Vegetables 60%. Purchased 1000 kilos of Carrots at STRAZEELE for division. 1st Inniskis attached to 55 Signals II Army received orders to rejoin 62nd Brigade. Reinforcements arrived as follows: 6 Leicesters 34; 1st Lincoln 125; 9 (KOYL) 72; 10 (KOYL) 71 O.R. | |
| | 24th | | 23 O.R. Arrived from 64th Machine Gun Co. D.E. Supplies from Railhead by M.T. & Draft Transport for H.Q.M. & Train Wagons drawn 1110th Bde. 15000 lb coke 13000 lb Charcoal drawn from Railhead. Increased Divisional Park to 10,000 rations. | |

**WAR DIARY**
or
**INTELLIGENCE SUMMARY.**
(Erase heading not required.)

Army Form C. 2118.

S.S.D. 21st Div.

| Place | Date | Hour | Summary of Events and Information | Remarks and references to Appendices |
|---|---|---|---|---|
| METEREN | 26th Sep | | Drew supplies from BAILLEUL by H.T. for 62nd & 64th Bdes. Hvy. N.T. for Div Troops & 110th Bde. Brigade moved to forward area by Buses. | 110 |
| | 27th | | Cleared 53½ ton load from Railhead & dumped at No. 1 Coy Train. No. 3 Coy Train moved to H.31.d.5.8. Sheet 28. Selby Torpedo Boat found to be amount rendered by A.D.M.S. Issued 2,400 gs modified alcohol & 4,000 p. of blowing guncotton to 110th Bde. | |
| | 28th | | Brew 50 th th of Railhead to office the unused quantity. Issued today rations to 50 Bm. Troops. 62nd & 64th Bdes. moved to forward area. Train containers No 2 & 4 moved in accordance with Brigade orders. Refilled 62nd Bde at M.5.a.7.1. 64th Bde at M.5.c.3.7. & th Division from H.Q. at M.5.c.3.7. | |
| ENING HEIST | 29th | | 97th, 96th, 126 Bde R.E. & H.Q. 110 R.E. & 14th N.F. (Pioneers) reported Division & attached to Division. 97 & 1 H.Q. R.E. to 62nd Bde group. 98th Co. R.E. 114th N.F. to 110 Bde group. 126 Bde R.E. to 64th Bde group. Drew supplies at Railhead for consumption 1st October. Drew from BAILLEUL for the last time. No Trp Artillery & 110th Bde. Train Wagons for 62nd & 64th Bdes. 4th Div Artillery att. to Div. 2317 | 2472 2317 |
| OUDERDOM RAILHEAD | 30th | | Drew supplies from OUDERDOM. Drew rum for 21st Div. Artillery. 64th, 110th Bdes. Received 51,000 lbs. Extra from dump at No 1 Coy Train drawn on by Supply Officer. Mobile bombing of area from 8.15 pm until 1.40 am, some casualties to men & animals. Drew 250 two bolted blankets to 110th Bde. | |

M.A. Plant Major
S.S.O. 21st Div

# WAR DIARY
## INTELLIGENCE SUMMARY

Army Form C. 2118.

1/10/17 to 31/10/17    S.S.O. 21st Division

| Place | Date | Hour | Summary of Events and Information | Remarks and references to Appendices |
|---|---|---|---|---|
| ENINGHEM | October 1st | | Supply Train late at Railhead. Drew supplies for 21st Div. by War Transport the 41st Div. Artillery attached to M.T. Drew drawn to 110th, 64th R.F.A., F.21st Div. Troops + to 41st Div. Art. Detachment 30 p. Heavy For 3 p. | |
| | 2nd | | 10 Ton Coal M.T. Van Up Cable train from R.H.A. Rent to M₂ F.S.D. for 300 heavy return to be equally divided between 63rd Hey Bde. Drew 5000 up solidified alcohol from X Corps Troops & Artillery attached. Corps Issued same to 64, 94, 110th Bdes & 21 D.A.C.; also 41st Artillery attached. Issued also to Guards 63rd Hey Bde. Rent Reg't Officer to DOULIEU to purchase same for Division. | |
| | 3rd | | M & B.C. drew supplies for 21st Division for last time, being transferred to VIII Division at STEENWERCK. | |
| | 4th | | M 50 issued divisional supplies at Railhead. On Issue arrival of 21st Supply Column which is returning to Division. | |
| | 5th | | Went to M₂ F.S.D. + drew 300 Uh Oats. Iron Rate Reserve, issued 100Uh to each Brigade. S.O. wired Results 62, 64, 110th Bde + 21st Artillery. | |
| | 6th | | No Oats arrived at Railhead. Drew 41,600 Uhs of oats from 21st Reserve Park. Rent to M₂ F.S.D. for 500 Ulb Rum. 230 Heavy required for day's ration X Corps Authority being obtained to make full issue to 21st Div. & same to 41st Div. Arty. attached. 315th Army Field Artillery Brigade transferred from VIII Division. Issued supplies for first time today; comprising est. strength 947 men and 920 animals. | |

# WAR DIARY
## or
## INTELLIGENCE SUMMARY

Army Form C. 2118.

S.S.O. 21st Divn.

| Place | Date | Hour | Summary of Events and Information | Remarks and references to Appendices |
|---|---|---|---|---|
| REMINGHELST | 4th | | 4th Div hty drew supplies from rail for last & were proceeded to refurn their division | |
| | 8th | a.m. | 6th Rde marched to EBBLINGHEM area. Loaded supplies by MT & transport to new area. M.T. Coy Train proceeded by road. Remainder portion of Brigade by rail. | |
| BLARINGHEM | 9th | a.m. | 6th Rde moved by rail to SEROUS area. Infantry Entrained at OUDEZOM. N° 2 Coy train marched by road. Units loaded f.m.t. supplies by MT and moved to SEROUS. Train HQ moved to BLARINGHEM. | |
| | 10th | | Drew supplies today by Rlwy from EBBLINGHEM. Divl Troops 110th Rde & 31/35 A F.A. Rde transferred to this Divn at OUDEZOM 15/13 M.F. 18th Bn. & 11 Yorks & Lancs transferred to 18 New Zealand Bhowed S.Y. road and reformed up to & including 11. transferred to 19 New Zealand from 14th Copr.15 & subsequently 9 Royd L.S. & 6 Leicesters moved to S.O. all these areas referred to to & including 13th. transferred Wrote to S.O. 21st Bn Troops to 13th & onwards — 75% Fresh Meat Bread drawn from RAILHD | |
| | 11 | | 110th Brigade moved from present area to WARDRECQUES and entered supplies at OUDEZOM Gr. 12 h time by 23rd Bn. polis Rgt. Dropped by Lorries at RACQUINGHEM, where Sy Train. 12 h till 1. 75% fresh meat bread drawn from Railhd also full reserve rations | |
| | 13th & 14. | | All groups drew by Horse Transport permitted. Nothing to record. Nothing to record except that RES 4th Can. Divn drew 11 Tons Coal — | [signature] |

Army Form C. 2118.

# WAR DIARY
## or
## INTELLIGENCE SUMMARY.

(Erase heading not required.)

SSO 21st Div

| Place | Date | Hour | Summary of Events and Information | Remarks and references to Appendices |
|---|---|---|---|---|
| BLARINGHEM | Oct 15th | | 7th Brigade detached to forward area, 2 miles distr of O.R. Supply Transport detached from 23rd per Inst. A.A Q 7th & R. 55 mules. 8th Decoder Bn attacked to 7th Bn for rations consumption. 17th Hants S.B.O. O.R. animals S.T. Transport & supply wagons proceeded by road. One half tone Rumts units in rest area. 80% Bech dud. 750 other ranks & 90 vehicles. Received back 11 Tm Cont loaned to 4th Canadian Divn. | |
| | 16th | | M. Train proceeded aw/escort to U.K. pro/days - assumed command of Train pr detm - | |
| | 18th | | 3 Bn Train Hq & 10 lorries proceeded to new area - 2358.I.2 - light tps & light tps 118th Inf rest reinforced. accompanied this camp. Loories taking rations on foot to Train Col Rfte H.Q. 9th Decoder returned to 23rd Div. Ammunition 2nd (Can)anda 6205 Train for drawn from Poelkent Returned at 6pm. of 4 Cy Train S.BRANGHEM. | |
| | 19th | | 14th Cy Train proceeded by passed units VIA ECCKE to RENINGHELST - hulling forth night of ECCKE. | |
| | 20th | | 64th Bde moved from 4 Blk area to forward area, headquarters Henry at CHATEAU-SÉGARD - 64 Pk Rfles 164th Bde Wyls. | |
| ZEVECOTEN | 21st | | N.2 Cy Train moved to RENINGHELST by march rote. M.1 & 2 out M.6 & 9.4. Indent complete at EISBURGHEM thereafter in present area. Replenished 64 Bde links twice - rations by Train HQ moved to ZEVECOTEN. Replenished 64 Bde links twice - 3rd Australian L.A Bde drew rations for 4th line in consumption 22 - Streyf 1036 men and mules from CAESTRE - 23 - Strgt.h. 62 & Bde 1V9 & 1/4 Ry. 3rd HD 7th LD 111 Mules - Dar sipples in this word + 64th Bde NQ & WQ Cy. R.T. Rjlmd.h. R. full nauy sent twice 9 Fay 29 1st 4x.29 64th Bde NQ & WQ Cy. |  |
| | 22nd | | Operation permits to Trenches taken Ten Hupr - 9shies Ratified rtur'd to Ommoments - Drew battles from CAESTRE for 62rd - 64th Bdes +3rd Army O.T.A Bde - Replenished certain reins of 64th 1 Bde Forcd - Drew ample lodging hostile aircraft. WM |

# WAR DIARY or INTELLIGENCE SUMMARY

Army Form C. 2118.

280 21st Division

| Place | Date | Hour | Summary of Events and Information | Remarks and references to Appendices |
|---|---|---|---|---|
| CHATEAU SEGARD | 23rd | | Train HQ moved from ZEVECOTEN to CHATEAU SEGARD. Biscuits from OUDERDOM for all Division by MT. No forward wurde attached draw rations for first time. Consumption 25th – 151st Field Amb. Men 182, animals 68; 70 K.M.G. Coy. Men 197, animals 67; Consumption 24th – 315 Army F.A. Bde Men 926, animals 996. Animals 981, 88th Lab. Coy Men 1039, animals 4. Biscuit full ration if Rum for all ranks. | |
| | 24th | | Biscuits fullies from OUDERDOM by Horse Transport for 21st Div, & 315 & 113 Army F.A. Bdes. 3rd Australian Army F.A. Bde by MT. Issued 1200 lb extra frozen to each of the 3 Army F.A. Bdes. Jam extra frozen received at Railhead. Biscuits established above (is 6x by two R/W 600 g/s each. Biscuit Ration of Rum to all troops. Jam Rations issued as follows – 62nd Bde Inft 376, 110th Bde 305, 64th Bde 191. Issued 1 ton Straw to 10th Field Ambulance. Apples Issued from 64th Army Artillery. | |
| | 25th | | 64th Bde Inf Regt received 3days rations today for consumption 27, 28 + 29th. 1 Cldr Bale of 10 × Collinsh. Reserve 3days rations on entry into the front line. Brew Rum from Divisional issued 108 gal alcohol. Installation - bogs Bde 700 gls, 64th Bde 600 gls, 110th Bde 600 gls, 315 (inc 63" FAR) 100 gls. Issued 50 gallon Whale Oil as follows: 18 Fd Amb 6gls, 64th & 110th Bdes 15 Gls+, 21 Div Artillery Attached Troops. 3rd Australian A.F.A. Bde received 10 gallons. Area bombed at night by hostile aircraft. | |
| | 26th | | Rations (consumption 27) 18 & 19th 4.15 PM issued to 7 decrease of 7th December. 18 of 7 trucks 2/ drew full care of Division & Troops strength Rations Rations in addition issued Soldiers Absence a full day - of Rum. Bread Rations og. 110th Bde 1700 og. 1000 Bde 1200 og. 1tripled in this large perforation of Checked were issued. | |
| | 27th | | Train arrived at Railhead containing no Rind & only Biscuit packed. Sent to RENINGHELST for 26,675 lb. Pieces of 537th Coal long lives meal to Oct, to DICKEBUSCH for 2300 lb MICAESTRE for al new Arrival Hospital Arrival | 41,000 |

Brew Rum (intake of Division)

# WAR DIARY or INTELLIGENCE SUMMARY

Army Form C. 2118.

SSO 21st Division

| Place | Date | Hour | Summary of Events and Information | Remarks and references to Appendices |
|---|---|---|---|---|
| CHATEAU SEGARD | 28th | | Loading & loading Railhead through new receipt of Hayfield. Reduced successor insurance. Usual preparation of truck head braked. Drew Rum for which Drawn received in addition Railhead all men in trucks including O.R. Pty. - Replaced 31 rations of 9th 7A who destroyed by shell fire | |
| | 29th | | 101st Field Coy RE received orders to rejoin division. Drew supplies Railhead from one 30th. (looktime) I Corps Troops supplied rations for 1st Mor to onwards. Drew Rum in whole division & per ship for Trench Strength. Sent to CAESTRE to be sorted. Drew 5000 ozs Soldiers Alcohol from X Corps Troops S.C. Issued a quantity to 62nd & 110th Bdes. Area heavily bombed by hostile aircraft during the night. One aerial torpedo struck outer portion of Train HQ Hut but failed to explode. | |
| | 30th | | Drew 6 sacks of Braziers from CAESTRE issued 1 each to 21 Div Troops, 64th & 2nd Bdes. 315 of A.Bde. 113 O.R. Bde. 13 Dwgts of A.Bde. Issued Rum to whole division (prevalent in addition to Trench Strength) - 62nd & Bde partially relieved by 64th. (2half) Drew 5000 ozs Soldiers Alcohol from X Corps Troops S.Col Ref D | |
| | 31st | | Drew 21,113 lbs of Extra Hay. Plans for fraye. Normal supply of Trench men drawn from Drew 3rd Thur Cwt to 24 Tons worth from Railhead. 161st Hoz Bde completed. 101st Field Coy RE Transport & X Corps Troops supply Colm for consumption 1st Nov. Area again bombed during the night by hostile aircraft | |

M.Elliott Major
SSO 21st Div

# WAR DIARY

**Army Form C. 2118.**

"Nov 1st – 30th 1917"

**S.S.O. 21st Division**

## INTELLIGENCE SUMMARY.
*(Erase heading not required.)*

Instructions regarding War Diaries and Intelligence Summaries are contained in F.S. Regs., Part II. and the Staff Manual respectively. Title pages will be prepared in manuscript.

| Place | Date | Hour | Summary of Events and Information | Remarks and references to Appendices |
|---|---|---|---|---|
| CHATEAU SÉGARD | NOVEMBER 1st | | 315 Army Field Artillery Bde moved to 5th Army Area. Draw supplies for last time for consumption 2nd Nov. Strength 901 men. 906 animals. Lent to CAESTRE in 2 Tons Forge Coal to Supply Col No Two (Cavalry). | |
| | 2nd | | Forge Coal 10 Tons. Oats 42 Tons. Word of Two Extra forage Shaw 5,719 kilos & Hay 10,974 kilos drawn from Railhead. Near black Bread from No. 2 FSD. Issued to units of Division on certificate of DAPVS. Issued down to strip pulphood. | |
| | 3rd | | 52nd Army Field Artillery Bde drew rations for consumption 5th inst. Str 1 Field Coy. – Strength 977 men. Animals 935. Previously rationed by 39th Divn. Issued Army to send standard loading of otherwise. | |
| | 5th 6th | | Nothing to report. 20 Divl Troops proceeded to U.K. on leave, his duties being taken over by 211 L. of C. Ry. Reg. Officer. Draw from No. 2 FSD. 12,000 gr solidified alcohol, rationing 400 or to S.O. L.O.C. Troops, being quantity received in at last issue. Issued to each of Divl + Gen. Hos. Bdes. 1,000 Gr. | |
| | 7th | | Went to HQ II Army Hear DADS reference request of Genl Whil Led give rations in the Railway Mdcds by Twelve Klass been cleared at OUDEZEEM on 7/10/17. The quantity 3½ tons was not claimed by 21st Divn. Branch Solidifies alcohol 1000 gr each to 62 & 110 Fdos. Issued be Sun Rations from Reserve Stock to 1st Division. Nothing official to record. | |

M.A.K.

Army Form C. 2118.

# WAR DIARY
## or
## INTELLIGENCE SUMMARY
*(Erase heading not required.)*

S.S.O. 21st Division

| Place | Date | Hour | Summary of Events and Information | Remarks and references to Appendices |
|---|---|---|---|---|
| CHATEAU SEGARD | October 9th | | Drew 16SD Rations from OUDERDOM to replace ammo destroyed by shellfire - See Intelligence of 1015 lb Biscuit. 19s Two Feed Meat, 50 lb jam - Authority DADST II Army B21. 4/11/19. Mule supplies handed over to Capt. MAUGHAM 2nd Grenade Office at Derby Dump - I Do. A.I.I. | |
| | 10th | | Issued 53 Iron Rations to 9th Leicesters to replace those lost & destroyed in action. Drew 3000 as of 64th Fde 2 batty carried off front line & Solidified Alcohol and I Corp Authority from X Corps Troops Supply Colm. 16SD Rams Rations sent up to I 20.A.I.I. moved to Dump. The two battns in support moved to Reveir. Returned 703 lb Dripping to Railhead (DERBY DUMP). Handed over to Divisional Grenade Officer (Capt. MAUGHAM) 21 Div Mining all solidified Alcohol - 64th Fde relief completed - | |
| | 11th 13th | | Issued 1000 go each to 62 & 110 Bdes (Solidified Alcohol) - 64th Bde relief completed. I Cav. Inf Bde Dump strength 24 men & L.D. Nothing to record. | |
| | 14th | | Drew supplies (main Rations) & rations - consumption 16th - Iron 52nd, 113th & 3rd Australian Army Field Arty. Bde + 2nd Lahore Cav. artravite Hqrs. New Zealand Div. Handed over 21 Div Iron Dumps to Sqm 1st New Zealand Div. as follows - Corb 173 Tons. Wood 150 Tons. Oats 114 Tons. Charcoal 1 Ton. Inglat 2 Tons. | |
| | 15th | | Drew supplies for first time at WIPPENHOEK. Loaded 21 Artillery Rmt Inform dispatched to forward dumps. In Nouestonk - MORBECQUE Road - M.T. Cny Train proceeded by Road march to MORBECQUE. Loaded 110 Fde Grup by lorry + 62 Fde Adv.pt H.T. Returned 740 lbs Dripping Railhead. Camel drawing Rum Incident. | |
| VIEUX BERQUIN | 16th | | Drew supplies for 21 Inf. Bdes. from WIPPENHOEK. Moto Artillery from CAESTRE, all by M.T. Filled up with 3 days atts. to VIEUX BERQUIN. 21st Div relief completed. Relieved by N.3 Div. | |

# WAR DIARY or INTELLIGENCE SUMMARY

Army Form C. 2118.

210. 21st Divn

| Place | Date | Hour | Summary of Events and Information | Remarks and references to Appendices |
|---|---|---|---|---|
| VIEUX BERQUIN | Nov. 17th | | Issued supplies to the 3 inf. Brigades of WIPPENHOEK, infantry & Artillery at CAESTRE, all by M.T. Dumped to follows: Artillery at OUTERSTEENE, 62nd at LA COURONYE, 110th at DOULIEU. 104th at WIPPENHOEK. 110th crossed S. of BAILLEUL-OUTERSTEENE Road. Drew from Rail from M.T. at CAESTRE. | |
| BARLIN | 18th | | Transfer moved to BARLIN (1st Army Area). Div. Troops Group landed at BARLIN. 62nd & 110th Bdes at WIPPENHOEK all by M.T. dumped supplies & stores. 62nd at GONNEHEM, 64th at LA COURONNE, 110th at DOULIEU. I remained behind at VIEUX BERQUIN. 51 bales of extra frags drawn @ 103 to sack, 19 one sold the. | |
| | 19th | | Drew supplies at WIPPENHOEK for 64th, 110th Bdes, dumping at VENDIN and LA COURONNE respectively. 21 Div Arty & 613 Nde drew from 31st Div at ECURIE all by M.T. | |
| | 20th | | Drew supplies from Railhead as follows :- by 62nd & 110th Bdes from BARLIN, 110th from WIPPENHOEK, and Artillery from 31st Div at ECURIE. | |
| | 21st | | 64th & 110th from BARLIN, 62nd Artillery from 31st Div at ECURIE. Took over 47th Div. Fuel Dump at Ste ST. CATHERINE quantity as follows :- Coal 28 Tns, Wood 12 Tns, Charcoal 29 tons. also ALUM 240 lb. "C" Solution 5 galls, Lime juice 4 galls, Whale oil 7 galls, Lime 500 Kilos. | |
| MADAGASCAR | 22nd | | Took over attached units from 47th Divn. | |

W.W.

# WAR DIARY
## or
## INTELLIGENCE SUMMARY

Army Form C. 2118.

A.D. 31st Divn.

| Place | Date | Hour | Summary of Events and Information | Remarks and references to Appendices |
|---|---|---|---|---|
| MADAGASCAR | November 22nd | | 116 Tren Coy. 699 men 10 animals, below Str. 40 men, 1st Field Survey Co. 32 men, 159 Lab Coy. 4100 p.m. 10 animals, 157 Lab Coy. 33 men 4 animals, YMCA ROCLINCOURT 4 men, Town Major ANZIN 16 men, 25 M.A.C. 62 men, Tomahawk St. CATHERINE 11 men, 131 Cpl Cafe Camp. 98 men animals, 9 Aux. Steam Coy 35 men, Townhaps ST. AUBIN 12 men, No. 5 Area Valley Cobaret 11 men. Took over I Army Coal dump at 11 A.8.6 from S.S.o. 47 Divn. Quantity 660.6 tons. Supplied 110th Rde N.F. from ARRAS | |
| | 23rd | | Breastuffe supplied 110th Rde N.F. from ARRAS, other troops from 31st Divn at ECURIE. 110th Rde drew hay but from Mont ST ELOY. Rest of Divn from ECURIE. Received 10-0-0 Rations Hay returned from ECURIE to dumps distributed to Divinal Strength. Sent Planness lorry to LE COMTE | |
| | 24th | | | |
| | 25th | | Supply train late did not draw until 2 p.m. from Railhead owing to awkward of R.O.T. who sent train to ARRAS in mistake. Loaded Divn HQ supplies on lorry & despatched it to VILLIERS CHATEL forward place. Divn HQ drew 2 days rations to day. Sent supplies of 14th N.F. by lorry to LE COMTE. Isupply of coal. Loaded 110th Rde supplies by lorries at MONT ST. ELOY. Supply column supply personnel 50. O.R. Joined Train + attached to No. 4 Company | |
| | 26th | | Drew 10 Tons coal from I Army dump at 11 A.8.6. Issued 18 Tons to XIII Corps Troops. 178 Tons to 31st Divn. from I Army ammt. 110th Rde drew supplies for last time from MT. ST ELOY | |
| | 27th | | Drew supplies whole Divisions from ECURIE. Sent supplies for 4 R.E. & R.F.A. by lorry to BERLES and BETHENCOURT, 110th Rde supplies to ROCLINCOURT. Drew 4600 lbs Straw from Special S.D. ECURIE forward 110th Rde & 14th N.F. sleeping in mud floors - Ackley PDFT I. Army. | |

Sch. 82 Forms/C2118/14

# WAR DIARY
## or
## INTELLIGENCE SUMMARY.

(Erase heading not required.)

Army Form C. 2118.

220 21st Divn

| Place | Date | Hour | Summary of Events and Information | Remarks and references to Appendices |
|---|---|---|---|---|
| MADAGASCAR | November 28th | | Drew supplies from Railhead ECURIE by M.T. for Br. Bn. R.A's & Hd of Divn Tps. by M.T. for 110th Bde - sent 2 Loads to 111 Rde - Drew full issue Rum for divison on XIII Corps authority. Handed over library Coal dump at 2.111.6. 8.b. to 220 31st Divn. Quantity handed over 6,354 Tons. | |
| | 29th | | Nothing to record. | W.P. Allison Major 220 21st Divn |

# WAR DIARY
## INTELLIGENCE SUMMARY

Army Form C. 2118.

Dec 1917

| Place | Date | Hour | Summary of Events and Information | Remarks and references to Appendices |
|---|---|---|---|---|
| MADAGASCAR CAMP | 1st | | Proceeded with which proceed to Italian front. All arrangements for advance party are to be passed onto to proceed by train at 8 a.m. from ARRAS to 2.. O1 4 pm all ration supply advices but Ad.S was hurriedly advanced in III Army. No Artillery Transport for train. Division concentrated around TINCOURT, BOIRE - COURCELLES and preceding by road. Train HQ opened at BOIRE - Div Hd opened at TINCOURT. During the difficulty supplies in duty the big 11th Div Rdes to train 7 Capt Davis 8eo Sup Officer MMC was to supplies arranged. Drew supplies from Rdes Div. TINCOURT to last 2nd and 3rd Brigade bivouacked. Drew supplies Rdes transferred to 21 Div. Headquarters to places close by III. III Div kitty Cabs being transferred to ITALY. A.D.C. Unit had proceeded by road to ITALY. | |
| BUIRE-COURCELLES | 2nd | | Train HQ & preparation. Drew supplies from PRIE & Mk 3 infantry Brigade by M.T. Artillery proceeded at BAPAUME. 14th M.T. drew rations from ARRAS Railhead - arranged tobacco fuel from SSD 55 Amm. Withdrew | |
| TINCOURT | 3rd | | Moved office to TINCOURT, Mobile aeroplane supplementing train in locality. for R station at Railhead 50rs complete para rations temoniqued to 67 N° 8 F.S.D. PERONNE. Auxiliary M.P.T. train III Army 2nd - 7th Corps W.C 2nd - 108 Army F.A T.D. applied for ad wig where bread with rejoined rations drawn from M.G F.S.D. PERONNE a 33rb - 0th and receipts R 55 pm QMS - Drew 12 Tons Coal from 7 Corps T.S.C. | |
| " | 4th 5th | | Railhead moved to ROISEL three supplies by MuchTransport - Drew 10 Tons Coal from RSO Lists 8 & SD for 10 Tons draw for Rlt. Attached amongst unit of 62 - 110 Rdes. Draw 6 Tons of charcoal from Railhead, Rum ration issued. Div drawn. | |

# WAR DIARY or INTELLIGENCE SUMMARY

Army Form C. 2118.

| Place | Date | Hour | Summary of Events and Information | Remarks and references to Appendices |
|---|---|---|---|---|
| TINCOURT | 6th | | Drew 12 Tons Coal from 7 Corps Supply Col. | |
| | 7th | | Drew 6 Tons Charcoal from R.S.O.; 30% Haywheat, 30% Haywheat, 30% Oatwheat. | |
| | 7th | | T.O.R. attached unit to 110th Fd. Coy. R.E. 30% Oatwheat. 60% Oatmeal. 1st Motor M.G. Batty. att. to supplies struck off. | |
| | 8th | | 5 Tons Coffee arrived at Railhead, distributed amongst units of Division. Drew 6 Tons Charcoal from Railhead & 9 Tons Coal. | |
| | 9th | | 1st Echelon relieved by 4th in the line. Asked D.D.S.&T. to send up 60% Haywheat beat & 20% of the bread. Ration in flour (to be drawn on Saturday). Late today laundry congestion in Railhead yard. | |
| | 10th | | Nothing to Report. Late in loading caused congestion in Railhead yard. | |
| | 11th | | Drew 5 Tons Coal & 16 Tons Coke from Railhead. | |
| | 12th | | Issued Straw to units of 9 Corps — Woods 16th Regs. 1100lbs, 94th Fd. R.A. 1000lbs, 9th Fd. R.F.A. 1000 lbs. 121 R.A.C. as per above the issuing to units drawing on us being on basis. Draw 50 Tons of Coal from Railhead. | |
| | 13th | | Moved Advanced Coal Dump from RUYRE to LONGAVESNES. 50% Flack Meal & 60% Bread issued from Railhead — also 6 Tons Charcoal. | |
| | 14th | | 2.30 Rolling Turnips handed over to 16th Div. R.O. Distributed these among 4 Regts of the Div. | |
| | 15th | | 108 of A.P.de drew 975 + 933 animals; 283 A.F.A.Bde 948 men & 894 animals drew supplies for one (consumption 174) on transfer from VII Corps T.S.C. Drew 9 Tons Coal, 14 Tons Coke & 6 Tons Charcoal from R.S.O. M.L.L. | |

**Army Form C. 2118.**

# WAR DIARY
## or
## INTELLIGENCE SUMMARY.
*(Erase heading not required.)*

Instructions regarding War Diaries and Intelligence Summaries are contained in F. S. Regs., Part II. and the Staff Manual respectively. Title pages will be prepared in manuscript.

AD 37th Divn

| Place | Date | Hour | Summary of Events and Information | Remarks and references to Appendices |
|---|---|---|---|---|
| TINCOURT | 18th | | Moved Divisional Fuel Dump from SUIRE to LONGAVESNES. | |
| | | | Supp. Train very late. Arrived at 6.30 pm. before returned to Camp at 1 A.m. 19. Roads very bad though thick covering of frozen snow. Cold but fine. 65th S.A. Transport like TII coln Tpt. | |
| | 19th | | Train Issues 1d nil rations to units but 1st line Transport came to Railhead for Company Coys & draw supplies. 58 Tons Cnl & 20 Tons Coke drawn by 1st Line Transport at Railhead. Issued 3000 6m Asphol II army units to 2 batns 62 Adv 1 batt. 110th Rde. Weather very cold but fine. to send up troops. 3500 Tons messes to on Saturdays + to both Cavalry daily. | |
| | 20th | | Drew 96 Tons Wood, 20 Tons Coke. 6 Tons Charcoal by 1st line. Manifested at LONGAVESNES forward 15 loads from SMTD [...] purpose. Sent to 1 RE & FSD for Rum - [...] sandbag shank 222 AT | |
| | 21st | | Sent to No. 8 FSD for 10000 Rations. Supply Train arriving. Discontinued Dropping off Cay RE 21 OR; 15 Labour Cy 260 OR; 162 Lab Cy 420 OR 12 TO Party of trunks Sent 27 OR; Tramway DETACHMENT 1 OR, & Issued in detail from Army. Supplies taken from Railhead by Train Transport. 60% Fresh Meat. 50% Bread. Reminded brass rank. | |
| | 22nd 23rd | | Train Companies prepared SUIRE to AIZECOURT-LE-BAS. Sked 50 Tons Coal from Pipes. 15m Wood from Avesnes. 20 Tons Coke & 7 Tons Charcoal. Loaded supplies for division on 60 Cm. railway & dumped down to 1st line Rde at E15 a.11.5 62 H64 Trucks at E15 a.4.4. Used 20 Trucks - 60% fresh Meat, 70% Bread. Rum issued to all Ranks. Issued SD Dept & army for Troth Cavalry devs. Bread 2 AB - Xmas pudding for man. Frozen Peas - | |
| | 25th 26th 27th | | Nothing exceptional to report. Drew fuel from Railhead. Usual proportion of fresh meat, bread, fresh vegetables | |

W.M.W

# WAR DIARY / INTELLIGENCE SUMMARY

Army Form C. 2118.

H.Q. 21st Division

| Place | Date | Hour | Summary of Events and Information | Remarks and references to Appendices |
|---|---|---|---|---|
| AIZECOURT LE-BAS | 28th | | Train H.Q. moved to AIZECOURT-LE-BAS from TINCOURT. 4½ Tons Coal, 17 tons Charcoal, Wire Cake drawn. Extra Trench Rations to-night 6,777 O.Rs drawn, full issue Rum. 355 O.R. arrived from Reinforcement Depot. About ½ millions of Rum. | Weather bitterly cold. |
| | 29th | | Extra Trench Rations issued to O.Rs to-day about full issue of Rum. Weather very cold. 159 O.R. arrived for 63rd Bde; 146 O.R. for 110 Bde — Sewer/own Rations in replacement of Jumpsteads — 62 Bde, 28; 64 Bde 80; 110 Bde 20; 108 A.F.A. Bde 80. Weather very cold | Drew 66 Tons Wood |
| | 30th | | Issued 116 pas trusses hay to — lifted DEPOT to other trucks of officers cottage to issue through Special Need IIG Bde 29th trucks return to be set up as flow. Cold continues. Prev 80009. | |
| | 31st | | Rail Line Depot to open Fresh from Railhead. Potatoes Rations from Railhead. Reduced by Depot St. Army hd potatoes reduced to 2 pr daily. Issue very much up by fried fuel, minor fried vegetables. 282 A.F.A. Bde left Division men being sickroom families transferred III Corps Troops R.C. | |

W.R.Robertson Maj.
G.S.O. 21 Divn.

**Army Form C. 2118.**

# WAR DIARY
# or
# INTELLIGENCE SUMMARY.
(Erase heading not required.)

No 39th Division

| Place | Date | Hour | Summary of Events and Information | Remarks and references to Appendices |
|---|---|---|---|---|
| MEZEROURT LE-BAPS | Jany 1st/18 | | 60% fresh meat, 50% bread. Vegetable rations made up by 2 captured fruits. | Issued 22/12/18 |
| | | | Billed strew to 10th K.O.Y.L.I. | |
| | 2nd | | CQMS moved from Line to AMIENVILLE area for transport rebuilt after knockabout. 3rd. | |
| | | | Returned party to be on Carpet T.S. cloth. Issued billet stores to M.G. Coy. Issued D.S.L.I. stores | |
| | | | to 300 Trench kit bags for Eston. | |
| | 3rd | | Nothing of importance to report. | |
| | 4th | | Produced 10,550 kilos of trench bombs and arranged to have | |
| | | | more 10,000 kilos to arrive by Rail. Arrived to draw 80 tons | |
| | | | of wood from 7th Bn Suffs Rgt. | |
| | 5th | | Drew 8 ton lorries from R.S.O. la on APPREETE. | |
| | 6th | | Nothing of importance to report. | |
| | 7th | | Cleared 20 Trucks Wood from Gort Dump to D'll Trench dump and | |
| | | | thence to full dump. | |
| | 8th | | Ordered 4 in planks while old and Oruy bales | |
| | 9th | | Petrol on the came up again. Cleared balance of wood from | |
| | | | Gort Dump. | |

Army Form C. 2118.

# WAR DIARY
## or
## INTELLIGENCE SUMMARY.
(Erase heading not required.)

S.S. Div 1st Division

Instructions regarding War Diaries and Intelligence Summaries are contained in F. S. Regs., Part II. and the Staff Manual respectively. Title pages will be prepared in manuscript.

| Place | Date | Hour | Summary of Events and Information | Remarks and references to Appendices |
|---|---|---|---|---|
| AIZECOURT LE-BAS | Jan 1918 10th | | Nothing of interest to report. | |
| | 11th | | Received orders to draw Fuel Wood from MANANCOURT WOOD. Arranged with O/C to draw to our own dump at roadside and from there to Sup Fuel Dump. | |
| | 12th | | 60 % Bread 30 % Meat drawn at Railhead. 33rd M.T. Coy Sect moved to Peronne owing to that the Supply Column should draw their rations Issue 2 tons billet straw and 13,000 9/3 sulated rations. | |
| | 13th | | Nothing of importance to report. | |
| | 14th | | Truck of Biscuit from M/W Gorentin arrived. Out very dirty & opened to take same [?] which use unsatisfactory. | |
| | 15th | | New consignment of buildings for Railhead. | |
| | 16th | | 100 Tons load drawn by Supply Railway to Sup Truck dump owing to thaw beginning. | |
| | 17th | | Nothing to report. | |
| | 18th | | Meat and Bread 60 % | |

**Army Form C. 2118.**

# WAR DIARY
## or
## INTELLIGENCE SUMMARY.
*(Erase heading not required.)*

S.S.O. 2. I. S. [illegible]

| Place | Date | Hour | Summary of Events and Information | Remarks and references to Appendices |
|---|---|---|---|---|
| AZICOURT LEVAL | 19th 1918 | | S.S.O.O. F.L. Du5 sent at Railhead to be made of known | |
| | 20th | | Shipment of the Ullit to Rally [illegible] returns for storing sheen drawn from VII CTSC at | |
| | | | [illegible] in closis. 11 P & M Rale dhipsulle sim by hy 14 Rale | |
| | 21st | | S.S. Trubel & Pty. Two takes drawn at Railhead ehoupored at O.L. 357 Refillingh'd of Div Tp. | |
| | 22nd | | No Reson received at Railhead. [illegible] what was available at M & 2.S.P. | |
| | 23rd | | Telliverine of Rum sent up by trains, before that next, 75% Bread to fullvegetable issue drawn from Railhead - draws Tonsmart from Corps Dump at MARIEUX. | |
| | 24th | | Draw 7on Iron Ration for "reserve of resistance" arranged storage as follows :- 200 at No Pole HQ Eq & 7.5 at GAULCOURT & 500 at GUYENCOURT - Authority DD.P.T. str 220 of 14/11/18. 60% Frozen Meat & 75% Bread, fullvegetable Ration drawn from Railhead - 8'o or OR | |
| | | | Op 163 Det Coy attached for rations - [illegible] 5P Two loss at Railhead transferred at Div.Tp. drmp. | |
| | 25th | | 60% Frest Meat 80% Bread - Draw no vegtable ration from R.A.P. in order to adjust ordnance consist through puchase of fresh vegetable. | |
| | 26th | | 50% Frest Meat & 75% Bread - no issue of [illegible] drawn no party vegetable return - | |
| | 27th | | Drew supplies for 106 A.T.A. Pole (R.F.A.) for last time exchange to 7th C.T.S.C. stained 445 Us Hay from Railhead in exchange provinder granted, embarrassed by N.O. 17 Train Who cleared | [illegible] |

Army Form C. 2118.

# WAR DIARY
## or
## INTELLIGENCE SUMMARY.
(Erase heading not required.)

llo 21st Divn

| Place | Date | Hour | Summary of Events and Information | Remarks and references to Appendices |
|---|---|---|---|---|
| AIZECOURT LE BAS | Jany 1918 29th | | Visited refilling points & Railhead with Major July 21st Divn & Colonel of U.S. Army. Perfected system of moving supplies. 60% Fingstead & 90% Meat. 13500 orangs arrived as party Fresh Vegetable Ration. Issued supplies to 282 A.F.R.P.s and ourfp from 7th Corp Tranp S.C. strength 958 men, 970 animals. attached to 3rd Tranp Fuelp. 20th Divn Cele down from Div and transfered to 2nd Suppy Column. | |
| | 30th | | Owing to troop movements division were moved to CV 14 in Centricule line E 15 e 5.5 as a temporary measure. Supplied during 10 hr hrs 117 fres MANTHCOURT BDE to 155 th Refilling points moved to 14th 2nd Col by Lorry heavy rains. Mancea. Re-drew forage from BAS Col by Lorry. Hard established Mancean cross roads. | Maff Sheet maps llo 21 Divn |
| | 31st | | | |

Maff Sheet maps
llo 21 Divn

# WAR DIARY or INTELLIGENCE SUMMARY

Army Form C. 2118.

**LLO 21st Divn**

(Erase heading not required.)

Instructions regarding War Diaries and Intelligence Summaries are contained in F. S. Regs., Part II. and the Staff Manual respectively. Title pages will be prepared in manuscript.

| Place | Date | Hour | Summary of Events and Information | Remarks and references to Appendices |
|---|---|---|---|---|
| AIZECOURT LE-BAS | Feby 1918 | | | |
| | 1st | | No potatoes received. Vegetable ration made up by onions & dried fruits | |
| | 2nd | | 159 O.R. of 3/4th Queens transferred to 33rd Divn. returned up to 4th. 159 O.R. of same batt proceeded join 4th. | 41. O.R. |
| | | | 14th Divn returned up to 4 pm 5th. No potatoes sent up by Base. Vegetable ration in Onions & dried fruits to 10th Yorks issued from Base. Mixed DB+T to increase weekly issue of flour to 2400 lbs. | |
| | 3rd | | 14th OR 1st 15th DLI arrived returned up to 4 pm 4th. No potatoes issued out of packet. 6th to Royal Munst + 15th Bread sent to PERONNE for Avre to Supply Depot a Supply Train. 2nd Lincoln Rgt arrived at transfer from 8th Divn to 62nd Rfle Vice 3/4th Queens. 116th Yorks 10th being broken up. Strength 740 men transmitted. 159 3/4 Queens transferred to 13th Divn. 159 OR to 33rd Divn returned up to 4th + 6th = | |
| | 4th | | No potatoes. 4500 Kilo A.P.B. Cabbage arrived at Railhead Haut-Allaines 5 Ton Lorries Oake asked SPB both am. Baca issued forward as Trench ration to 110 Rfle. Asked SPB to 13 B.M.F. 159 OR to 14th M.F. 200 OR have | |
| | 5th | | 178 OR arrived from 31st Divn. transferred to 10th RG4h + to 9th RGth. Only 30lb of flour requirements been transferred from 10th RGh. | |
| | 6th | | Changed distribution of bread from Reycet - Two 11th Fld Amens add. Bare arrived by 62 Fd Ambe No OD for Russ and bay Amens. Thee in first consignment of potatoes received p arrived thru Rail. | 6 up |

W.H.

# WAR DIARY
## INTELLIGENCE SUMMARY

(Erase heading not required.)

Army Form C. 2118.

220  21st Divn.

| Place | Date | Hour | Summary of Events and Information | Remarks and references to Appendices |
|---|---|---|---|---|
| AIZECOURT LE-BAS | 7th | | Relieved 10th Yorkshire Regt. Since 110th Bde relieved in line by 62nd Bde. Imp't kept Bd sent to 6th R.O.R. Drew 37 Mins Carts from Railhead. Handed at Divl Fuel Dump. Transferred following units from 6th Bty A.m.b. to Divl Troops Group – 152/1 Labour Coy, Divl H.Q., Hqrs. R.E., 21 Divl Signal Coy & A.P.M. (M.M. Police). 52 O.R. 10th York L.I. transferred to 31st Divn. retained up to 9th inclusive. 210 O.R. 9th LEICESTERS transferred to 6th Divn retained up to 9th inclusive | |
| | 9th | | Sent two Cars for Railhead stuffs but not at Div. Dump. Drew full issue of Rum for Divisions, there being a large stock at Railhead. 315 O.R. 10th Yorks. Regt. transferred 50th Divn retained up to 11th inclusive. 13th – Usual percentage of Fresh Meat, Bread & Vegetables. | |
| | 10th | | 241 O.R. 10th K.O.Y.L.I. transferred to 32nd Divn retained up to 15th. Cleared Fuel work train at FINS, loaded into Caterpillar line transfered at Divl Fuel Dump. Quantity drawn = 50¾ tons. Wired Army for authority to obtain 5 Tons Jrunged Cake through Purchase Board. | |
| | 11th | | Owing to large arrival of Vegetables rations eased usual special Number – 100% Vegetables drawn for Railhead today. 70% Fresh Meat & 66⅔% Bread. | |
| | 13th | | Attended Cond. of Supply at H.Q. 7th Corps Rebyd- the Redrawal of actions by 21st Divn Gave evidence to the effect the order to draw Rations from 7th Corps by wire resulting in delayed more to Railhead of unit. | |

M.C.T.

# WAR DIARY
## or
## INTELLIGENCE SUMMARY.

Army Form C. 2118.

WD 21st Divn

| Place | Date | Hour | Summary of Events and Information | Remarks and references to Appendices |
|---|---|---|---|---|
| FREVILLERS LE-RAS | Feby 13th | | Drew only 50% of Vegetable ration to allow withdrawal. Drew 75% vice Overtime Resilient dump at Fuel Dump. Co/y Paper Rest & 75% Bread. Party of 47 OR 2/4th Queens proceeded to Corps Reinf. Camp returned Feb 14th. | |
| | 14th | | 50% bread drawn from RMP dumped at Divl Field Dump. Veal loaf in lieu of Cheese. Ration in lieu of Jam. Full Vegetable ration drawn. Usual proportion of Ingredient Bread. | |
| | 15th | | Veal loaf cut up in lieu of Cheese again. RD Visited AMIENS. Purchased for the Divisl Canteen. | |
| | 16th | | Received Cheese in usual proportion. Other Rations normal. 1 A.T. of Batty transferred to 3 — | |
| | 17th | | Corps dues rations for conveying this 17th to last time. Trucks promised by Light Rly to transport Coal from Railhead to Fuel Dump did not arrive. Complained to Corps "Q" | |
| | 18th | | Nothing to report excepting that 24 Tons Coal drawn from Railhead & dumped at Fuel dump. | |
| | 19th | | Truck containing 3800 kilos Cabbage held up from S.P.B. Distributed according to strength. DCos rations for 7th Cav. Field Station (but 8th F.A.) for issue 20th February came on transfer from VII Corps Troops. Strength 1297 OR + 48 animals. Drew 15 Tons wood from MARAMCOURT forest dumped at Fuel dump. | |
| | 20th | | Had Vista nomenclature FAMECHON to serve or left column. AD coffee ready for issue. Party of 103 OR b/15 N.F. attached to work under 16th Divn. Received 16 Tony Carrots & Purchases at AMIENS to Supplement rations. Off ration. Received 5 Tons Sucker (Cabbage) to Troops — | |

# WAR DIARY
## INTELLIGENCE SUMMARY.
(Erase heading not required.)

Army Form C. 2118.

Instructions regarding War Diaries and Intelligence Summaries are contained in F. S. Regs., Part II. and the Staff Manual respectively. Title pages will be prepared in manuscript.

A.D.S. 21st Division

| Place | Date | Hour | Summary of Events and Information | Remarks and references to Appendices |
|---|---|---|---|---|
| AIZECOURT LE BAS | Feb. 21st | | Nothing to report. | |
| | 22nd | | 1800 lb Mutton short on train received by Rlys. Find this probable make up on 23rd. | |
| | 23rd | | Shortage of above Mutton made good, but a further shortage of 7,770 lbs on pack train. Arrange this should fall on Div. Tps for future. | |
| | 24th | | Shortage of 1700 lbs. Meat on Pack Train's first made up. Supply Train arrived short of 1670 lbs. Mtn. Fractions truck having received of the Divnl Groceries from detail who excepting Tea, Suga & Candles. Sent to LA CHAPELETTE for these commodities up to 14.00 hrs the 25th. | |
| | 25th | | Drew 2090 kilos Cabbage from Railhead. Train arrived 2800 lbs Meat short. Drew this from TINCOURT. Usual proportion of other supplies. | |
| | 26th | | Usual proportion of Bread Meat. Fairly Vegetable Ration received in Orange (13,000). 53 Tons coal drawn from C.O.T. Tincourt Transport Fuel Dump. 1st Sqd Yorks Regt drew it from Railhead. | |
| | 27th | | Usual detail. 6 bottles at HAUT ALLAINES. Through 2760 kilos drawn from Railhead, found to be much too hurtful for consumption owing to frost. | |
| | 28th | | 1000 tubs of Butter drawn from Railhead. 1800 Oranges rec. as part of Vegetable Ration: only had to received the ration from Supply Train as had had one drawn (awd) through S.P.B. vegetables (no potatoes) 110th Bde delivered 49th Bde (16th Div) & 5th Bde reched 27th Bde (116th Div). Sent to LA CHAPELETTE for 110th Hd Hd's share. | |

Walpott Major
A.D.S. 21 Div.

# WAR DIARY / INTELLIGENCE SUMMARY

Army Form C. 2118.

March 1st – 31st

No. 21st Division

| Place | Date March | Hour | Summary of Events and Information | Remarks and references to Appendices |
|---|---|---|---|---|
| AILLECOURT LE BAS | 1st | | Drew rations from Railhead. Forwarded transport for 108 AFA Bde. Strength Intn HQ LT 9th 3U gun for new 2nd March. Ser/6. | |
| | | | LACHAPELETTE for 3600 lbs Hay, 72 cwm bulk (30 lb Tea 36x 16) Railhead. Sky Coy. Maunfont arrived at Hallnoil, sent 3 Tons to Villeups Reste Hell. Attempted remounts at Prvd Drnup. Dir Runner took him to 6th Bde. Dis Tpr + blow officer took it to 6 + 11th Pates + Div Tpr (Strengths on Trunder). Drew 2 Graphite Rates. | |
| | 2nd | | At LACHAPELLETTE for 300 lbs Hay, 6th Bde Trpd Head 175 lb Bread – Rel to LACHAPELETTE for Oats and water. Tidence. | |
| | 3rd | | Supply Train arrived containing only Rackhorse Bread Ration. Direct supplies. Rest to LACHAPELETTE for Biscuit 58 x 50, Fur.D meat 113 x 48, Jam 63 x 50, Sugar 113 x 60, Tea 56 lb, Milk 30 x 48, Salt 41 x 50, Rum 43 gall. Hay 76 lb 61 lb, Oats 57,873 lb, Petrol 615 galls, Lub Oil 30 gall, MSO 57 pkt, Cigarettes 25 pkts, MPO Small Matches. Spirit 30 pkt, Whole Flat 25 galls, Coal to HAH for 1000 lb. Candles – Butter not available. Brace Runner not available. No light Railway truck available. Ditto Supplies from ROISEL by M.T. returned to LACHAPELETTE. | |
| | 4th | | Drew field dried bread Ration 3 made up by MT. + Cheese from ROISEL loaded on light Railway. Set to LACHAPELETTE for Flour 117 x 64, Biscuit 61 x 50, MV 47 x 48, Jam 35 x 60, Sugar 43 x 60, Tea 14 x 30, Milk 30 x 48, Salt 3 x 50, Rum 57 gall, Hay 70,149 lb, Oats 59,403 lb, MSO 40 gall, Petrol 316 galls, Lub Oil 40 galls, Cheese 10 galls, Candles 247 lbs, MPO 40 pkt, Whale Oil 20 gall, Officers Press Meator 6 lb of each, and 6 Tons of Coal Wheel Drnup. Drew all house supplies by lorries. | |

**Army Form C. 2118.**

# WAR DIARY
## INTELLIGENCE SUMMARY.
*(Erase heading not required.)*

Instructions regarding War Diaries and Intelligence Summaries are contained in F. S. Regs., Part II. and the Staff Manual respectively. Title pages will be prepared in manuscript.

220   21st Division

| Place | Date | Hour | Summary of Events and Information | Remarks and references to Appendices |
|---|---|---|---|---|
| AIZECOURT LE-BAS | Month Sept 5th | | Issued to LA CHAPELETTE Hay 70,517 lbs, Oats 50,391 lbs, P.Meat 116x6 lbs, Bisct 62x50 lbs, Peas 91 galls, Rum 776 galls, Salt 35 galls, P.Beef 110 lbs, Cheese 110 lbs, Candles 110 lbs, W.P.O 35 galls. Whisky 15 galls, Oxford Lodge, Epsom Salts etc, Iron Rations 1256. Remainder of supplies from ROISEL by Light Railway. | |
| | 6th | | Drew supplies from ROISEL by M.T. transport no Light Railway trucks being available, drew Preserved Meat Biscuit Rats from LA CHAPELETTE. Linseed Cake drawn from LA CHAPELETTE 4400 lbs, distributed thus as follows:- Div Troops 3080 lbs, 62nd Bde 640 lbs, 110th Bde 390 lbs, 64th Bde 290 lbs. Rectbiot distributed (1500 kilos per animal) drawn & working at 8½ kg per horse. Drew 15 Tons coal from LA CHAPELETTE | |
| | 7th | | 5,000 Kilos L.P.B. Corods arrived at Railhead. Cleared these the same supplies by Horse Transport. | |
| | 8th | | 6½ M. Gill Bent moved to MARICOURT decorating for this unit & had time preparing to transport. | |
| | | | Corps Troops. 16,800 Kilos Corods Arrived at Railhead from AMIENS when they were produced & issued there on behalf to Div Gps Offices. Drew 15 Tons coal from LA CHAPELETTE | |
| | | | Issued 6½ lbs Chloride of Lime to Div. Gp. Offices. 115 Ton Wood from VII Corps dump at FINS. Supplies Div Troops Group loaded on Light Railway | |
| | 10th | | Motor Group by Horse Transport. Completed the drawing of 100 Tons Wood from MARANCOURT Forest. 100 Ton Coal cleared from Railhead by lorries & dumped at Fuel Dump. Began the drawing of 100 Tons. | |
| | | | Wood from MARANCOURT Forest by Horse Transport. Loaded supplies at Railhead for Div Troops Bde. | |
| | | | 110 Bdes by Light Railway. H.Q. Bakery H.T. | |
| | 11th | | Base Kilos. MT Corods cleared from LA CHAPELETTE. 5,000 Kilos of Corods to keep clearing from TINCOURT | MA/3 |

# WAR DIARY
## or
## INTELLIGENCE SUMMARY.

Army Form C. 2118.

(Erase heading not required.)

| Place | Date March | Hour | Summary of Events and Information | Remarks and references to Appendices |
|---|---|---|---|---|
| AILECOURT | | | | |
| LE-BAS | 13th | | Issued Goggles Lubricant Hypo to Bde Gas Officers also 67 N Sections Alarms. Discs etc Tin etc | |
| | | | Coal Railhead returned to trot Dump. One RFA returned from it. Also RFA RFA parcels | |
| | | | K2 Ammon below. Photograph new guns in trench | |
| | | | | |
| | 14th | | Gunner Toohey taken to hospital suspense tus at N°1 A S Dept. LA CHAPPELLETTE for M.P. Railway to | |
| | | | Amiens — Forth & 50 prs Peas Haricots Bacon Bister Tea Sugar 236 Pos Cattle — No Sacks — Potatoes | |
| | | | B. Distribution foul RFA Parties from Div. Meat by day Bread 1 in × 50. Ran to Cello Mule O/c 10 Cells. | |
| | 15th | | Cavalry fresh 7h. Sent LA CHAPPELLETTE to take Carts — None available. Potatoes not av. 4PM | |
| | | | 38,000 lbs Turnips Reed. from DPR for forage. Attempted to get animal strength. Drew 10 tons Cake from | |
| | | | LA CHAPELETTE. | |
| | 16th | | 36½ Tons Oval drawn from Railhead about 12½ Tons E.P.R. 3500 Kilos Carrots & Frags. from LA CHAPELETTE. | |
| | | | 5000 Kilos Carrots (vegetables). In DADT ambulant drew 11,250 lbs Lub. oil. 16 Attached Infantry to Reserve to Bacon | |
| | | | Rations received. Other half received by rail. | |
| | 17th | | Sent LA FLAQUE for 55,000 lbs Biscuits. Oats 9076 lbs deficient on Supply Train. | |
| | 18th | | Sent to Tincourt for 36 lbs Biscuit & 5000 lbs Whale Oil. — 2 Tons Chloride of Lime drawn from | |
| | | | LA CHAPELETTE & delivered to Div Gas Officers. | |
| | 19th | | Sent for Cart draws from LA CHAPELETTE & issued to Div Gas Officer. | kak |

# WAR DIARY or INTELLIGENCE SUMMARY

Army Form C. 2118.

2nd Division

| Place | Date | Hour | Summary of Events and Information | Remarks and references to Appendices |
|---|---|---|---|---|
| AIZECOURT LE BAS | August 20 | | Brigade HQ left Park Farm LA CHAPELETTE (K.34.d.1.1.) at 2 p.m. officers 26 OR & 5 Animals arrived AIZECOURT LE BAS 2 | |
| | | | Arrangements for R.R. | |
| | 21st | | Hostile Counter barrage of the position commenced at 3.30 a.m. half an hour's shelling H.E. Gas + Shells | |
| | | | Brigade moved to TIVENCOURT (approx.) location to wait in TIVENCOURT (strong) - where we had debussed by H.T. | |
| | | | Obtained SS to add D/s spare 14 HAROLETTE for Bde HeadQrs. | |
| HEM | 22nd | | Orders to Bde recd. Moved to HAUT ALLAINES bringing with Bde from LA CHAPELETTE. Public call was Talies Cnp | |
| BLAKES | | | HEM + AINES + CORT LE BAS of Gd EN HAUT ALLAINES Brigade in Single Halbine 28? | |
| CLERY + HARICOURT | 23rd | | N - A Bde 1. 24th Div HAULT 030 OR 1730 arrived. Droall draws of night. | |
| | | | Relieved continues moved to CLERY subsequently moving back on the ETRICOURT. WOOD SUPPLY Dm | |
| | | | PLATEAU pulled by M.T. Ambulance 2500 rations received 41 casualties. Train Cnp moved to CURLU | |
| | | | at SP ref to RULE W.d. [?]ARICOURT. Forward 2 day Supplies and 1 day Supplies to 2nd Heavy Bde R.A. | |
| | | | 130 OR 10 LP 130 HT shaded [?] aled to 173 labour Cnp 160 OR who were also stranded. Small supply it | |
| | | | mules. | |
| BRAY Somme | 24th | | Bde shelled from PLATEAU (HARICOURT) by HT. Weather very fine. Supplies dumped direct to Train Conforms Cnps | |
| | 25th | | As usual. | |
| | | | Armistice horse BONES by M.T. returned near SAILLY-LE-SEC, removed from HQ at night from BRAY to SAILLY LAURETTE | |
| | | | Bde returned | |
| BRESLE | 26th | | Was shelled by HELIN by H.T. Burnt at BRISUX. Train Cnp moved 4 a.m. to CONTAY. HQ remaining at BRESLE | |
| | | | mule | |
| | | | Wirally dealt with chy hostile artillery. Retirement continued | |

# WAR DIARY
## INTELLIGENCE SUMMARY

Army Form C. 2118.

110  21st Divn

| Place | Date | Hour | Summary of Events and Information | Remarks and references to Appendices |
|---|---|---|---|---|
| BEAUCOURT | March 27th | | Went to VIGNACOURT and supply train had been diverted to FIESELLES - Lorries, wet - Motherfine. Motor supplies from FIESELLES by MT transported to AGNICOURT. 40% Fresh Meat & Bread received. | |
| NEAR BEAUCOURT | 28th | | Railhead VIGNACOURT. Drew 90 galls Rum - drove to where division sent to BELLE EGLISE. Dumped In 3 Mm Coal. Visited III Army HQ. DRT arranged to get coal sent up on pack train. Supplies at AGNICOURT. 40% fresh Rations, drew 2 days pea soup per man. Italians billed by both artillery fairly quiet Observer - motor bus with some men - Issued (659 rations to stragglers) | tylers locally - also L.M.G. dittos during night. Sent to |
| BEAUCOURT | 29th | | Rations = 62 Bde 319, 110 Bde 1444, 64 Bde 196 - To adjust drew 2 days supplies from Railhead & that 90 galls Rum to the various groups for distribution to SO's - (all 3 envel. set). Train HQ moved to ALLONVILLE. Railhead HANGEST-SUR-SOMME. Loaded supplies again by MT. DOULLENS for hay unit having arrived at Railhead, also 91 galls Rum to complete full issue for division - Dumped supplies refilled at a civilian MOLLIENS-AU-BOIS. Capt P St J Findlater Commanding N° 1 Coy Train was Killed on night 28th/29th - buried in church cemetery at MOLLIENS-AU-BOIS. In The Civil times (wart Railhead | |
| ALLONVILLE | 30th | | Railhead HANGEST-SUR-SOMME, drew supplies by MT send to DOULLENS for rum to complete full issue for division. Dumped 62 Bde at POULAINVILLE, 110th Bde at CARDONETTE, 64th Bde at PETIT CARDONETTE. | |
| | 31st | | Drew supplies by MT from HANGEST, dumped 62 Bde at BOURDON, 110th Mob. Bths & Divl Troops at AMIENS RAINNVILLE Road, Issued 3 horse Rum allowance. 62nd Bde HQ Rum Train marched to HANGEST. Preparatory to entraining for II Army area. | |

W. Gilbert Knoop  
SSO 21 Divn

Army Form C. 2118.

1st - 31st April 1918

Original

# WAR DIARY
## INTELLIGENCE SUMMARY
(Erase heading not required.)

No. 21st Division

| Place | Date | Hour | Summary of Events and Information | Remarks and references to Appendices |
|---|---|---|---|---|
| | April | | | |
| KLONVILLE | 1st | | Drew supplies by MT from LONGPRÉ-LES-CORPS-SAINTS, dumped supplies for units entraining later in day at HANGEST and at ST.ROCH. 62nd Bde by MT Bde proceeded to II Army area staged for night near BAILLEUL. Div: transferred to Australian Corps & concentrated around LOCRE DRANOUTRE & KEMMEL. Proceeded by car to new area & remained for night at CAESTRE. | |
| DRANOUTRE | 2nd | | Train HQ moved to DRANOUTRE, dumped 62nd Bde Hoy supplies at Church LOCRE then refilling four place. Drew supplies by MT from LA CLYTTE for the three infantry brigades thence by MT. 110th - 61st DRANOUTRE Church, 62nd Bde at LOCRE Church - refilled there. Met SSO 1st Australian Div. Took into ABCD rations of P.B. meat & Biscuit stored at MACONOCHIE SIDING as a reserve. Sent up Meat HW Cutbill 20 bi. Bde to check quantities & arrange for guard. Took over fuel Dump also Coal 120 Tons, Coke 70 Tons dumped in LOCREHOF FARM. 599 o.r. arrived for our fourth Bde. | |
| | 3rd | | 623 o.r. arrived for Division for that. | |
| | 4th | | Drew supplies for the following Units handed over by 1st Cavalry Div. by MT Dranoutre & MACONOCHIE 4th Res Regt. 693 o.r. 1262 animals, 12th B.R.E.A. 987 o.r., 18th Trans Coy R.E. 535 o.r. 16 I.D. + 16 L.D., 14th Field Survey Co. 44 o.r., II Anzac Mobile School 101 o.r., 295 Rly R.E. 216 o.r. 2 L.D., Tonchaye DRANOUTRE 81 o.r. 14 L.D., 5th R.M.A. Bde 91 o.r., "B" HorseA.C. R.E. 35 o.r. 3 L.D., 167 Co R.E. 92 o.r. 137 animals, 3 Aust A.F.F.B.L. 107 o.r. 940 animals, 34th R.Clay R.E. 160 o.r. "71 animals, 6th m.G. Ballooks M 139 o.r. | |
| Aust Ht. Cafe Heavy Ttus | | | 80 A.B.M. 39 yr. Div 111 o.r., 86 o.r. 11, 495 ox. pole drs Bath Sea Parks C/2 anaher 22 o.r. | |

# WAR DIARY
## INTELLIGENCE SUMMARY.

Army Form C. 2118.

WO 21st Division

| Place | Date | Hour | Summary of Events and Information | Remarks and references to Appendices |
|---|---|---|---|---|
| | April | | | |
| DRANOUTRE | 5th | | Drew supplies from LA CLYTTE by H.T. Obtained 2 Tons hay from Railhead. Drew 4920 lbs of linseed cake from RLO VLAMERTINGHE. Withdrew 1 amongst units of Divn attached Amm. Sent to 9th Corps M.T. Coy for 500 gls solidified alcohol. Re 29th Div L.O. rpts Tms observed. | |
| | 6th | | Drew 5 tons hay from Railhead. Also 100 Tons coal from BAILLEUL issued by Horse Transport. | |
| | 7th | | Numerous O of Ms sent, units at present attached to SCO 9th Divn. | |
| | | | 50.23 D.R. 366 HD 1051 L.D. Drew 2500 gls solidified alcohol from 9th C.T. M.T. Coy. Present. | |
| | | | 110th Fde LO issued supplies at BRULOOZE by Horse Transport. Am. bn 7A return to service to Position MONT-DES-CATS | |
| | 8th | | Loaded at Railhead by H.T. Rest of 110 Fde Supply Lorries. Handed over to SSO 19th Divn. 16000 rations | |
| | | | Pres Meal Present. RSO on a recce at MACONOCHIE SIDING. | |
| | 9th | | Loaded at Railhead by H.T. Rest LO b/2 Fde rations are rations left in Support Points. By LO | |
| | | | 38th Fde rations. 23.00 returns in all (Pres Meal Present) | |
| | 10th | | Nothing today except fresh rations. Arrange H10 Fde lorries shifted. | |
| | 11th | | Pulled LA CLYTTE dump supplies by Horse Transport. Hadn't won Pros Dump at LOCKE MOF. | |
| | | | Pres R SCO 19th Divn Coll Ha Ton. Coll 20 ins, Mont 20 ins, Charcoal 2 Tons & Tooth con Fuel Dumps. | |
| | | | 6am. DO of A Divn at EEDENWARLE 16f OUDEZOM. Quantity 150 Tons Coal | WAM |

Army Form C. 2118.

# WAR DIARY
## INTELLIGENCE SUMMARY.
(Erase heading not required.)

No 21st Division

| Place | Date April | Hour | Summary of Events and Information | Remarks and references to Appendices |
|---|---|---|---|---|
| HEKSKEN | 12th | | Train HQ moved from BRAMOUTRE to HEKSKEN. Left previous night. Drew supplies for Rations & RENINGHELST by M.T. Drew supplies to find strength of 49th Division apart by H.T. strength 3548 OR + 3071 animals. Drew attacks from LA CLYTTE. | |
| | 13th | | Railhead ABEELE drew supplies by M.T. a fresh strength amounted to over 3300's & 1430 animals had to send out for cordivals, quarters & supplies. Drew Bread, Dried Fruit, Cheese, butter, Biscuit, P.Meat, M.V., Candles, Tobacco from OUDERDOM. + Bacon, Rum, Pickles, Straw, Sugar, Tea, Butter, cheese, Bread, & fresh meat from WIPPENHOEK. Drew stores on solidified alcohol from WIPPENHOEK. | |
| | 14th | | Railhead ABEELE. Train did not contain enough supplies for strength of Div. Sent to OUDERDOM for Bis 719 lb, P.Meat 1308 lbs, Jam 115 lbs, Dried Milk 74 lb, Rice 165 lb, Oatmeal 162 lb, Candles 190 lb, Oats 1500 lb. To WIPPENHOEK for Jam 219 lb, Dried Milk 83 lb, Candles 650 lb, M.V. 229 tins, Sugar 249 lb, Cheese 229 lb, Bacon 2450 lb, Rum 127 galls, Iron Rations 480, Straw 8605 lb. | |
| | 15th | | Railhead ABEELE drew supplies for division. Meat delivered to their own Divisions. Dumped 62nd & 110th Bde supplies for division (less billeting) by M.T. 49th Divl Troops did not draw from us. Bde supplies on Reninghelst - Canada Corner Road. 110th Bde at G.20.c.5.B. Divl SEARLE inspected supplies to support points at I.30.a.8.7. 640 I.R. 5lb Biscuit 1200 also P.Meat, I.29.d.6.3. Biscuit Rtn 500, P.Meat 620, Mutton 21 tins, I.30.c.3.6. 300 I.R. Biscuit 150. | |

W.A.A.

Army Form C. 2118.

910 21st Division

# WAR DIARY
## or
## INTELLIGENCE SUMMARY.
(Erase heading not required.)

Instructions regarding War Diaries and Intelligence Summaries are contained in F. S. Regs., Part II. and the Staff Manual respectively. Title pages will be prepared in manuscript.

| Place | Date | Hour | Summary of Events and Information | Remarks and references to Appendices |
|---|---|---|---|---|
| | April | | | |
| HERKEN | 15th (cont) | | Inspected billets, tailors, baths in support points | |
| | | | 9.20 a.m. 3 p. mid; 2/Lt Thompson. J19a58. 300 I.R., J19b26. 1020 I.R., J20b64. 500 I.R., J13d52. 380 I.R. Biscuit 75. Pachart 39. HOOGE CRATER 800 Biscuit, Pachart 1020, Tiffeny 2180 I.R with SSO. | |
| | | | Halfway House I19.c.37. MIL All in good condition. Issued 1090 Iron ration to 110th Bde MG, 4090 | |
| | 16th | | Iron Ration to Hq 39th Composite Bde for storage in support points. Receipts obtained from Staff Captains. | |
| LISSENTHOEK | 16th | | Drew supplies from ABEELE by MT dumped near Train camp. Lead away to WIPPENHOEK | |
| | | | for Pirm & Straw | |
| | 17th | | 226 OR arrived from 62nd Bde, 365 OR to 6 4th Bde 1359 to 110th Bde, distribution from Railhead for | |
| | | | issue 18th | |
| | 18th | | Railhead to record exceeding in Scarcity of all in transit ABEELE Station Serving London | |
| | 19th | | Lil Train may late at Railhead loaded by M.T at 4 pm transferred to 15 pm rifilled | |
| | | | Shrapnel fired over Artillery (rough) fin first time where leaving the train area 2082 | |
| | | | Went to 10/20 Dinners | |
| | | SHELLHOEK | Much hostile shelling of back areas, also some bombing | |
| | 20th | | Lent to WIPPENHOEK 39,048 4.9 Pile, 67 pelle Ruin, 97 Mo Tobacco trip Mo Chards, 9 Ricons, | |
| | | | 1 rifely train again late | |
| | 21st | | Lent to WIPPENHOEK for 140 pelle Petrol, 46 pelle Petrol, 46 pelle Ruin, 7889 Mo Straw forage 141,073 Mr Oats deliverer on Supply | |
| | | | Train | |

# WAR DIARY or INTELLIGENCE SUMMARY

Army Form C. 2118.

**21st Division** No.

| Place | Date | Hour | Summary of Events and Information | Remarks and references to Appendices |
|---|---|---|---|---|
| 4th A.Q. | April 22nd | | Nothing to report. | |
| | 23rd | | Sent to WIPPENHOEK fr Rum 36 galls, Pepper 26¾ lbs, Oats 2400 lb, Straw Eggs lb, M.V 763 tins, Jam 436 lbs. Cheese 319 lbs, Sugar 1015 lbs, Milk 343 tins, Glaxo 114 lbs, Butter 112 lb, Tea 102 lb, not available at railhead. Oranges part line of Vegetables received. Locally killed thronted at night by hostile planes. | |
| | 24th | | Sent to WIPPENHOEK fr 32⅓ lines M.V., 37 galls Rum, 15 lb Jam 10 6lb Cheese, 227 lb Sugar, 41 lb Tea, 36 lb Dried Milk BR, 250 lb Biscuit, 110 lb Candles, 60 lb Oxford powder. Some shelling of locality by H.V. grenades, night. | |
| | 25th | | Sent to WIPPENHOEK fr 2414 lb Biscuit, 59 lb Unsweet Milk, 297 lb Sugar, 216 lb Candles, 85 lb Butter, 127 lb Wheat, 10 galls Rum, 432 lb Tea, 1511 lb Jam, 114 lb Cheese, 4688 lb Steam. Locally heavily shelled by H.V. guns. | |
| | 26th | | Unloaded at REMINGHELST Suit Trumps by M.T. the 3 Brigades by Horse Transport. No supply train Arrived. Supplies were drawn from R.S.O's Depot supplemented by 25505 lbs Hay, 7743 lbs Oats, 9033 lb Maize, Candles Extra, Butter 56 lb, Sugar 160 lb, Tab Oil 60 galls, Whale Oil 10 galls, all drawn from WIPPENHOEK. Locally shelled at intervals by H.V. guns during day. | |
| | 27th | | Army made railhead ROOSEBRUGGE what there I found no arrangements made for no supply train. Marshall, drew supplies from ABEELE by M.T. dumped the 3 Brigade groups at L.I.C. & Dirt Trumps at STEENVORDE. The 3 Brigade Train Coys marched to L.I.C.9.1 (3.Coy) & F25.d.3.3 (2 Coy) Sent to WIPPENHOEK fr 448 galls Petrol, 150 Pun Rolin fr 1915 NR, 116 lbs Carbide 60 lb Chloride of lime, 15 galls Jam. | |

15 F.mills, HR/C.67, Loudoght/L., 99883 [illegible] 354,000 6/17 Bogg [illegible] /C2141/5

Army Form C. 2118.

# WAR DIARY
## INTELLIGENCE SUMMARY.
*(Erase heading not required.)*

110. 21st Division

| Place | Date | Hour | Summary of Events and Information | Remarks and references to Appendices |
|---|---|---|---|---|
| | April | | | |
| | 28th | | Rubbish ABEELE. Issues 150 Iron Rations to 1/15 D.F. Nth Wing of attack crew. | |
| | 29th | | 2/3 Coy. moved GODEZEELE | |
| J.13.b.59 | 30th | | Totally under Wilver still [illegible] on shifting. Moved Train HQ to van N° 2 Coy at K.16.9.1. Drew supplies from ROUSBRUGGE by M.T. Attached supplies at Church to 62nd Bde Brighton. Other personnel on wards HQ to van N° 2 Coy at K.16.9.1. Drew supplies from ROUSBRUGGE by M.T. Bivi bi-lang probst to deliver 230 th. | |
| | | | Took 100 Iron Rations [illegible] made up Lost at Regt | |
| | | | Walltort hear? | |
| | | | 110 21st Div | |

Original

**WAR DIARY**

**INTELLIGENCE SUMMARY**
(Erase heading not required.)

Army Form C. 2118.

1st to 31st May 1918

30th Division

| Place | Date | Hour | Summary of Events and Information | Remarks and references to Appendices |
|---|---|---|---|---|
| B.E.F. | May 1st | | Div. artillery HQ. from ROUSBRUGGE, diverted 110th Bde at STEENVOORDE, 62nd Inf Bde at LEDERZEELE and Div.Tp at TERDEGHEM. Enemy artillery & A.A. Cpl. obtained. hit the ammunition dump night of 30 April they exposed 15 to WATOU area. 65th F.A. moved to LEDERZEELE. Into WIPPENHOEK 1830h Div arrived. PROVEN for D50 H. Bisent. | |
| RUBROUCK | 2nd | | Division relieved by 16 Div. Two HQ moved to RUBROUCK. Infantry moved to arrived LEDERZEELE | |
| | 3rd | | 6th Bde rear supplies train from ST OMER by M.T. Artillery 110th Bde from BLENDECQUES. Bldgs refused to join 9th Corps in 6th British Army. Area entered at 4th. | |
| | 4th | | Drew supplies from ST OMER by division by M.T. proceeded to render aux 6th French Army. Div. Moved to IX British Corps. landed POIX at 8.30 pm stopped the night Mud L.H. & W. cav. Division started entraining at ARQUES, STONER & WIZERNES | |
| ROMIGNY | 5th | | Arrived at FERE-EN-TARDENOISE reported to ADST. IX Corps did not draw supplies 8230, transport ran with train HQ. staff at ROMIGNY. | |
| | 6th | | Drew supplies by elements of Div. arriving from ST GILLES to division 7.– Distribution by elements of 6 battle Bde arriving near Div. jun. by M.T. Douglas 65 Bde at JHERY 64th Bde at ROMIGNY. 110th Bde near JARGEAU. Div. Trps VILLERS-ARGON | |
| | 9th | | Div Reinforcement arrived. Draw supplies short of Cheese, Bacon, Milk, & Jam. | [signature] |

Army Form C. 2118.

# WAR DIARY
## or
## INTELLIGENCE SUMMARY.
(Erase heading not required.)

No. 21st Division

Instructions regarding War Diaries and Intelligence Summaries are contained in F. S. Regs., Part II. and the Staff Manual respectively. Title pages will be prepared in manuscript.

| Place | Date | Hour | Summary of Events and Information | Remarks and references to Appendices |
|---|---|---|---|---|
| ROMIGNY | Sept 9th | | Showers of rain. Chops milk & jam as & 8th replenished. Drew 100000 litres Cast Horse Fdr West firm Trade tendencies Non Qualities Rice returned later. Jas ADC & Q. Corps talked that fresh | |
| | 10th | | supplies might be obtained from Paris district. Drew Canned Cake from Railhead Q Tow | |
| | 11th | | New supplies by H.T. from B.H.O Advt M.T. (no rest of) division | |
| | 12th | | 2 by pre train moved to ?? Sdg & near BOUVANCOURT. 4 Cn's near TROUILLY. dumped supplies near these places. | |
| | 13th | | No 1 Coy moved from LT. GEMME to TRIGNY. No 3 Coy moved from ADVERY to camp between JONCHERY and MUIZON, with supplies. Main Divn Dec 7000 & off between JONCHERY and MUIZON. R.Q. to GILLES. Established Dv.dd.Par R.Q. & GILLES | |
| | 14th | | Drawn supplies by M.T. from PROUILLY thought supplies as follows – Am.Tn. TRIGNY, 64 Bde. near BOUVANCOURT. 110 Bde at FIREWORKS near MUIZON. 64 Bde near JONCHERY. Devt.n. ST.GILLES. In return Coke, 50 lb hotch Stores, 300 lb candles, ICOURLANDON fr. 50 galls donkey'd. Stills Wash Bd. 6470 lb. Oats | |
| | 15th | | Issued by Rly Tranft. May 14th drawn by M.T. Issued to Units Supplies Rors for 600 th Bde. Sty the Bolk 100 lb jam 50 galls lubricate Still Wash oil, A.M. | |

(A7283) Wt W309/M1672 350,000 4/17 Sch. 52a Forms/C/2118/14
D. D. & L., London, E.C.

**Army Form C. 2118.**

# WAR DIARY
## or
## INTELLIGENCE SUMMARY.
*(Erase heading not required.)*

SOISSONS SHEET

31st Division

| Place | Date | Hour | Summary of Events and Information | Remarks and references to Appendices |
|---|---|---|---|---|
| PROUILLY | 16th | | Moved from ROMIGNY to PROUILLY. Strength Return as follows. Divr. Troops 196, 62 Bde 485, 110 Bde 654, 64th Bde 1007 ; Total 4064. | |
| | 18th | | Issued supplies at night Railway for full train sent up mixed groups to TRIGNY station, & VAUX VARENNES. Rationed Artillery horse after arrival in rest at hay. | |
| | 20th | | MK II Rifles for use from Lewis gun mountings — sent to COURLANDON for distribution. | |
| | 21st | | Railway opened to VAUX VARENNES & up line to TRIGNY railhead. Also am rehearsal, cleared railhead at CAMP CUISSAT. Handed Civilian & Indust Armand between those 2 railheads. | |
| | 23rd | | Dressed up & made present rations for Divisn to arrive at Railhead on 26th. Rations will be held by Divr M.T. Coys in reserve. | |
| | 25th | | 10 tons Oat Ration to 9th Locethe fractional number as pr GS. Corps Authority made enquiries in Reilly | |
| | | | as to purchase & supply of GConsumables. Quantity small & price excessive. | |
| | 26th | | Heavy attack by enemy, not possible to load supplies at PROUILLY to line out, but supplies to limits by Train from Drew supplies from FERE-EN-TARDENOIS. Mobile Field Canteen sold in Brds area to civil refugees. | |
| SERZY | 28th | | Moved SERZY - MONNAY this am. DORMANS to M.T. reduced strength by 400 horse return, to should steam plus | |
| PARADIS | 29th | | Moved PARADIS near JANCOURT. Churnel washflesh frame or DS on JONDREVILLE Road Bridge refuse. | |
| | | | In M.T from DRAMER divisional strength down to 2000 horse previous day. Supply now party Bridle Hay | Well |

# WAR DIARY
## INTELLIGENCE SUMMARY

Army Form C. 2118.

| Place | Date | Hour | Summary of Events and Information | Remarks and references to Appendices |
|---|---|---|---|---|
| PARIS (CUMIÈRES) | July 30 | | Draw rations from EPERNAY [Night]. Population 140. Obtaining all requirements everything. Oats 30m/t. Ran 20,000 lb Potato soon fell, drawn from other supply [train] at EPERNAY gate. Train HR moved & unloaded off train 2nd near BRUGNY. All Train Coy [unloaded] in FORÊT D'EPERNAY. Ripple [hamper] here. Suffr. train moving late from Rx. | |
| CHALTRAIT AU-BOIS | 31st | | Train HQ moved to CHALTRAIT-AU-BOIS. Draw rations from CUMIÈRES (EPERNAY) by M.T. all Suppl. train having late for have rcvt to CRACHER & DAHENS. Train Coy billeted as follows: No 1 ST MARTIN D'ABLOIS. No 2 (d.h.q.) No 2 SOUVIÈRES, No 3 S.E of ETRECH?, No 4 E of CHALTRAIT-AU-BOIS. | |

W.R.Flint Major

ADO 21 Division

Original

1st to 30th June 1918

Army Form C. 2118.

# WAR DIARY
## INTELLIGENCE SUMMARY
(Erase heading not required.)

No. 21 Div.

| Place | Date | Hour | Summary of Events and Information | Remarks and references to Appendices |
|---|---|---|---|---|
| CHÂTEAU au BOIS | 1st | | Drew supplies but unfortunately trains running very late. Composite present up to defend river crossing at DORMANS; HQ at IGNY-LE-JARD approx strength 2200 men Transport. | |
| | 2nd | | 9th Train arrived | |
| | 3rd | 10 a.m. | Drew supplies but from MORAINS-LE-PETIT. Train ran 24 hours late, arrived at 10 a.m. dumped supplies received as follows :- 21st Independent Bde. near IGNY-LE-JARD - 64th Bde. at CONGY. 110th Bde. at COURTONNET; Divl Troops at clearing in FORÊT-D'ENARNAY. Attended conference at HQ 9th Corps; subject "supply situation". | |
| | 4th | | Drew supplies but from MORAINS-LE-PETIT; Transport as before. | |
| | 5th | | Drew supplies but from MORAINS-LE-PETIT and from CONNANTRE. 1000 from Rations drawn same to Q.M. of 21st Independent Brigade for distribution. May dump went Gaulding, that to be abandoned. 1000 Iron Rations sent up to 21st Indept. Bde. | |
| | 6th | | Drew supplies but from MORAINS-Transports before. Dumps on train drawn from CONNANTRE. Complaint of 64th Field Ambulance at non receipt of groceries from CONNANTRE totally unfounded. | |
| | 7th | | Communications moved on investigation to be totally unfounded. Group Iron Ration as follows :- 110 Bde 507, 64 Bde 478, 54 NF 240, 64 Bde 579, 17/8/4 400. | |
| LA NOUE | 8th 9th | | Moved to LA NOUE | |
| | 10th | | Drew supplies from LE GAULT-EN-FORÊT, dumped 110th Bde supplies in MONTMIRAIL - ESSART Road 64th Bde at LES BORDES. | |
| | 11th | | Sent to CONNANTRE for 360 Iron Rations for Divl. Arty, sent 20 in all 440 to complete held. | |

Army Form C. 2118.

# WAR DIARY
# INTELLIGENCE SUMMARY.
(Erase heading not required.)

No 21st Division

| Place | Date | Hour | Summary of Events and Information | Remarks and references to Appendices |
|---|---|---|---|---|
| LA NOUE | June 12th | | 64th Field Ambce returned to Division from 9th Corps troops — posted as 110th Bde Amb for Consumption 1st. | |
| | 13th | | Addition to existing Suppl. Train at Railhead, drew 1 days Train Ration for elements of the Division entraining at 4th for II Army area. Animals 1305 | 4733 OR |
| | 14th | | MT drew supplies from HEGUILT-EN-FORÊT proceeded to 4th Army area beyond, proceeded road to OISEMONT proceeded. | |
| OISEMONT | 15th | | Drew supplies by MT from MARTAINNEVILLE; dumped 62nd Fld. at VIAMMEVILLE & 4th at TOEUFELS. | |
| | 16th | | | |
| | 17th | 2.4.00 | Reinforcements arrived for Division from base, drew a days rations before BATTACHES to pack kourpoiels to rest this number. No 3 Coy Train moved to VILLEROY. | |
| | 18th | | 7th reinforcements arrived for Division from Base. Orders received for the two BATTACHES. No 4 Coy Train moved to near ARGUEL. | |
| | 19th | | 115 OR arrived for 1st W.R. & 1st S. Lanc preparatory to these units being transferred to 21 Div from 25 Div. Drew Special issue of Tobacco from WOINCOURT for 4766 OR on IV Army authorities. | |
| | 20th | | No 1 & 2 Coy Train arrived from IX Corps area handed to BOUTTENCOURT and MESNIL respectively. | |
| | 21st | | No 2 Coy Train marched to LE HAMEAU — 63rd Field amp moving into training area. | |

Army Form C. 2118.

# WAR DIARY
## — or —
## INTELLIGENCE SUMMARY.
*(Erase heading not required.)*

Instructions regarding War Diaries and Intelligence Summaries are contained in F. S. Regs., Part II. and the Staff Manual respectively. Title pages will be prepared in manuscript.

      21st Division

| Place | Date | Hour | Summary of Events and Information | Remarks and references to Appendices |
|---|---|---|---|---|
| GAMACHES. | June 22nd | | Moved from OISEMONT to GAMACHES; No. 1 Coy to EU, H.Q. & 2 Coys to LE HAMEL, 3 Coys to BROMESNIL, No. 4 Coy to LONGROY. Rifles ammunition to be drawn by B.M. at BOUTTENCOURT. No. 4 Rfles at VILLEROY. H.Q. at LE HAMEL. | |
| | 23rd | | Drew supplies from GAMACHES by M.T. Ind. Troops, by high Indians by A.T. 61st & 62nd Rfles. 2/Squad F&Wells Jones Division from 25th Div. Received rations on 23rd at presumption 2350. No. 1 Coy Train moved from EU to MESNIL VAL. — | |
| | 24th | | Following units transferred fruitfully prepared to Div. from 30th Div.: 97 F.Amb.: to Div. Pole. 3rd Sany. Sec. to Div. Tps.} Detachment moved by M.G. Pole.} Reinforcements from 96th F.A. Ambulance to GUERVILLE. Ambulance EU | |
| | 25th | | Instruct received in the night & has taken over by 30th Div. Owing to supply Train being shortloaded at Rouen Rec sent to ABBEVILLE for 3000 rations — Drew rations from 220. O.R. of 33rd American Division. Presumption 25th & 26th. Published same at EU. | |
| | 28th | | Follow received in Transport vehicle of 8th Leicestershire Regt. to leave Division — Retained until rept. Aur 30th. | |
| | 29th | | Orders received for Division to proceed to III Army Area. Transport to go by rail on 30th dismounted portion by rail on 1st July. | |
| | 30th | | All Transport marched at 6 a.m. staging at OISEMONT for night | |

M.F. Shorthager
ADC 21 Div

Original

# WAR DIARY
## INTELLIGENCE SUMMARY

Army Form C. 2118.

1st to 31st July 1918.

220  21st Division

| Place | Date | Hour | Summary of Events and Information | Remarks and references to Appendices |
|---|---|---|---|---|
| AMIENS | July 1st | | Movement Order of Division — Transport stayed tonight at BOURDON. Infantry and dismounted taken entrained for II Corps Reserve area. Train HQ moved to BEAUQUESNE. Dismounted Artillery Stephens entrained in division. Artillery M.T. Coy Train remained in BOUTTENCOURT area at this moment. | Appended |
| BEAUQUESNE | 2nd | | 62nd Bde concentrated in Intrd BEAUVESNE. 64th at POCHEVILLERS, 110th at RAINCHEVAL Northern Road III Army for 3 Rdes. Moved for Div Troops | |
| | 3rd | | M.T. Coy at TRAMAS. Felt unwell. Capt Urquhart took over duties to S.S.O. Artillery Still at Rouvillan except from gunnery and showing 7 either now reserved 7 M.T. | |
| | 4th | | Sick. | |
| | 5th | | Sick. Did Much transferred from 64th Bde to Intd in — Sin gnps, also 126. R.E. transferred Dist Coy Spiers 62nd Bde to Supply Cols. | |
| | 6th | | Dist Coy Jones to Pochevillers [...] Coy Adams to [...] 164 Bde. For Commander [...] 110th + 64th Tn. Reles [Company] to 62 Rdes. | |
| | 7th | | by tr. T.M.Baker of transferred to Suffs. Charged So Su Rdes at POCHEVILLERS. + 21st Buttalion | |
| | 8th | | 126. R.E. transferred to Suffs Charge so Su Rdes. | |
| | 10th | | Capt Urquhart Rct ill. Capt Short took over Duties of S.S.O. | |
| | 12th | | Weekly Green forage for animals of Division obtained through [...] & Distribution Completed | |
| | 13th | | First issue of Supplies to 3rd & 7th Bdes RHA. DID Coy in charge of 21st Dn Ammn Supply | |
| | 14th | | tonight ex motor F.S. BEAUQUESNE to TOUTENCOURT. RS from Charge & Bn 216 lookd Rd 3D | |

Army Form C. 2118.

SS0 21st Division

# WAR DIARY
## or
## INTELLIGENCE SUMMARY.
(Erase heading not required.)

Instructions regarding War Diaries and Intelligence Summaries are contained in F. S. Regs., Part II. and the Staff Manual respectively. Title pages will be prepared in manuscript.

| Place | Date | Hour | Summary of Events and Information | Remarks and references to Appendices |
|---|---|---|---|---|
| BEAUQUESNE | July 15 | | Capt Short sick. Lieut Cottrell took over duties as S.S.O. | |
| | 16 | | 6000 Rations of Preserved Meat drawn from ROSEL to Div Reserve. "held on MTCo" Supply Column. 110th Bde moved from RAINCHEVAL to ACHEUX ASA 5000 og of Solidified alcohol drawn from E Coys | |
| | 17 | | 110th Bde returned to RAINCHEVAL Area. 2 tons of pressed cal drawn for RHA Brigades attached to Div | |
| | 18 | | 62nd Bde moved to RAINCHEVAL area. 110th Bde to ACHEUX. Preserved Meat Ration issued from MT Co, to each | |
| | | | 62nd Bde. 1700, MG Bde. 450, "Pioneers 450. Div Wing transferred to OMTCo for rations. | |
| | 19 | | 23,000 Kilos of Seton Forays ordered for Divisions & Wings started. | |
| | 20 | | 3rd Batt RHA drew supplies for last time. 1500 lbs of Bran drawn from SCMTCo – allowed to 33rd MVS | |
| | 21 | | 500 lbs of Fresh Meat condemned on 62nd Bde Dump, replaced by RSO ROSEL | |
| | 22 | | 5030 Kilos of Oats drawn from Railhead for Division | |
| | 23 | | 3 Transferences Cabs drawn from No 5 F.S.D issued as follows on recommendation of DDMS. 62nd Bde 8½ cut. 110th Bde 8½ cut, 64 Bde 2¾ cut, Div Troops 20 cut. | |
| | 24th | | 110 IR arrived in 21 Div Area, 50 Tons Wood & 40 Tonsford drawn from Railhead (transport Div Supply) RAINCHEVAL. 7th HLNM left area these supplies for last time consumption 26th following | |
| | 25th | | unit transferred from 63rd Brown Pumuation 27th onwards – left Half 3rd Pontoon Park RE 112 OR 113 HP, 16 OD; 17th Aux Hosp Depots 42 OR 14 LD, Tam Major FORCEVILLE 14 OR, Oues(null) ACHEUX 64 OR 2HR 13 ID; Let Areals (null) ARQUEVES Schreiben rations to Bird Reception Camp TALMAS by lorry 1250 OR. No 2 Coy Train | |
| | | | 19 OR – moved to O 3 d.2.6. N.U Coy. O 3 a 5 2. Brown released 63 Div to line – Div HQ moved to RAINCHEVAL Train HQ unmoved at BEAUQUESNE. No 1 Coy Train arrived from 4th Army ment compiled at N 3 A 7 6. Rso repleased to the Ration & Med 125th Rest released on 26 by nuc DT Vegetable Ration + TFN Potatoe 400, Onion 13, Dried Veg Y's 3. Issued 25 Am Ration to troops. | |
| | 26th | | Q.K.N.U.Q.2 t 21 1st Lynd Cy. | W.Re |

Army Form C. 2118.

# WAR DIARY
## INTELLIGENCE SUMMARY.
(Erase heading not required.)

S.S.O. 21st- Division -

| Place | Date | Hour | Summary of Events and Information | Remarks and references to Appendices |
|---|---|---|---|---|
| BEAUQUESNE | July 27th | | Drew 78 galls Petrol under V Cpts Authy Q 8057 dt. 14/7/16 And issued as follows -: 64th-Bde 25 galls, 110th-R.F.A. 21 galls, Div. Trn 9 galls. | 62nd-Bde 23 galls |
| | 29th | | May drawn from Railhead at flat rate of 9lbs per animal. Decided to issue on refilling points as for following scale -: H.D. 11 lbs ; L.D. Riders 9 lbs ; Mules 8 lb ; Tent over. Fuel Supply of 63rd Divn Coal 30 tons Wood 15 Charcoal 2½ Also 5000 ozs Solidified Alcohol Issued will be retained in a reserve by D.D. 63rd Mule - also 154 galls Rum Retained in reserve in M.T. Coy. | |
| | 30th 31st | | Nothing to record | |

M.A.S. Kent Major
S.S.O. 21st Divn.

Original
1/23rd Aug - 1918

# WAR DIARY
## INTELLIGENCE SUMMARY
(Erase heading not required.)

Army Form C. 2118.

A.A.O. 21st Divn

| Place | Date August | Hour | Summary of Events and Information | Remarks and references to Appendices |
|---|---|---|---|---|
| BEAUQUESNE | 1st | | Visited D.D.S.T. III Army. 63rd Div Coly drew supplies for first time. Strength 2362. Arrivals 1903. Issues 1211 Cells. Return of Horsed strength of Division - Return this from reserve M.T. Coy. Made arrangements with Purchase Board to cut green fronj at I.27.6.2.1 and allotted this to 21 Divl Arty. 500 lb Linseed Cake drawn from (HDAS) & issued as per Animal Strength. | |
| | 2nd | | | |
| | 3rd | | Drew 1 ton Chloride of Lime from AUXI-LE-CHATEAU Hauled over to Div Gas offrs. | |
| | 4th | | Handed over Fuel dump on ARQUEVES-LOUVENCOURT Rd to 120 63rd Divn - Wood 29, Charcoal 1½ Tons. Truck of cabbage drawn from Railhead & issued between the 4 groups. | Gen'l S.E. between the 4 groups of DADVS. |
| | 5th | | Sack of Linseed = 119 lb - Issued to B/94 & No.1 Section BAC recommendation of DADVS. Arranged with Purchase Board office to visit farmers in LOUVENCOURT area with a view to purchase of green fronj for Divl Troops & 62nd Rde. | |
| | 6th | | Drew supplies at Railhead for last time for 63rd. Divl Arty group prior to returning to their own Division. | |
| | 7th | | Drew 2 days to line fire issue to division. | |
| | 8th | | 3600 lbs cabbage received at Railhead distributed amongst all 4 groups. | |
| | 9th | | Sack of Linseed issued to B/94. 75% Rd and 60% Field Het 50% Field Coy as 1.8 Ton 81 road drawn from at Railhead. Unit testd Purchase Board if nec from J. Green Forage arrived & rtn detail of 63rd | |

Army Form C. 2118.

S.S.O. 21st Division

# WAR DIARY
## or
## INTELLIGENCE SUMMARY.
*(Erase heading not required.)*

Instructions regarding War Diaries and Intelligence Summaries are contained in F. S. Regs., Part II. and the Staff Manual respectively. Title pages will be prepared in manuscript.

| Place | Date August | Hour | Summary of Events and Information | Remarks and references to Appendices |
|---|---|---|---|---|
| BEAUQUESNE | 10 | | Bread & Gro. 75%. Fd Meat 60%. Coke 6¾ Tons drawn for Railhead. | |
| " | 11 | | Took over Fd Sup. & 63rd Divnl Amn Col. 80 Tons Wood 50 Bushels Oats & Bran to Tns. | |
| " | 12 | | Bread 75% & Meat 60%. Coke 6½ Tons drawn 11¾ Tn drawn from Railhead. | |
| " | 13 | | Fd Wood & H² Tns Tractors 8732 lbs drawn at Railhead. Gutted Produce Bread moved further up 60 Tns green forage at BELLE EGLISE farm. | |
| " | 14 | | Drew at Railhead & Meat 60% Bread 75%. Cabbage 2340 lbs & Meat 60%. Coal 9 and Coke 10½ Tns drawn at Railhead. | |
| " | 15 | | Coal 10¼ Tns, Coke 9 Tns, Charcoal 26¾ Tns drawn at Railhead. Fed into section of 18th A.F.A. Bde. Visited ADS dept of S.S.& T. | |
| " | 16 | | 3rd Army report. | |
| " | 17 | | Nothing to report. | |
| " | 18 | | Coal 33.42 lbs drawn at Railhead. Fed. 1756 Trench Engrs and 199 L. Trench Company. | |
| AMMERVAL | 19 | | Bread 80% Cabbage 2290 lbs drawn at Railhead | |

Army Form C. 2118.

# WAR DIARY
## or
## INTELLIGENCE SUMMARY.
(Erase heading not required.)

S.S.O. 1st Divison

| Place | Date | Hour | Summary of Events and Information | Remarks and references to Appendices |
|---|---|---|---|---|
| RAINECHERAL | Aug 20 | | Replenished all M.T. Bicycle Tires. Drew 10,000 rds of S.A.A. for 1st Bn. M.T. Lorry. | |
| " | 21 | | Drew and issued Rum Ration to men in trenches. | |
| " | 22 | | Railhead moved to BELLE EGLISE. Worked at 9 am to three Transport. | |
| " | 23 | | Nothing of importance to report. | |
| ACHEUX MAILLY | 24 25 | | Drew 10,000 rds of S.A.A. Ur. Am. from 1st Bn. Transport M.T. Bn. | |
| MAILLY | 26 | | Railhead moved to BEAUSSART. Drew & Issued Transport. | |
| " | 27 | | Drew 105 Trg Rnd at Railhead. Drew 10,000 rds S.A.A. ditto. | |
| " | 28 | | Fed the 17th M.A.S. on Supt. Trnsp. group. Drew 10,000 rds SAA absorbed for 1st Bn Transport M.T. Bn. | |
| " | 29 | | Nothing of importance to report. | |
| GRANDCOURT | 30 | | Drew supplies & M.T. Spares at dumps and helped at GRANDCOURT | |
| " | 31 | | Drew extra 1lb of Oats to artillery horses on att. of B' Amm. | |

John Archer Lt.
S & o

# WAR DIARY

**Army Form C. 2118.**

1st K 3rd September 1918. Original

**INTELLIGENCE SUMMARY**

S.S.O. 31st Division

| Place | Date | Hour | Summary of Events and Information | Remarks and references to Appendices |
|---|---|---|---|---|
| GRANDCOURT | 1st Sept | | Drew Supplies at AVELUY. Train did not arrive until 8.30 p.m. at first, then next morning. Drew 15,000 ozs Schiedhal alcohol for 5th Bn Tank M.T. Coy. | |
| " | 2nd | | and 3 Tins of Cordite from III Army frames. Train arrived emp. Lorries took place at 9.30 a.m. and all parts dumped on ALBERT-BAPAUME road. Drew 282 gallons of Rum for the balance of the week's Divnl allowance. | |
| " | 3rd | | Nothing to report. | |
| ES ARC | 4th | | Drew 11,250 lbs of Bacon & Butter from 1st Bn Troops Tanks M.T. Coy. | |
| " | 5th | | Drew Supplies at BEAULENCOURT at 6 p.m. Drew 10½ Tins of Cordite. | |
| " | 6th | | Drew by Horse Train at Beaulencourt at 11 a.m. Sent away for 200 gallons of Rum. | |
| ES BOEUFS | 7th | | Drew 15,000 ozs Schiedhal alcohol for 5th Bn Troops M.T. Coy. Drew Returns from 31st Draughter Camp who arrived at Beaulencourt. | |
| " | 8th | | Drew by M.T. from 31st Tank Troop & 64th Bde. Both dumped at LE MESNIL | |

heals

**Army Form C. 2118.**

# WAR DIARY
## or
## INTELLIGENCE SUMMARY.
*(Erase heading not required.)*

S.S.O. 21st Div.

Instructions regarding War Diaries and Intelligence Summaries are contained in F.S. Regs., Part II. and the Staff Manual respectively. Title pages will be prepared in manuscript.

| Place | Date | Hour | Summary of Events and Information | Remarks and references to Appendices |
|---|---|---|---|---|
| LES BOEUFS | 9th | | Packs did not arrive until 3 pm. | |
| | 11th | | No gems arrived with Supply Train, attempted requisite quantity from DOULLENS. Drew 1500 go fillip Ration from MIRAUMONT, drew 200 galls from DOULLENS. | |
| | 13th | | Loading at Railhead did not commence before 4 pm. | |
| | 15th | | Left to Doullens for 10 galls Rum. 110th Bde relieved by 19th Bde (33 Div) | |
| | 16th | | Reinforcements arrived as follows :– 12/13 R.F. 37; 1 Yorks 10, 9 KOYLI 21, 10th DLI 60, 6 Leicesters 99, 7th Leicesters 25, 10th Yorks 39; 14th R.F. 20 returned up to 16th. Drew 2 days supplies for these – Also returned up to 17th – 1, 1 Yorks 93, 15 DLI 223 – | |
| | 17th | | Led to DOULLENS for 249 Jm Rations for 63 Bde & 400 for 110th Bde. delayed there to repair lines direct. Drew 5000 rations of Rations from S. Corps Troops not distributed – Division attacked, attained objectives. Over 700 prisoners of 17 June taken by 21st Div. | |
| | 18th | | Supply Train did not arrive at Railhead – ROCQUIGNY – until 6:30 pm – by 53rd Div in line – No 2 & 3 Sup Train moved to ROCQUIGNY. 21st Div relieved | |
| ROCQUIGNY | 20th | | Drew supplies by Horse Transport. All reinforcements Details of Reception Camp returned to units. | |
| | 21st | | | |
| | 23rd | | Drew 4,730 kilos lettings from Railhead, also 6 Tons Coal – loaded supplies at Mildrey. | |

MW

Army Form C. 2118.

# WAR DIARY
# or
# INTELLIGENCE SUMMARY.
*(Erase heading not required.)*

Instructions regarding War Diaries and Intelligence Summaries are contained in F. S. Regs., Part II. and the Staff Manual respectively. Title pages will be prepared in manuscript.

SS.O 21st Divn

| Place | Date | Hour | Summary of Events and Information | Remarks and references to Appendices |
|---|---|---|---|---|
| LES BOEUFS | Sept 24th | | 64th Bde marched from LES BOEUFS to forward area - Issued Rum to 62 & 64 Bdes & Intendent Ration. 10 a.m. hd qrs. - Indentures 1 days veg ration. 64th Bde Sup. Intendent Railhead. Div marched at night. 95th Bde RFA & Ser: DAC temporarily attached to Guards Div. Drew 6 Motor Lorries Railhead. Sent to REAULENCOURT for 10,000 lb Oats. | |
| | 25th | | Noted III Army HQ (DSNT) 62nd & 110th Bdes & 31 Dft/Div went up to the line in relief of 50th - 51st Bdes of 17th Division. Drew up 1000 lb Iron Rum. Have been twice nearly in the line. Ordered to move Wednesday to Katredsay at Railhead. Issued Rum to Reinforcements. 64th Bde went off march to arrive Wednesday at Railhead - | |
| | 27th | | Sent to REAULENCOURT for 9000 lb Hay & 3000 lb Oats deficient on train. Into line. Issued Rum Polished Alcohol to 62, 64 110 Bdes. Drew 131 gals Rum from V Corps M.T. Coy. - | V36 and |
| LE MESNIL EN-ARROUAISE | 29th | | Moved Office to LE MESNIK-EN-ARROUAISE. Transp Companies moved to NE of ETRICOURT. Drew Supplies from Railhead by M.T. and dumped at new Camp. V3e (last STC). | V36 and (last STC) |
| | 30th | | Drew Rum 124 galls from VII Corps Troop M.T. Coy des Pendant. Drew 7 Ton coal from ROCQUIGNY. Relieved Area Command to LESBOEUF and SAILLY SAILLISEL until 31st Nov inclusive prior to handing over to V Corps S.O. Strength 25 OR & 1 LD each. Railhead Fins. Drew supplies by Horse Transport Issued Rum Polished Alcohol to 62, 64, 110 Bdes. | Fins |

WL & Stock pages
S.S.O 21 Divn

Original

# WAR DIARY / INTELLIGENCE SUMMARY

Army Form C. 2118.

1st to 31st Oct. 1918

S.S.O.  21st Division

| Place | Date | Hour | Summary of Events and Information | Remarks and references to Appendices |
|---|---|---|---|---|
| LE MESNIL EN ARROUAISE | 1st | | Drew supplies from FINS by horse transport. | |
| | 2nd | | Drew 185 galls Rum & 2500 rations Pea Soup from II Corps MT Coy, & Timber(oak) from ROCQUIGNY. Reinforcements from base as under :- 1 Lincolns 100 O.R., 1 Yorks NF. 13 O.R., 9&10 RF. 25, 12/13 NF. 13 O.R. | |
| | 4th | | Reinforcements arrived as follows :- 1 Lincoln 179, 2nd Lincoln 167, 12/13 NF 22, 1st E Yorks 33, and 9 KOYLI 37 - added these numbers to indent. No foragem purchasem sent to ROCQUIGNY for straw 5800 lbs. Oats 30,000. Hay 19,900 lbs. | |
| NEAR EQUANCOURT | 6th | | Drew 12 n galls Rum from II Corps MT Coy - Train N.R. moved to near EQUANCOURT | |
| | 7th | | 9th & 2nd RFA & tr of DAC returned from 2nd Div. Supply wagons failed to arrive. So supplies & rations to be drawn the drawn of Railhead at 9am returned at W.g.&L.O. from 915 O.R. & 820 animals the scheme of Railhead being moving forward. Supplies public front were again drawn of Railhead horse lines. Drew 3 two horsed of Railhead sadly a part of Hay ration + 1 om saddled | |
| | 8th | | 21st Division attacked Named objectives. Drew 46 galls Rum 1500 rations Pea Soup from II Cps MT Coy. Dumped 67, 64, 110 E Bde supplies a ordinance South of GOUZEAUCOURT. V Corps MT Coy - dumped at FINS - GOUZEAUCOURT Rd.- Issued all Cmfs of Railhead by M.T. Brie Troop en FINS-GOUZEAUCOURT Rd. | |
| West of GOUZEAUCOURT W.11.C.u.8 | 9th | | 4 gov R.ln lettys received at Railhead detailed according to time. 77 O.R. arrived for 1st/15 NF. 105 O.R. for 1st East Yorks. Drew supplies probable Divisional MT Dumped as previously | W.M.M |

# WAR DIARY

## INTELLIGENCE SUMMARY

Army Form C. 2118.

S.S.O. 21st Division

| Place | Date | Hour | Summary of Events and Information | Remarks and references to Appendices |
|---|---|---|---|---|
| M.32.b.7.2 (57.B) | October 10th | | Moved from N.11.c.4.8 (57.c). Division HQ moved to WALINCOURT. Drew 125 galls. Petrol from V Corps M.T. Coy. + 250s Rations Pers Coys. Following Reinforcements arrived: (Lincolns 114, 2; Lincolns 11, 1; 13 N.F. 175, 1; 9 Yorks 181, 15; D.L.I. 135, 9 K.O.Y.L.I. 129, 6 Leics 117, 7 Leics 122, 1 Wilts 146, 222 Empl. Coy 6). Drew 2 days rations for all Pers. Dumped supplies (drawn from R.H.) by M.T. as follows:— Divnl Troops at N.24.a-2.5; 62nd, 64th, 110th Bdes moved in M.32.C. (Refs: 57.B). Issued 16 Rations to French civilians in WALINCOURT for French Mission attached Divn – arrangements as per A/Q/M/T memo noted dated April 1918. |  |
| WALINCOURT | 11th | | Moved to WALINCOURT. Loaded supplies at 11am by M.T. dumped all supplies at WALINCOURT (walkout). M.T. Train Coy located here. Sent to ROCQUIGNY for 13000 lbs Oats deficient in supply train. |  |
|  | 12th | | Train late at Railhead – dumped supplies by M.T. at 4.30 pm. Same refilling points as previous day. |  |
|  | 13th | | Drew rations to French Mission for civilians – 15 full British rations = (60 men.). Drew Petrol from ROCQUIGNY. Issued 58 British rations to French Mission for civilians. |  |
|  | 14th | | Railhead SOREL – loaded by M.T. |  |
|  | 15th | | Railhead MASNIÈRES – drew 3200 kilo biscuits from Railhead – loaded by M.T. Billions of Rum. |  |
|  | 17th | | Notified above delayed arrival of supply train which was unloaded at FINS at 3.30 pm – M.T. |  |
|  | 18th | | Drew supplies again from MASNIÈRES line being repaired. Obtained 7,100 lbs forage (new) in WALINCOURT. Arranged payment with NATIVE. Loaded by M.T. |  |
|  | 19th | | Supply Train did not arrive until 3.30 pm. Loaded by M.T. |  |

Wall

Army Form C. 2118.

# WAR DIARY
## INTELLIGENCE SUMMARY.
(Erase heading not required.)

no 21st Division

| Place | Date | Hour | Summary of Events and Information | Remarks and references to Appendices |
|---|---|---|---|---|
| WATRINCOURT | Oct. 20th | | Supply Train did not arrive. | |
| | 21st | | Supply Train due 20th. arrived at 6.30 a.m. loaded by M.T. - 4 Tom bakings drawn from Railhead. Sent to HAVRINCOURT and ACHIET-LE-GRAND for 1200 Iron Rations & Issued nil 80 pdlr. | |
| | 22nd | | Divisional Train moved to MONTIGNY, refilled at WATRINCOURT and marched Beaurains with full guns rations when Units received Interim presumption 23rd. Drew 350 galls Rum & 10,000 lbs solidified alcohol from V Corps Troops S.O., also 500 rations of Tea Soup. | |
| BEAUMONT by INCHY | 23rd | | Train HQ moved to outskirts of INCHY. Supply Train did not arrive. | |
| | 24th | 4 am | Supply Train due 23rd arrived at 4 a.m. dumped & refilled on BEAUMONT-BETHENCOURT Road. Maps of 3rd Hussars arrived & the attached to D.A.P.M. issued 19 O.R. & 20 2nd annual Returns for consumption 25th. Issued rations to 1st O.R. G.HS & 61st Dn North Irish Horse (Cyclists) attached to D.A.P.M. presumption 24th to 25th. Discussioned (600 Rations for French Civilians to Liaison Officer 21st Div.) (Iron Rations, Mess Compounds of British ration) carried there to VENDEGIES MAIRIE. 10 Tom Coal drawn from Railhead | |
| | 25th | | Drew rations to French Mission 27/00 rations for Civilians at PONT-DU-NORD & sent by lorry to VENDEGIES. Refilled on BEAUMONT-BETHENCOURT road. Supply Train due 24th arrived at | |
| | 26th | 2 am. | Supply Train due 25th arrived at 6 a.m. to-day. | |

Army Form C. 2118.

# WAR DIARY
## INTELLIGENCE SUMMARY.
*(Erase heading not required.)*

S.S.O. 21st Division

| Place | Date October | Hour | Summary of Events and Information | Remarks and references to Appendices |
|---|---|---|---|---|
| INCHY | 26th | | 21st Div: relieved in line by 17th Div. Supply Train cleared by 2 a.m on 27th. Units at Railhead by Horse Transport for 3 inf: brigades start for Div: Troops, M. Transport & Divn: Amm: Pk at Railhead. | Noted |
| | 27th | | Moved to Railhys from I Corps Vegetable Dump near FRESNOY. The following reinforcements arrived from Base: 62nd Bde. 294 O.R.; 64th Bde. 325 O.R.; 110th Bde 184 O.R.; Div Artillery 22 O.R. added 2 days rations to supply. Sent up 2500 rations to French Curtains to POIX. Loaded by MT for Div Tps, 62 & 110th Bdes, 64th Bde by H.T. Cleared Supply Train at 3 a.m. 28th. | |
| | 28th 29th | | M. Supply Train arrived – 21 Tons Coal drawn from Railhead & dumped at INCHY. A.M. Supply Train arrived. Drew 1 days Preserved Rations from Army Reserve dumps at CAUDRY. Dumped 62 & 110th Bde: at NEUVILLY Station, Div: Troops at INCHY – all by M.T. 64th Bde: by M.T. & H.T. & transport to N°4 Corps Camp at NEUVILLY. 62 & 64th Bdes moved into line in relief of 17th Div, 110th Bde in reserve. Delivered 70 complete returns to French Mission at NEUVILLY for Civilians. Divisional Reception Camp moved from MARCOING to MONTIGNY. | |
| | 30th | | Supply Train due on 28th – arrived at 2 a.m. Loaded all dumps by M.T. and dumped 3 infantry brigades at NEUVILLY, Div: Troops at INCHY. Supply Train due 29th arrived at 3 p.m. Loaded by H.T. not dumped. 11 Tons forage drawn from Railhead – Drew 500 lbs Cakes from I Corps Reg: Dump. | |
| | 31st | | Supply Train due 30th – arrived & cleared at 8 a.m. I Corps Train moved from INCHY to NEUVILLY – dumped supplies for all front there – 150 Italian personnel notified as leaving Base for B.A.C. Dress 2. days rations for future – 20 O.R. for 62 Bde, 336 O.R. for 64th Bde, 16 O.R. for 110th M.E. & 20 O.R. for M.G. Bn – all added to indent. | |

W.A. Stuart Major SSO 21 Divn

Army Form C. 2118.

1 - 30 Nov. 1918.

# WAR DIARY
## INTELLIGENCE SUMMARY.
(Erase heading not required.)

21st Division -
D.S.O.

Instructions regarding War Diaries and Intelligence Summaries are contained in F.S. Regs., Part II. and the Staff Manual respectively. Title pages will be prepared in manuscript.

| Place | Date November | Hour | Summary of Events and Information | Remarks and references to Appendices |
|---|---|---|---|---|
| INCHY. | 1st | | Supply Train due on 31 Oct. arrived, dumped all groups at NEUVILLY. Attended conference at V Corps HQ re requisitioning of forage & vegetables in area. Decided that certain places should be used as dump & terms made for another officer to deal with the matter. Sent up to FRENCH MISSION 30 rations for civilians. MT to Marcs at VENDEGIES as requested by Liaison Officer. Added to present remounts 80 LD, 21 LD for MG Bn. | |
| | 2nd | | Supply Train dump't arrived at 5 a.m. - drew by MT transport as before. Reinforcements as follows arrived - 1 Wbn 105 OR, 6 Lewis Sgt OR, 7th Lewis 57 OR. Added ment & groups concerned. | |
| | 3rd | | Railway Bridge at CAUDRY blown up by delayed action mine, drew supplies from CAMBRAI Annexe by MT transport at INCHY. | |
| | 4th | | Railhead CAMBRAI VILLE. Sent to V Corps Troops Column for 340 galls. Rum 110,000 cigarettes (also 5000 rations Cocoa & Milk. Dumped at INCHY. Train HQ moved to POIX DU NORD | |
| POIX. du NORD | 5th | | Railhead CAMBRAI VILLE - Issued Rum Rectified alcohol to infantry, R.E.s, Pioneers 21 Div Arty being in line. | |
| | 6th | | Train Coys moved to LOCQUIGNOL (FORÊT-DE-MORMAL) Dumped supplies near the village full four groups. | |
| LOCQUIGNOL | 7th | | Drew supplies from CAUDRY - Moved to LOCQUIGNOL. | |
| BERLAIMONT | 8th | | " " " Moved to BERLAIMONT, dumped 3 brigades near LOCQUIGNOL and Div. Troops in FORÊT-DE-MORMAL. Drew 50 galls. Rum as an extra from V Corps Reserve & distributed among the 4 groups. DSR Coy moved to TÊTE-NOIRE. | |
| | 9th | | Drew supplies 3 brigades on GRAND CARRIÈRES - BERLAIMONT Rd, Div. Troops near TÊTE NOIRE. DSR Coy Div Arty 63, 64 Fld 128, 110 Fld 321, Dtmr 2 days rations to all units. | |

Army Form C. 2118.

22.0. 21st Div.

# WAR DIARY
## INTELLIGENCE SUMMARY.
(Erase heading not required.)

| Place | Date | Hour | Summary of Events and Information | Remarks and references to Appendices |
|---|---|---|---|---|
| | | November | | |
| BERLAIMONT | 10th | | 'N' Special Coy RE. 160 O.R. attached fumigation to 64th Bde. drew interview from 12th. New Zealand Tunn Coy. 150 men attd to 62nd Bde. positions, drew rations for same 12th. Delivered to Marie AULNOYE 50 tins milk for French Civilians (to Marie AYMERIES 387 full British ration bags supplies for 3 days). Obtained receipts from French Admin att'd to 21st Div'n. | |
| | 11th | | Armistice declared. | |
| AULNOYE | 12th | | Moved to AULNOYE. Train cups moved - No 2 t AYMERIES, No 3 to near BEAUFORT. Dumped supplies at these places. | |
| | 13th | | Delivered 359 full British Rations to AULNOYE Marie and 1721 Litre AYMERIES. for issue to French Civilians. Obtained receipts from French Marie. | |
| | 15th | | Supplies dumped down by M.T. Coys. As 2 Supply Trains arrived at Railhead (CAUDRY) in late afternoon & during night of 13-14th. No 1 Coy Train moved back to NEUVILLY. Transferred 'N' Special Coy RE. to I Corps for rations Consumption 17th. Drew 12000 lbs Cabbage from I Corps Veg. Dump. | |
| | 16th | | 105 OR Fm. 1st SR. J. - After 2 days return to Sec.. Transferred Mob. Vet Secn from 64th to 62nd Bde. Visited III Army HR. (DAP+T) LE MASNIERES. | |
| | 17th | | Drew 270 palls Rum from II Corps - Underwing 200 battle strength return No1 & No 2 HQ by HQ 1st Corps. | |
| | 18th | | Railhead moved from CAUDRY to SOLESMES issued Run to 63 by the 1st HT Corps. | |

# WAR DIARY
## INTELLIGENCE SUMMARY.
(Erase heading not required.)

Army Form C. 2118.

1910 21st Division

| Place | Date | Hour | Summary of Events and Information | Remarks and references to Appendices |
|---|---|---|---|---|
| AULNOYE | 19th | | Issued Routine Order. Hoxe with 2 days rations previous to mid leaving Corps Area. Issued SD return held in readiness by 8.30 P.M. 21 Div in Shapples t prisoners returned by Germans. Immediate return to Marcus AULNOYE on by 11.10. Orderly Officers: Delivered 2080 full rations to Marcus AULNOYE. Appendices. 3. | |
| | 20th | | New Zealand Travelling boy drew rations upto 23. flat piece and gehaty to II Army. Issued SD return to Do P.M. brakers t prisoners returned by enemy. Drew Ems Hay t Straw t Firewood. In Prov. Troop lodge from Stephs Dump at NEUVILLY. Issued Rum made to all ranks. 1 blanket per plr issue from not by small ranks. Retained | |
| | 22nd | | A Train Coys as reserve. | 45 OR arrived |
| | 25th | | Drew Cabbage. 6 Tons t from II Corps dump, issued units all group. | |
| | 26th | | Railroad changed to SASSESCHES. Drew 138 full Rum from II Corps H.T. Cay. first D.I.I. added 2 days rations to by t Base Intent. | |
| | 27th | | 186 falls Rum drawn from I Corps Troops H.T. Cay. Lent 3 Tons coal to SD Dw Tp at NEUVILLY | |
| | 28th | | Supply Train arrived 2 am on 29th, loaded at 6 am 29th | |
| | 29th | | Drew 6 Tons Cabbage from Firing Mean. Drew & cleared 165. by 11.10. Adler. | |
| | 30th | | 180 men and 211 animals at 97, 98 + 116 Engr RE proceeded by march route to NEUVILLY. Supply Train + supplies then for consumption up to 31st. Sent 3 Tons Coal to S.O. Dw T.B. at NEUVILLY. Drew 6 Tons Cabbage. for each Bigde lent Individually. Drew 3 days rations for SS OR. | |

A.S.C.04. W. W17772/A2551. 750,000. 9/17. Sch. 52. Forms/C.2118/14

C O N F I D E N T I A L.

WAR DIARY

OF

Senior Supply Officer., 21st Division.

FROM:- December 1st.   TO:- December 31st 1918.

Original

# WAR DIARY
## or
## INTELLIGENCE SUMMARY.

*(Erase heading not required.)*

Army Form C. 2118.

1st to 31 Dec. 1918

120. 21st Division

| Place | Date | Hour | Summary of Events and Information | Remarks and references to Appendices |
|---|---|---|---|---|
| AULNOYE | 1st | | M.T. supply Train arrived and nearly 3 s/s all just supply situation which has 1 day ahead of normal. Supply Train one day previous contained no food or potatoes which enabling these supplies having been cut off. Preserved meat has been drawn from SOLESMES Train. Parties of R.E. Coys moved to ENGLEFONTAINE en route for AMIENS area - Draughted returns left including Crew after 4th at SOLESMES railway station 33 O.R. | |
| | | | fr. 12/13 N.F. onward. | |
| | 2nd | | 326 falls Rum drawn from V Corps Troops M.T. Coy. Held in M.T. Coy as reserve. | |
| | 3rd | | 11 O.R. [14th] N.F.; 29 1st D.G.; 13 9. Roy. F.A.; 23 7 Leic; 15 & 6th Leic. two days rations attack in each of these. | |
| | 4th | | Transferred to M.T. from 110th Bde to 62 Pde preparing to move to AMIENS area. | |
| | 5th | | 14th N.F. left area for work in CAVILLON area, returned up to 8th inclusive, including 1 day supplies dumped at SOLESMES. | |
| | 6th | | Transferred "Examining Post" K.O.Y.L.I. to XIII Corps Troops S.D. Party of Murris left Division for Base. | |
| | 7th | | 25 O.R. arrived fr. 14/13 N.F.; 36 O.R. for 1st Wilts; 7 Leic 20 O.R.; 8 O.R. 7 Leic. | |
| | 8th | | No cheese or Oatmeal arrived and supply Trains, drew Cabbage 6000 lbs from AU TERTRE Farm. | WAK |

Army Form C. 2118.

# WAR DIARY
or
## INTELLIGENCE SUMMARY.
(Erase heading not required.)

No. 110. 21st Division

| Place | Date | Hour | Summary of Events and Information | Remarks and references to Appendices |
|---|---|---|---|---|
| AULNOYE | 12th | | 64th Bde Grp marched from LEMONT-FONTAINE area to BERLAIMONT; supplies dumped there and supply wagons refilled. Transferred personnel, MMP, equipment Coy from 62 Bde Grp to 10 Ton supply wagons & Area Court A/trucks transferred to 38th Divn - returned upto 14th inclusive. - Dumped rations of 21 M.G. Bn at VENDEGIES presumption 13th – | |
| | 13th | | 64th Bde continued march to VENDEGIES where supplies dumped refilling took place. Duc Troops Grp including Artillery moved from NEUVILLY to WALINCOURT - dumped supplies at NEUVILLY. Issued 4 days rations to 146 OR of 21st Th.Rde at MONTAY. Supplies of 21 M.G. Bn dumped at INCHY Church, presumption 14th. Artillery Grp supplies drawn from ROISEL. | |
| INCHY | 14th | | 64th Bde continued its march, supplies for 2 days dumped at INCHY. Also 21st M.G. Bn. 110th Bde marched from BEAUFORT to BERLAIMONT, supplies dumped there. 21st Div Artillery Column 62nd Bde Grp still at MONTAY supplies drawn by supply officers Duc Troops at PERONNE. AULNERIES. Train HQ moved from Aulnoys to INCHY. | |
| | 15th | | Moved from INCHY to AILLY-SUR-SOMME. Drew supplies there for br by Bde advanced parties, Rear party drawing from PERONNE. 110th Bde supplies dumped at INCHY. 62nd Bde dumped at AULNERIES. Div Tps dumped near PROYART after drawing from LA FLAQUE. | |
| MOLLIENS VIDAME | 16th | | Drew by Bde Rear parties supplies from AILLY. Transport from LA FLAQUE - 62nd Bde dumped at ENGLEFONTAINE - Div Tps drawn from CORBIE | W.P.L. |

D.D. & L., London, E.C.
(M5091) Wt W1771/M2031 750,000 5/17 Sch. 52 Forms/C2118/14

# WAR DIARY / INTELLIGENCE SUMMARY

Army Form C. 2118.

No. 110. 21st Division

| Place | Date | Hour | Summary of Events and Information | Remarks and references to Appendices |
|---|---|---|---|---|
| MOLLIENS VIDAME | Sept 17th | | Drew supplies for Div. Troops & 64th Bde. Pack parties from AILLY. 64th Bde. Transport from CORBIE's Rest. 110th Bde. Transport from PERONNE on I.C.T. Dumped Coal & wood for Div Tpo (110th Bde as shown) | |
| | 18th | | Div. Troops, Whole of 64th Bde. Pack Party. Pack part of 110th Bde. drawn from AILLY. – 110th Bde. from pt. FLAQUE. 62nd Bde at IRCHY. Obtained straw for billets of 64th Bde & 110th Bde & Div Tpo. Sent to ST OUEN for wood 10 Tons. | |
| | 19th | | Div Troops, 62nd Bde Pack party, 64th Bde front, 110th Bde Brig. HQrs supplies all drawn from AILLY-SUR-SOMME. 110th Bde Transport from CORBIE. 62nd Bde Transport from PERONNE. Dumped 17 Tons Coal at CAVILLON for 62nd Bde. Drew 21 Tons Wood from Railhead. | |
| | 20th | | Div. Troops, 64th Bde, 110th Hd. Bde party, 62nd Bde Pack party. supplies drawn from AILLY. 62nd Bde Transport from PERONNE. – Dumped 20 Tons Coal at FLOXICOURT for 64th Bde. 1500 lbs billet straw for 62nd Bde at CAVILLON. Full bread, meat & vegetable Ration drawn from R.H.d. Sent to ST OUEN for wood 10 Tons. | |
| 1st Fy RE reported from detachment | 21st | | All supplies drawn from AILLY (except party those for 62nd Bde Transport party which was drawn from CORBIE.) Full bread, meat & vegetable Ration drawn. Sent to ST OUEN for wood 10 Tons. | |
| | 22nd | | Div Troops, Whole Divn drawn from AILLY-SUR-SOMME. Sent to ST OUEN for wood 10 Tons – 9th Coy RE rejoined. 110th Bde from detachment. Only 50% Bacon & Cheese drawn from RHd, Oatmeal not available. | |
| | 23rd | | Full ration landed on the various Groups for issue 23rd. Full Bread & fresh meat, 75% Veg, 30% Butter, Ration, Xmas Pudding 50% Jam, nil, 70% lieu of Butter. | |

M.W.W.

Army Form C. 2118.

# WAR DIARY
## INTELLIGENCE SUMMARY.
*(Erase heading not required.)*

Instructions regarding War Diaries and Intelligence Summaries are contained in F. S. Regs., Part II. and the Staff Manual respectively. Title pages will be prepared in manuscript.

A.A.O. 21st Div.

| Place | Date | Hour | Summary of Events and Information | Remarks and references to Appendices |
|---|---|---|---|---|
| MOLIENS VIDAME | Dec 26th | | Frozen meat 70%, Fullbread. Only 20% Butter ration net MR in lieu. Veg 6 oz. BPws 17.9.20 of Meat from A GRAPELETTE + Mitins Swedes from Railhead supplement Ration. No oatmeal available. Candles difficult to obtain in adequate quantities. | |
| | 27th | | Oatmeal not available; Bread 16 oz, Frozen meat 8 oz, 6 oz Potatoes. No margarine Mr V in lieu. | |
| | 28th | | Bread 75%, Frozen meat full. Potatoes 6 oz. Margarine 2 oz, rest M.V. in lieu. Rice Oatmeal not available - 10 bdgs Kiln Swedes as extra frops received - | |
| | 29th | | Frozen meat 10 oz, Potatoes 6 oz, Full Margarine, Tobacco + 50% - Linseed 180 lb - Bran 16 oz | |
| | 30th | | Frozen meat 8 oz, Bread 13 oz, Potatoes 6 oz. Transferred M.V.S. funds to 110th Fd Pk fump. | |
| | 31st | | Nothing to record. | |

W.A. Stewart Major
S.S.O. 21st Division.

**CONFIDENTIAL.**

**WAR DIARY.**

OF

Senior Supply Officer., 21st Division.

FROM:- 1st January 1919.   TO:- 31st January 1919.

Army Form C. 2118.

# WAR DIARY
## or
## INTELLIGENCE SUMMARY.
(Erase heading not required.)

January 1919.   220.   21st Divn.

| Place | Date | Hour | Summary of Events and Information | Remarks and references to Appendices |
|---|---|---|---|---|
| MOLLIENS VIDAME | 1st | | No Jam available, dried fruit drawn in lieu. Bread 80%, Flour 12½%, Biscuit 7½%. | |
| | 2nd | | No fresh Vegetables available, dried Veg drawn in lieu. No petrol arrived from base. Other Commodities Satisfactory. | |
| | 3rd | | Nothing to report. | |
| | 4th | | 1 Ton Oaten Mpack Iron no potatoes. Sent to CORBIE for 3 Tons Horse Coal & 2 Tons Fog Coal. | |
| | 5th | | Sent to FDVY for extra forage as follows:- Divn Tps 304 lb, 62nd Bde 564 lb, 64th Bde 766 lb, 110th Bde 992 lb. = 1 kilo per animal. 20,000 lb Linseed Cake drawn from Railhead & issued at per animal strength the Cmdr. Vegetable Ration of potatoes & onions supplemented by Bread Veg to complete. Sent to CORBIE for 1st Wks. 20,000 lb dinner Cake | |
| | 6th | | Sent to FDVY for extra forage as follows:- Divn Tps 304 lb - 62nd Bde 568, 64th Bde 782 lb. 110th Bde 984 lb. - Oatmeal not available Full issue of all other components of ration except bg only & oz Rice not available. | |
| | 7th | | Full Wheat, 1 oz Macaroni, 1 oz Rice, No Oatmeal, Full Vegetables. 10 Ton Coal | |
| | 8th | | Full Bread, Vegetables. 4790 Kilo Cabbage, 1 oz Butter, 2 oz Rice & Oatmeal, Dried fruit lieu Jam and 18½ Tons Coal. | |

MAR.

Army Form C. 2118.

M.D. 21st Divn.

# WAR DIARY
## or
## INTELLIGENCE SUMMARY.
(Erase heading not required.)

| Place | Date | Hour | Summary of Events and Information | Remarks and references to Appendices |
|---|---|---|---|---|
| MOLLIENS VIDAME | Jany 1919 | | | |
| | 9th | | Similar from Railhead. Full Bread, Meat Mtyblatte rations. | |
| | 10th | | Full Meat, Mtyblatte Bread rations, 70% hardtack 7/8", 17% two Cwt, 4% Steam Coal, | |
| | 11th | | Full Meat, Bread 65%, Biscuit 25%, Flour 10%, Fuller. Tobacco/Cigarettes obtainable – 16 Firewood. 6 Two Steam Coal. 4 Tons Linseed Cake distributed – Followone Rum – | |
| | 14th | | 9000 Feb Ruts received at perm. | |
| | 15th | | Soap Candles drawn in lieu of Paraffin Candles. 1 Km Tobacco issue made – Dried fruit in lieu of Jam. Veg Ration 16 ozs – Sacks of damaged flour issued to 110 to dio. | |
| | 16th | | 600 Mtyblatte drawn from A.R. – Dried fruit iss'y to complete ration. 1/2 oz Tobacco drawn. | |
| | 17th | | 10,706 lbs of Bran and 140 lbs Linseed drawn at Railhead. | |
| | 18th | | 62,893 lbs of Locust Beans drawn at Railhead. Reported low stock of Fennel to 21st Division. | |
| | 19th | | Drew 22 Tons of Coal, 5000 Kilos of Cabbage and 10,000 Kilos of Roots drawn from Railhead. Reported a Supply Service. | |
| | 20th | | A/m the 22 Tons of Coal drew from Railhead which moved to HANGEST-SUR-SOMME | |

Army Form C. 2118.

Instructions regarding War Diaries and Intelligence Summaries are contained in F. S. Regs., Part II. and the Staff Manual respectively. Title pages will be prepared in manuscript.

# WAR DIARY
or
## INTELLIGENCE SUMMARY.
(Erase heading not required.)

S.S.O. 21st Div.

| Place | Date | Hour | Summary of Events and Information | Remarks and references to Appendices |
|---|---|---|---|---|
| MOLLIENS VIDAME | Jany 1919 21st | | 1st Tons bread drawn at Railhead & 10788 lbs of Sweeds. | |
| " | 22nd | | Stopped loading of Bacon & Milk until Reserve Stock is exhausted in accordance with Army Instructions. Bread as Tons drawn. Saw Deputy Ast'l Officer with reference to allied increase of Wood. | |
| " | 23rd | | Forty and Lard 6½ Tons. Cabbage 3340 lbs and Sweeds 17670 drawn at Railhead. Wood 40 Tons and Coal 64 Tons. | |
| " | 24th | | Arranged that loading should commence at 10.30. 5½ Tons of Wood drawn. Full vegetables drawn at Railhead. Again repeated the low state of bread to the Senior Supply Officer. | |
| " | 25th | | 87½ lb Bread. Full vegetable drawn at Railhead. Saw D.A.D.S. 3rd Army and arranged loading of 90 Tons of Coal. Arranged with D.S.Q. to begin unloading on the 28th in accordance with Army Orders on the 28th. | |
| " | 26th | | 6 lb Veg & 10970 lbs Swedes Tons of bread drawn at Railhead. | |

Army Form C. 2118.

# WAR DIARY
or
## INTELLIGENCE SUMMARY.
*(Erase heading not required.)*

S.S.O. 21st Div

| Place | Date | Hour | Summary of Events and Information | Remarks and references to Appendices |
|---|---|---|---|---|
| MOLLIENS VIDAME | Jan 27 1919 | | Nothing of importance to report. | |
| " | 28 | | S.B's 33, 24 & Front Room out. 10,000 25 issued & run. | |
| " | 29 | | Obtained authority from D.D.S.&T. to draw 20 Tons of Coal for Army Tpt. dump. | |
| " | 30 | | Nothing of importance to report. | |
| " | 31 | | Completed withdrawal of Vim Return in accordance with D.D.S.&T. No S/84/13 of 21.1.19. Drew 58½ Tons of Coal from Railhead. [illegible] | |

[signature] Major
S.S.O. 21st Div

CONFIDENTIAL

WAR DIARY

OF

Senior Supply Officer., 21st Division.

FROM:- 1st February, 1919.   TO:- 28th February 1919.

Original

1st to 28th Feb 19.

Army Form C. 2118.

# WAR DIARY
## or
## INTELLIGENCE SUMMARY.
(Erase heading not required.)

S.S. O 2128 Summary

Instructions regarding War Diaries and Intelligence Summaries are contained in F. S. Regs., Part II. and the Staff Manual respectively. Title pages will be prepared in manuscript.

| Place | Date 1919 | Hour | Summary of Events and Information | Remarks and references to Appendices |
|---|---|---|---|---|
| MOLLIENS VIDAME | Feb 1st | | 53 Trs of Coal drawn at Rubked. Received report a Supply Services | |
| " | 2d | | Ordered all tied in to refit to be helpful at so 110th A.b's dept | |
| | | | AILLY to west of further concentration of the Division. Ordered up | |
| | | | forage equivalent urgent. | |
| " | 3d | | Commenced forming ted dump at POUCHES to west of by S.M. | |
| | | | Corps | |
| " | 4th | | Refits to refit | |
| " | 5th | | Removed cattle at 11 refits 1 mag to 1 down at Railhead station S.S.S.O.T. | |
| | | | S.S.O. 4.2.19. | |
| " | 6th | | 6. Of of Vegetable drawn at Railhead | |
| " | 7th | | Refits move of + ret dumps | |
| " | 8th | | Coal 262 and West so Trs drawn at Railhead | |
| " | 9th | | 8650 Rds of Turnip drawn and Smith and 6 Trs . | |
| " | 10th | | Trolley of infantance to refit | |
| " | 11th | | 8 op of Vegetables and 22 Trs Coal drawn. | |

(A7853) D. D. & L., London, E.C. Wt W809/M1672 350,000 4/17 Sch. 52a Forms/C/2118/14

# WAR DIARY
## INTELLIGENCE SUMMARY

Army Form C. 2118.

S.S.O. 21st Divn.

| Place | Date 1919 | Hour | Summary of Events and Information | Remarks and references to Appendices |
|---|---|---|---|---|
| MOLLIENS VIDAME | 12th | | Rutland moved to AILLY-SUR-SOMME. Infantry at 10.30. 64th Bde Coy & loaded by M.T. the rest by H.T. 48 Tons of Baggage and livestock in lieu of rations. | |
| " | 13th | | 17 Tons Coal. 7 op vegetables drawn. | |
| " | 14th | | Coal & ITons and Charcoal 12,000 lbs drawn. | |
| " | 15th | | Three Frenchmen came into Force and 64th Bde drew by those Transport. | |
| " | 16th | | Rations to infant. | |
| " | 17th | | Bacon and milk issued. | |
| " | 18th | | 6 op vegetables drawn. | |
| " | 19th | | So Bde Coy 6 Lbs thick drawn. Issued first in lieu of Jam and 6 op vegetables. 2 × Tons Coal issued at Railhead | |
| " | 20th | | 74 galleons of Rum drawn which included 10 for men on nights duty. 6 op vegetables drawn | |
| " | 21st | | Rations of infantry issued to infant. | |
| " | 22nd | | 60 gallons Rum drawn and 6 op vegetables. | |

**WAR DIARY**
or
**INTELLIGENCE SUMMARY.**

Army Form C. 2118.

SSO 21st Divison

| Place | Date | Hour | Summary of Events and Information | Remarks and references to Appendices |
|---|---|---|---|---|
| MOLLIENS VIDAME | Feb 1919 23rd | | 100% Field Meet down. Units asked to note the Jnt att. drew fuel from dump of S.O. 110 Side at AILLY. | |
| " | 24th | | Thaw preventin any work. Drew billet straw at LONGPRÉ | |
| " | 25th | | Drew 40 Tons of wood from St Ouen | |
| " | 26th | | 8 op. vegetable drawn. | |
| " | 27th | | Issued three days rations at Railhead to dept (193) of 1st Fields Regt. being the Divisional Amn. Col. moved to Reserve Stock. | |
| " | 28th | | Double park of Field Meat received at Railhead. | |

Major
RASC